Valuable Partnerships

Valuable Partnerships
Cooperation, Innovation, and the Future of Municipal Texas

Robert J. Sullivan

RESOURCE *Publications* • Eugene, Oregon

VALUABLE PARTNERSHIPS
Cooperation, Innovation, and the Future of Municipal Texas

Copyright © 2019 Robert J. Sullivan. All rights reserved. Except for brief quotations in critical publications or reviews, no part of this book may be reproduced in any manner without prior written permission from the publisher. Write: Permissions, Wipf and Stock Publishers, 199 W. 8th Ave., Suite 3, Eugene, OR 97401.

Resource Publications
An Imprint of Wipf and Stock Publishers
199 W. 8th Ave., Suite 3
Eugene, OR 97401

www.wipfandstock.com

PAPERBACK ISBN: 978-1-5326-0794-3
HARDCOVER ISBN: 978-1-5326-0796-7
EBOOK ISBN: 978-1-5326-0795-0

Manufactured in the U.S.A.

Contents

List of Tables | ix
List of Illustrations | xi
Preface | xiii

Part I: The Current Texas Municipal Structure | 1

Chapter 1—Managing for Change | 3
    Local Challenges   3
    Modern Crises and Challenges   7
    New Challenges for Municipal Texas   8
    Innovative Responses   10
    Measured Improvement   11
    Evaluation Criteria & Methodology   12
    What You Will Learn From This book   14
    Local Government Axioms Driving book   15
    Book Structure/Flow   15

Chapter 2—Municipal Fragmentation and the Changing Face
       of America | 18
    Fragmented Government Structure   18
    My Two Cents   24
    Fragmentation and its Challenges   25
    Summary: Consequences for Twenty-First Century Texas   28

CONTENTS

Chapter 3—Why Texas? | 30
    Explosive Population Growth   30
    Political Culture   34
    Political Culture and the Texas Economy   38
    Changes that Demand Attention   41
    Summary   42

Chapter 4—Profiles of Urban Texas | 44
    Characteristics   44
    Characteristics Creating Profiles   46
    Statewide Results   50
    County Profiles   53
    Summary   63

Part II: Candidates & Criteria | 65

Chapter 5—Candidates for Selection | 67
    Regional and Consolidated Structures   68
    City-County Consolidation   71
    Benefits of Regionalism and Consolidation   73
    Interlocal Contracts & Other Examples of Functional Regionalism   74
    Summary   80

Chapter 6—What Do We Want from our Local Governments? | 81
    Methodology   81
    Policy Criteria   84
    Democratic Criteria   87
    Report Results   92
    Results   97

CONTENTS

Part III: Policy Prescriptions: Case Studies Incorporating the Best Practices Involving Cooperative Regionalism and Innovation in Texas | 99

Chapter 7—Cooperative City Management | 107
    The Scope of City Managers   108
    What City Managers Do   109
    Does a City Manager Provide Benefits for Citizens?   111
    Challenges to the Traditional Model   111
    Innovative Structure   113
    Results   116
    Analysis/How   117
    Summary   117

Chapter 8—Terrell-Economic Development and Water | 119
    The Typical Water Delivery Process   121
    Water Source/Acquisition   122
    Innovation   124
    A Brief Summary of the TIF Process   127
    Layering Statutes for Maximum Revenue   127
    Terrell Report Cards   134
    TIF Report Card   135
    Summary   136

Chapter 9—Lean Six Sigma & Analysis of the Service Provision Process | 139
    The Rise of Efficiency Analysis and Lean Six Sigma   139
    Gainesville commitment to Six Sigma/Analytics   141
    Wastewater Case Study   144
    The Lean Six Sigma Process: Identifying Steps Critical to Quality   146
    Outcomes   150
    Report Card   150
    Summary   151

Chapter 10—Medstar and Emergency Innovation | 152
    EMS History   154
    The Traditional EMS Delivery System   156
    Medstar   157
    Innovative Solutions   160
    Solutions   161
    Report Card   169
    Summary   169

CONTENTS

Part IV: Changing the Landscape: A Checklist for Reform | 171

Chapter 11—Synthesis of Results | 173
    Synthesizing the Results   176
    Barriers/Questions   179
    Summary   181

Chapter 12—Lessons Learned, Success, and the Future of Innovation | 182
    Lessons Learned   182
    How can Texas Advance Innovation?   185
    Why Discuss This Topic? Why Write About It?   187

Bibliography | 189
Index | 199

Tables

Table 2–1: Fragmentation Comparison for Largest American States | 21

Table 2–2: Comparing Fragmentation among Various Federations | 22

Table 3–1: Population Growth for Texas and United States 1950–2010 | 31

Table 3–2: Population Growth for the Ten Largest American States from 2010–2015 | 33

Table 3–3: Population Growth for Dallas, Houston, and Austin from 1940–2010 | 34

Table 3–4: State and Local Tax Burden Comparison between DC, Illinois, and Texas | 38

Table 3–5: Cost of Living Comparison between DC, Chicago, and Houston | 39

Table 4–1: Ten Largest Texas Counties' Population Increase | 45

Table 4–2: Socioeconomic Characteristics for Ten Largest Texas Counties | 47

Table 4–3: Harris County Socioeconomic Profile | 53

Table 4–4: Dallas County Socioeconomic Profile | 54

Table 4–5: Tarrant County Socioeconomic Profile | 55

Table 4–6: Bexar County Socioeconomic Profile | 56

Table 4–7: Travis County Socioeconomic Profile | 57

Table 4–8: Collin County Socioeconomic Profile | 58

Table 4–9: El Paso County Socioeconomic Profile | 59

Table 4–10: Hidalgo County Socioeconomic Profile | 60

TABLES

Table 4–11: Denton County Socioeconomic Profile | 61
Table 4–12: Fort Bend County Socioeconomic Profile | 62
Table 5–1: Urban Region Consolidations Since 1947 | 72
Table 6–1: Policy Checklist | 86
Table 6–2: Transparency Criteria | 89
Table 6–3: Democracy Questions | 91
Table 6–4: Regionalism Report Card | 97
Table 7–1: PRPC Contract Management Program Client List | 114
Table 7–2: PRPC Report Card | 117
Table 8–1: Terrell Water Source Options | 124
Table 8–2: Property Value/Tax Revenue Increases | 133
Table 8–3: Property Value Increase and Incremental Reimbursements | 134
Table 8–4: Water Delivery Report Card | 135
Table 8–5: TIF Report Card | 136
Table 9–1: Gainesville Socioeconomic Profile | 141
Table 9–2: Gainesville LSS Projects | 142
Table 9–3: Gainesville LSS Report Card | 150
Table 10–1: Socioeconomic Profiles of Medstar Client Cities | 158
Table 10–2: Medstar Resources | 159
Table 10–3: Medstar Budgetary Comparison | 162
Table 10–4: Response Time/Staffing Results 2012–2016 | 164
Table 10–5: Medstar Transparency Rubric | 167
Table 10–6: Medstar Report Card | 168
Table 11–1: Composite Report Card Results | 177
Table 11–2: Cluster Distribution for Five Largest Texas Counties | 180

Illustrations

Figure 6–1: Standard Water Delivery Process | 83
Figure 8–1: Standard Water Delivery Process | 121
Figure 8–2: Terrell Water Delivery Process | 126
Figure 8–3: How a TIF works | 130
Figure 9–1: Wastewater Treatment Plant Operational Process | 146
Figure 9–2: Post-LSS Wastewater Treatment Plant Process | 149

Preface

POLITICS AND POLICY INCITES passions. My students live to debate the merits of various political actors both human and organizational, as well as the policy decisions we live with daily. This is a small sect that squeezes every ounce of CSPAN coverage possible. The identity politics era has merely heightened this trend. Few people express indifference toward politics.

Additionally, the categories within political analysis enjoy high Q-ratings. Electoral politics is perhaps the most popular kid given its money, prestige, and coverage. Campaigns also shine the spotlight on people which always makes the story more compelling. Policy arenas such as international relations, foreign policy, and the economy generate interest simply due to their broad significance.

But the service side of local government? This is not the stuff of passion. There are several possible explanations for this apathy. For example, local issues rarely fall along partisan lines. American voters are accustomed (some say conditioned) to view policy arguments as two-sided, following a partisan script. The provision of utilities or EMS frequently fall outside the partisan realm. The fragmentation (a topic we discuss shortly) might also be a factor. The United States houses 90,000 plus local jurisdiction of various sizes. That is a large market to cover.

Perhaps the most compelling explanation is the simplest: local public services are simply boring, arcane topics. Whether a city adequately provides high quality water or spends too much money on libraries fails to move the needle unless the failure results in tragedy or compromises public safety.

The questions beckons: Why devote a full book to local government ,other than the obligatory, "My dissertation research addressed this layer so the next logical step is a book," response? The answer lies in the nature of

PREFACE

local goods and services. Public safety, education, and infrastructure are so basic that society takes them for granted. Yet these services are also essential in many cases—or have you not observed the stories of communities facing blackouts, a shortage of public safety personnel, or a dearth of clean potable water? Hard times await these communities.

And here is the rub: American municipalities remain at least ostensibly responsible for providing these services and are expected to guarantee availability to everyone regardless of income level.[1] Unfortunately, cities are struggling with funding these most basic and essential goods and services as revenue sources dry up and population shifts. This provides the drama of our work.

Most importantly, this work examines how cities (and local jurisdictions, generally) discover methods for overcoming these hurdles to provide critical services. We are so quick to praise private sector corporations that find ways to be leaner, meaner, and more productive. This book takes a moment to appreciate their public counterparts and the barriers they overcome in nurturing innovation.

So many people contributed in some way to this work. First, many thanks and warm thoughts flow to my dissertation committee chair, the late Dr. Richard Cole, who guided the foundational research of interlocal contracting and cooperation among Texas governments. Additionally, several of Dr. Cole's cohorts (in the early days of the Institute for Urban Studies) played critical roles. Many thanks to James Ray, Jay Stanford, and David Tees for their insight and support. I would also be remiss in failing to mention Dr. Enid Arvidson and her consistent support during my doctoral studies.

This work includes data, results, and thoughts culled from practitioners of the municipal arts. Many thanks to each and every city manager or staff member taking the time for interviews and data collection including Torry Edwards and Mike Sims from Terrell, Kyle Ingham and the PRPC folks, and Barry Sullivan (no relation, for which he is very thankful). The book is richer thanks to your contribution.

Finally, how can one adequately thank his family? Lea, Alec, and Cole comprise my foundation and primary source of joy. I love each of you more than my poor writing can fully express.

---

1. Customer funded utilities such as water and electricity, as well as ambulance/EMS to a lesser extent, could provide exceptions to this expectation.

Part I: The Current Texas Municipal Structure

WHAT DOES THE TRADITIONAL American municipal model look like, how does it operate, and what shifts are potentially altering the structure and its priorities? Which factors drive American municipal development and which realities mandate change? Additionally, what does the Texas municipal profile look like? How acute are the emerging challenges in Texas and how will local and state leaders respond? How has the state responded historically and does that provide insight for future responses?

Most nonfiction books addressing a problem (or opportunity for the-glass-is-half-full crowd) of this ilk follow a similar structure co-opted from the medical field. The author describes an illness plaguing a group, region, or society in general. This portion also provides a patient profile (as it were) so we understand who or what is under examination, and how certain characteristics impact the treatment phase. The next section prescribes a cure and treatment process. The book concludes with real life examples of the treatment in action bolstered by an analysis of whether the "medicine" cured the malady or at least mitigated the problem.

This study utilizes a similar structure. The book is divided into four parts (sections). Part I profiles our patient: the state of Texas, and more specifically, the 1,214 cities serving Texas residents.[1] Chapter 1 explains the challenges facing Texas leaders tasked with responding to a population explosion of a 30 percent increase over the next decade and a 55 percent increase over twenty years.[2] Such growth is remarkable considering Texas

---

1. U.S. Census Bureau. *Government Organization*.
2. Potter, *Population Projection*, 3–4.

has the second largest population in the country behind only California. Texas cities face challenges to their service capacities in meeting increased demand. The first two chapters examine the American municipal structure and the challenges flowing from said structure.

Chapter 3 serves as the "character profile" for the Lone Star state by tracing the historical development of the political culture and norms impacting government innovation. This chapter reminds readers that explosive population growth is nothing new to Texas leaders. Additionally, the prescription enjoys precedence among Texas local governments.

Finally, chapter 4 describes the current Texas urban structure with a socioeconomic profile of the ten most populous Texas counties. The chapter utilizes cluster analysis to organize each county based on socioeconomic data. This analysis proves beneficial later in the book as many of the regional agreements include a balance of wealthy, middle-class, and lower-income jurisdictions. Overall, this section not only sets the table for understanding the need for regional cooperation among Texas cities, but also highlights which type remains most viable.

1

Managing for Change

I welcome change as long as nothing is altered or different
RANDOM ANONYMOUS MEME

Local Challenges

HISTORY HAS AN ENDLESS array of mysteries. One of the biggest concerns is who or what caused the great Chicago Fire in 1871? The fire left a once proud, burgeoning city decimated with millions of dollars in property destroyed and hundreds of lives lost. However, history cannot definitely identify the cause of the fire.

However, the city's massive population growth created a long-term public health menace more difficult to fix than the fire. The Chicago population exploded from 1840–1880 as it transitioned from a tiny settlement of 4,000 to a booming metropolis of 500,000 by 1880. Then, Chicago really grew as the population eventually increased to one million by 1890. The population essentially doubled over the course of one decade![1]

Growth sounds great. After all, the city's economic profile attracted workers looking for jobs and opportunity. However, public services failed to keep pace. Several services suffered, like the water supply. Industry and manufacturing drove the business engine but also left toxic waste that businesses typically deposited in the Chicago River. And this is hardly the full

---

1. Hill, *The Chicago River*, 86.

story. Animal carcasses were added to the mix, but we will remain silent on the ultimate resting place for human waste.

While the fire remains a short-term (albeit high impact) tragedy for the generation that experienced it, water borne diseases proved to be more deadly. The Chicago River flowed into Lake Michigan which served as the city's water supply. Massive health problems ensued. For example, water borne diseases were thought to have killed thousands of people of the Chicago population in 1885 alone. The city faced a full blown public health calamity.[2]

City leaders shepherded the population through painful transition and adaptation. The aldermen assembly hired engineers and created a sanitation division to develop a solution. The hired experts quickly cobbled together a bold, innovative plan leveraging the technology and scientific expertise of the day.

The Plan—Reverse the Direction of the Chicago River

Reversing the direction of a river's water flow is a massive initiative requiring smart decisions, manpower, and time. The plan eventually mandated sanitary district engineers building three canals with dams and locks. The entire process lasted eleven years and required the services of 8,500 workers.

While the sacrifice was enormous, the measured results were clear and unassailable. The city experienced a massive decrease in water borne illnesses and health issues in general. Life expectancy exploded due to reduced health concerns. Overall, the Chicago water supply remains among the safest in the world.[3]

Also, what happens to Chicago as a destination city if leadership fails to effectively address this concern? Chicago enjoys its status as an international city due in no small part to a safer water supply as well as high quality public services in general. The author realizes city status and economic prospects pale in comparison to preserving and protecting human life. However, those topics remains part of this book and merit a mention.[4]

Why start a book about Texas municipalities with a story about the Chicago River and the impact of foul water? Well, good stories grab the reader's attention for one. The story also highlights the earliest phase of the city reform movement driven by an unprecedented combination of

2. Hill, *The Chicago River*, 116–19.
3. American Public Works Association, "Top Ten Public Works Projects."
4. American Public Works Association, "Top Ten Public Works Projects."

domestic migration from rural regions to urban enclaves such as Chicago (as well as Boston, New York, Philadelphia, etc.) and international immigration from Asia and Europe. The story proves a valuable introduction for these reasons alone.

The Chicago River reform also offers a wonderful illustration structuring the contents of this book. Our prioritized line of inquiry focuses less on the crisis itself and more the response. Here is a summary of the elements of the response:

1. Unsafe water presented a *crisis* or *challenge*
2. The city *responded* or *adapted*
3. The response relied on *innovations* driven by *professional expertise* and *technology*
4. The innovation *improved conditions in a measurable way*

Change is hard but inevitable. Preparing for and anticipating change is even harder. However, the world is changing while information and the way we do things is becoming obsolete at the fastest rate in history. Municipal governments do not enjoy immunity to this reality. This disruption forever alters local service provisions and the funding of server infrastructure. Therefore, our analysis follows the process modeled by Chicago:

1. Cities Face New Crises or Challenges

This book examines the challenges facing Texas municipalities including:

- Population growth
- The changing face of said population
- Fragmentation (more on that in a minute)
- Reduced budgets
- Trans-jurisdictional or multi-jurisdictional issues such as transportation or environmental problems.

2. Response/Innovation

While Chicago's response was impressive, it was ultimately reactive. Modern city leadership prioritizes proactive analysis of both opportunities and challenges including:

- Cooperation/intergovernmental contracts
- Regionalism
- Six Sigma
- Process analysis
- Data analytics

3. Measuring Improvement

Innovative responses prove fruitless unless the effort improves public service or solves lingering problems. *Valuable Partnerships* determines whether innovative tools yielded improvements by identifying criteria or goals leaders prioritize and measuring how effectively chosen innovations yielded desired objectives.

The term "municipality" fails to move the needle for most Americans. Local jurisdictions are like the football officials of politics. Nobody cares until a mistake is made that damages you or someone you know. Government functions such as waste removal, water, electricity, parks, and public safety are routinely taken for granted or ignored. Time and brain cells dedicated to politics and policy focus on the "horse race" context of federal elections or broad social issues. Local services remain largely ignored save the annual water rationing (if you live in southern states) or forty-eight hour blackout.

However, local government functions and services remain vital to every American citizen regardless of status or location. The quality, availability, and affordability of services such as public safety and utilities cannot be compromised. Across the nation, and especially in Texas, municipalities are experiencing the very challenges that put service delivery at risk. This book examines these challenges and explains the innovative tools local jurisdictions utilize to combat them. Most importantly, this study examines how these innovations are transforming the landscape of municipal America. My research career has focused on the how Texas municipal leaders face the expectations and challenges of building safer and stronger cities (as well as stronger counties, special districts, etc.).

Public sentiment has long viewed the delivery of local government functions as a static world comprised of bureaucrats carrying out or administering a rote task. Simply put, this picture needs adjusting. Public administrators, whether they be city manager or agency chiefs, manage dynamic organizations that must embrace innovation to continue functioning effectively.

Moderns Crises and Challenges

Like Chicago, modern cities and urban regions are facing unprecedented challenges. In fact, one of the primary challenges is structural. Municipal America is a fragmented puzzle linking over 90,000 local jurisdictions providing the most basic services to American citizens. Texas alone is home to over 5,000 local jurisdictions of both general and limited authority. The classic fragmented approach leaves each jurisdiction with the responsibility for public services to its citizens.[5] Local decision-makers proceed in the manner most beneficial to their citizens (and bosses). This is how they remain employed. Additionally, most of the 1,200 plus incorporated cities or towns are technically suburbs as the state has embraced urban sprawl.[6] Naturally, this situation can develop a competitive relationship between cities fighting for citizens and businesses, and the revenue that comes with both.

Local governments constantly battle for revenue. Many local jurisdictions are facing these problems with a reduced budget. Money remains the ultimate priority for municipal managers and the taxpayers they serve. The new fiscal reality hits as the American population grows and is becoming increasingly diverse. Citizens expect municipalities to accomplish more with less. Additionally, the American population is creating an ever increasing stress on social services due to increasing raw growth and diversity. Given these trends, a book examining local government innovation and the priorities behind those innovations must "follow the money," as it were.

Local leaders are always looking for opportunities to save money. However, any decision or innovation that compromises service quality should be avoided. The city managers, bureau chiefs, and fire chiefs the

---

5. U.S. Census Bureau. *Government Organization*.
6. Tannahill, *Texas Government*, 280.

author interviewed consistently stressed that their primary job was either building a more vibrant city or saving lives. Therefore, performance matters and agencies cannot sacrifice effective service provision to save a buck. Additionally, public agencies by their very nature serve an entire community as opposed to merely those customers who can afford it. Consequently, cooperation and innovation can also provide more effective government functions which can result in higher levels of quality from a suburb, or perhaps a small town with limited means. This is where my research evolved from the studies examining mere government efficiency to a broader canvas addressing additional criteria.

New Challenges for Municipal Texas

Why must Texas municipal leaders pursue innovation and cooperation in the first place? Their world is changing just like the aldermen leading industrial age Chicago. Individuals and organizations typically avoid adapting unless change is on the horizon. Municipal America is experiencing trends and challenges that mandate innovation.

Texas municipalities are experiencing these trends like few other states. For example, Texas is growing like no other state. A diverse, strong economy and cheap living costs attract new residents annually. Good weather doesn't hurt either. These attractive characteristics combined with high birth rates yielded the second largest population among the states. Furthermore, this trend was actually predictable and is expected to continue for perhaps the next twenty-five years.[7]

Economic growth and the increasing population that typically accompanies it obviously carry financial benefits for all realms of society including local governments. However, more people does not always equate to more money for the provision of public goods and services. Texas is also experiencing a shift in median household income and demographics which will impact public revenue streams.[8] This is especially true of larger cities, as a majority of the new Texans are flowing into the suburbs, which do not share their revenue with central cities (or poorer neighbors for that matter). It would behoove leaders to embrace regional cooperation and other innovative opportunities.

---

7. Gaines, "Looming Boom," 2.
8. Potter, *Population Projections for Texas*, 4.

Additionally, a growing population logically escalates demand for public goods and services. Transportation networks should experience increased congestion; school districts, which rely heavily on local tax revenues, will become increasingly overburdened; and local planning will become more critical and perhaps more politically charged. Additionally, several regions within the state could suffer from an inadequate water supply as well as experiencing increased costs for the provision of other utilities such as sewage service, natural gas, and electricity. These issues could adversely impact economic growth and quality of life for Texas residents.

The exploding population could also herald demands to regional planning over fragmented decision-making by individual cities. Local governments increasingly face public issues that are multi-jurisdictional in nature such as transportation, pollution, education, and crime. Individual municipalities eventually lose the capacity to manage complex policy issues with scopes extending beyond jurisdictional borders.[9] Therefore, city managers and public executives must leverage networks and alliances to nurture some form of intergovernmental cooperation.

Additionally, these alliances and agreements also provide opportunities in the provision of government functions. Tarrant County, the third largest Texas County with thirty-seven cities and towns ranging from Fort Worth (population 741,000) to Westover Hills (682), offers a prime example of public safety bloat.[10] Overall, thirty-four out of the thirty seven municipalities fund, manage, and staff both police and fire departments, while twenty-two have their own emergency medical services (EMS) and ambulance agencies.[11] Does the prospect of major cities and suburbs separately providing the same service within an urban region sound ideal? Does it truly make sense for a metropolitan region or county to have thirty-four separate police forces, thirty-four separate fire departments, as well as twenty-two separate EMS agencies, when a collaborative regional government that eliminates such wasteful duplication prove more productive and efficient? In fact, the sprawl-driven suburban wasteland hated by so many urban critics actually facilitates cooperative agreements as both wealthy and lower income cities can achieve vastly different objectives from the same contract. This book examines how those objectives are met.

9. Fredrickson, "The Repositioning of Public Administration," 877; Thurmaier and Wood, "Interlocal Agreements as an Alternative," 114–15.

10. U.S. Census Bureau, "American Community Survey."

11. U.S. Census Bureau, *Government Organization*.

PART I: THE CURRENT TEXAS MUNICIPAL STRUCTURE

The nature of Texas politics and its governing history challenges government innovation. The state embraces a hybrid of the traditionalistic/individualistic political cultures. Most Texans are skeptical of government and public spending at all levels. Recent political movements and trends within the state have only solidified this rugged individual climate. Local leaders should not expect increased funding given this reality.[12]

Given these issues, one must consider whether fragmented self-provision is the least expensive option and the best performance option. These challenges will not reduce the expectations of citizens regarding the quality and delivery of public goods. In fact, demand will increased exponentially. Which direction can cities follow to address this new world?

Innovative Responses

The Status Quo

Innovation, expertise, and technology saved the Chicago population by reversing the flow of water. Modern city managers and urban leaders enjoy access to ideas, innovation, and technology. While none of these tools will reverse the flow of a river, many take traditional city management practices in a totally new direction.

For example, the author briefly addressed the concept of fragmentation and sprawl earlier (and will go over it in further detail in chapter 2). Fragmentation—and its partner sprawl—has endured a wave of criticism over the years lead by reformers who identify it as both economically inefficient and unfair. Can poor communities actually provide government functions that perform as effectively as those serving higher income citizens? Is either scenario truly optimal?

Regional model advocates who have long dominated the reform option argue that their alternatives to fragmentation would prove far superior. Regional jurisdictions have various structures with authority over smaller jurisdictions, such as Metro in Portland, or city-county consolidations like Indianapolis or Louisville, that replaced the polycentric map with one government.[13]

---

12. Elazar, *American Federalism*, 85–87, 97.

13. Dolan, "Local Government Fragmentation,"43; Orfield, *American Metropolitics*, 10; Rusk, *Cities Without Suburbs*, 96–97.

This is the dominant debate within federal and local government: Does the prevailing polycentric fragmented municipal model remain most effective and efficient in the provision of public goods and services, or do regional jurisdictions provide a more optimal structure? Both structures have benefits and problems, yet these two questions have continued to dominate the debate.

Cooperation

The ongoing debate rarely considers intergovernmental cooperation or what I call voluntary regionalism. Functional regionalism also has a nice ring to it. Voluntary regionalism has found that structures produced by arrangements such as interlocal agreements or contracts can achieve the benefits of structured regional government while maintaining polycentricism. It remains feasible that municipalities and citizens can experience the best regionalism has to offer without experiencing the many challenges that complete structural transformation presents. However, while previous studies have examined interlocal contracting among Texas municipalities, research has yet to address whether the practice yields regional benefits and whether contracting cities prioritize intergovernmental cooperation.[14] This book asks these questions among others. Granted, local units have cooperated via additional structures including special districts and councils of governments. We will examine both options.

Measured Improvement

Outcomes and results are critical. History looks favorably upon the "river reversal" because it provided the Chicago urban region clean water and contributed to its growth and hallowed reputation. This author (and this book) argues that the "third way" cooperative option coupled with analytics is the most effective and feasible option for transforming Texas urban regions into hyperefficient machines producing high-quality services. That said, *Valuable Partnerships* rigorously challenges this working hypothesis by measuring and comparing all available options.

While this study will be a rigorous journey, two caveats are in order. First, the "best" option is a contextual standard. Federalism proves especially

---

14. Tees, Coles, and Searcy, *Durable Partnerships in Texas*, 13.

effective in diverse countries serving a diverse population with various beliefs, cultures, and priorities. This explains the success in America where the diversity is also regional and geographic. Therefore, regional consolidation proved feasible in regions such as Portland or Louisville. However, the context for this study is Texas local governments which serve a very unique populous that is very distinct for those two regions. Second, we must determine what makes fragmentation, regionalism, or cooperation the best option. What criteria do we use to evaluate and compare the options? We cannot examine structural options without identifying what we want out of our local governments in the first place.

Evaluation Criteria & Methodology

Given these expectations, this book adopts a policy analysis or evaluation methodology with four case studies embedded in the project that follow the same structure. The policy analysis process presumes a rational decision making model is a fit for public officials. The process includes five logical steps which are the typical steps for most any decision, although policy decisions can impact millions of people and affect access to public coffers.[15] Therefore, the process mandates extensive research into society and social issues. Most importantly, policy decisions impact generations an include consequences extending beyond the target population.

The book adopts the process model steps or stages of the policy process. Step one involves defining or analyzing a social problem. Part I defines the challenges facing local jurisdiction, specifically how the explosive Texas population is transforming the state and how Texas cities and towns must adapt and improve. Non-fiction works such as this project typically adopt a descriptive and prescriptive approach that includes describing a problem followed by the prescribed solution. Part I satisfies the descriptive phase.

The second and third steps of the process are truly the heavy lifting stages where policymakers and their staff work with policy experts (lobbyists, scientists, PhDs, etc.) to construct various solutions to the problem presented in stage one, and develop criteria for examining each alternatives and determining which is optimal given the situation and context of the times. Part II describes the many innovative options local officials can

---

15. Brewer and DeLeon, *The Foundation of Policy Analysis*, 17–21; Kraft, and Furlong, *Public Policy*, 78; Lindblom and Woodhouse, *The Policy-Making Process*, 83.

adopt and the criteria we will utilize to measure and compare said innovations.[16] The author applies the chosen criteria to each option to determine the optimal innovation for Texas jurisdictions.

Speaking of criteria, how do we measure structural efficacy? The public policy evaluation process provides a clinical approach to determining whether new innovations yield the local governance structure that produces the desired results. The policy evaluator initiates the process by asking what prospective policy should be accomplished and which outputs should be avoided. The author will examine cost savings, process efficiency, and high performance or effectiveness. These benchmarks remain priorities that drive innovation among local leaders. However, I value democracy and would prefer if the evaluation included democratic criteria, such as whether structural or functional options are also transparent, contribute to decentralization, and remain accountable to the citizens receiving the service.[17] Additionally, all citizens should enjoy access to quality public goods and services even if they cannot afford said services. Therefore, my evaluation examines whether the options equitably distribute service provision or equalize service availability. Finally, which policies exist much less thrive absent political feasibility. Therefore, we ask if the options would prove feasible within the Texas political culture.

Part III includes four case studies examining regionally structured interlocal agreements. Case studies structure deep examinations of an individual, group, system, or organization. Most students and readers assume that case studies are qualitative but these case studies are best described as mixed method in structure. In fact, the primary question each study addresses is whether the partnership under the microscope actually achieves the chosen criteria. Therefore, this part essentially includes four policy evaluations.[18]

Finally, Part IV incorporates the conclusion stage of the policy process. We synthesize the case study results to determine whether the regional cooperative model yields the results demanded by the policy criteria. This conclusion includes a consideration of impact on the future of Texas local government.

---

16. Kraft and Furlong, *Public Policy*, 78.
17. Kraft and Furlong, *Public Policy*, 152–59.
18. Yin, *Applications of Case Study Research*, 5.

PART I: THE CURRENT TEXAS MUNICIPAL STRUCTURE

What You Will Learn From This Book

This work bridges rich scholarship and practical application to produce an important reference for local government scholars and practitioners alike by covering the dynamic approaches altering how Texas municipalities operate. *Valuable Partnerships* investigates the efficacy of the American fragmented municipal model comprised of 90,000 plus jurisdictions. Critics consistently condemn this decentralized model while arguing for a regional structure that will yield greater efficiencies and scalability. They expect this regional structure to also solve the twin problems of equity and service delivery inequalities.

Conversely, *Valuable Partnerships* presents evidence that Texas local governments leverage regional cooperation and innovation to achieve these results without the political and structural upheaval. The author utilizes historic analysis, benchmark results, socioeconomic measures, and budgetary data to demonstrate how Texas governments increase service performance and reduce the burden to taxpayers. Such results support a counterthesis to the structural regionalism hypothesis by presenting findings that Texas local jurisdictions embracing regional cooperation and data analytics will experience the same benefits.

What assumptions drive municipal analysis and research? Every "scientific" finding flows from deeply held biases that mold and direct the method and framework driving every author/scholar. Municipal and city studies are hardly immune and, in fact, are shining examples. Like any writer/scholar (term used loosely), my worldview or strongly held beliefs influence my words, research, findings, and conclusions. The audience of readers (and this book itself) benefits from transparency. Additionally, I must address the beliefs and findings of other writers. While "bias" is unavoidable, we all endeavor to research our little niche and identify actual truth as best we can. After all, the ultimate responsibility of any "scholar" is determining whether what you believe about the world is right or wrong.

So, in the interest of full disclosure (and narrative structure), please allow me to introduce the accepted axioms/assumptions driving my deeper inquiry into this subject. These assumptions develop the structure and narrative for this book and provide as good an explanation as any for why this book needs to be written and this subject explored further.

Local Government Axioms Driving Book

1. Local public goods and service are for the most part essential and society must insure everyone has access regardless of income.
2. Fragmentation provides costs and benefits. One of the major costs is some municipalities struggle with providing adequate services.
3. Poverty is the key problem for many reasons. This is obvious, but the complexity extends beyond mere affordability.
4. Regional government is simply more efficient.
5. Transitioning to a regional structure remains unfeasible politically and the transition process could easily dilute any benefit. There are too many stakeholders with vested interests for an efficient transformation to occur. This is especially true in Texas. You might have an argument if a blank slate existed.
6. While Texas municipalities have no history of regional consolidation, there exists a strong history of cooperation. However, most of the contracts are between two parties where a large municipality utilizes excess capacity.
7. Following up on number six, multi-party contracts built on a regional structure is the optimal framework for meeting our chosen criteria to achieve successful service provision.
8. Finally, the solution lies with interlocal agreements among multiple (more than two) partners establishing a regional structure. Existing governments built on this basis reduce costs, nurture process efficiency, enhance service performance and effectiveness, and deliver quality services to low income communities.

Book Structure/Flow

These axioms provide the structure for the book. Social science research, like all disciplines, ponders difficult, complex questions. This book is no exception.

PART I: THE CURRENT TEXAS MUNICIPAL STRUCTURE

1. What is the historic American municipal structure and why is it in dire need of reform?

This question is intentionally hyperdramatic, an attention grabber. Municipal America essentially adopts a matrix structure loosely connecting 90,000 plus local jurisdictions. The effectiveness of this approach and the need for outright structural reform depends on the source of the critique. The regional school of thought calls for nothing less than full scale structural reform driven by consolidation or regional authorities. Conversely, this book argues that the matrix merely needs innovative tweaking.

However, why does the system need tweaking? Part I addresses this question by providing the "meat" of the trends facing Texas cities. Chapter 2 explains the prevailing American municipal model, chapter 3 introduces the characteristics and culture that makes Texas unique, and chapter 4 profiles urban Texas.

2. How are local leaders responding?

Part II is a relatively short section clocking in at two chapters. Part I rests on the position that seismic demographic changes are challenging the coffers and capacity of local jurisdictions, and the business-as-usual attitude provides a recipe for disaster. However, we need to identify what change needs to be accomplished before determining how to change. Chapter 5 fills this void by introducing the policy criteria needed to measure and compare the various reform options. Chapter 6 presents a more detailed explanation of the various innovative tools and structures for optimizing municipal performance and responsiveness with a focus on intergovernmental cooperation.

3. Are the responses innovative and effective?

How does innovative tweaking work in the real world of local governance? Part III introduces readers to city managers and local leaders conquering daunting financial and resource quandaries with innovative tools and techniques. This section highlights the complexity of city management in a state facing meteoric population growth while also illustrating the broad scope of local leadership by examining examples of several government function categories. Overall, Part III serves as a clarion call for dynamic, groundbreaking leadership most people attribute to the private sector. These reform examples meet exacting performance standards without compromising democracy as prescribed by the policy criteria.

4. Are the responses replicable in other urban regions?

Finally, Part IV synthesizes findings that hopefully yield a model structure for urban Texas. The final section synthesizes the case study findings to deliver meaningful results. Additionally, the compiled examination yields powerful lessons for government leaders who aspire to drive innovation in their processes, service delivery, and structure.

However, the journey begins with the history of municipal America and Texas.

2

Municipal Fragmentation and the Changing Face of Municipal America

WHAT DOES THE TRADITIONAL American municipal model look like, how does it operate, and what shifts are potentially altering the structure and its priorities? Which factors drove American municipal development and which realities mandated change? This chapter answers these questions by explaining the traditional (at least since 1945) fragmented American municipal structure and how this structure developed. However, the world is changing, thanks to numerous macro trends, and municipalities are hardly immune as explained in chapter 1. Therefore, we need to spend some time fleshing out these trends and their impact on local jurisdictions. This creates a template for examining what is specifically happening in Texas.

Our journey through these transformations should be interesting but first we need to consider some foundational questions. Specifically, what is meant by government fragmentation? Additionally, what is a suburb and how do you know if you live in one? Also, why are they evil, according to some scholars?

Fragmented Government Structure

The most basic definition for governmental fragmentation is "a system with a large number of local governments"[1] that individually provides services to citizens. Such structures exist on a subnational level (within one county, region, or state) as well as encompassing an entire sovereign nation like the United States. Fragmentation studies naturally dovetail at some level with

---

1. Dolan, "Local Government Fragmentation," 28.

suburban proliferation research. For example, studies have linked suburban causality with racism or at least what some scholars refer to as a NIMBYistic (not in my backyard) worldview that equates inner city "diversity" with the urban ills of crime, poverty, and ineffective schools.[2] The solution rests on exclusionary zoning which critics label as racially motivated.[3] Furthermore, suburban proliferation also carries the charge of moving jobs, training, and opportunity to the outer ring of most urban regions while increasing dependency on car ownership for socioeconomic groups that cannot afford private transportation.[4]

Conversely, fragmentation specifically refers to the number of local governments. Therefore, this chapter (and book) examines the consequences both positive and negative from thousands of local jurisdictions providing services to their own citizens. While this is probably the first time you have encountered government fragmentation in your lifetime, rest assured that this evolutionary development or structure receives substantial attention and analysis from several scholarly fronts. First and foremost, fragmentation is a federalism issue subject to examination and measurement for causation and impact by federal scholars in a comparative framework. A federation includes multiple layers of government (federal, state, and local), with each layer enjoying some level of unfettered policy authority. In other words, there are certain policy arenas where the central level cannot tell the subnational level what to do. Which arenas? The answer to that question not only varies among federations but can change or evolve over time within the same country. Essentially, a federation requires that subnational units enjoy some level of policy, political, and fiscal autonomy.[5]

Federalism studies remain concerned primarily with intergovernmental relations issues such as federal grant programs designed to support or (typically) direct state and local policy on an array of issues.[6] Overall, studies examine how state and local programs such as secondary education are funded, implemented, and delivered when multiple layers contribute to programs. Likewise, multiple disciplines under the large umbrella of urban affairs address fragmentation. Granted, most studies focus on causes

2. Denton and Massey, *American Apartheid*, 9–16.
3. Downs, "Some Realities about Sprawl," 960.
4. Kain, "Housing Segregation," 475; Wilson, *When Work Disappears*, 111.
5. Hueglin and Fenna, *Comparative Federalism*, 11
6. Elazar, *American Federalism*, 48–50; Kincaid, "Values and Tradeoffs in Federalism," 29; Watts, *Comparing Federal Systems*, 43.

PART I: THE CURRENT TEXAS MUNICIPAL STRUCTURE

and consequences of sprawl and suburbanization which is a topic for the next section. Conversely, urban economists analyze and measure the ability of municipalities to fund their own services.[7] Additionally, economics is a proper discipline for determining whether hundreds of smaller cities or towns can more effectively and efficiently provide public goods or services to an ever expanding metropolitan region than consolidated government.[8] Again, we get ahead of ourselves as this is a topic for chapter 5.

How do we determine whether fragmentation is prevalent at the national or subnational level? The many vested disciplines have provided numerous fragmentation measurements. Measurements typically determine either the total number of government units per metropolitan area or the total number of units per 100,000 people. Studies utilizing these tools determined that the midwestern and northeastern United States possessed the highest levels of American fragmentation while the West and Southeast possess were least fragmented. For example, 80 percent of the metropolitan regions (Pittsburgh, Minneapolis, St. Paul, St. Louis, and Cincinnati) with at least ten local governments per 100,000 people were midwest regions. These older studies identified the Midwest and the Northeast as the most fragmented regions. Conversely, the western region included several metropolitan areas such as San Francisco (1.7 per 100,000 people), Los Angeles (1.2 per 100,000), and San Diego (.7 per 100,000), which might be described as either monocentric or de facto monocentric regions.[9]

An additional, simpler measurement that also indicates the existence of fragmentation is local jurisdiction per capita. This involves simply dividing the total population by the number of local jurisdictions. Table 2–1 compares chosen American state regions utilizing both approaches. The statewide comparisons support the regional findings from earlier studies. The Midwest remains most fragmented as Ohio (33.31), Pennsylvania (38.56) and especially Illinois (54.20) lead the country in creating new municipalities. Conversely, California (8.78) and Florida (11.88) make do with fewer local jurisdictions while New York (17.82) and Texas (20.47) remain in the middle. Note that this is population divided by every county, city/town, school district, and special district in each metropolitan region.

---

7. O'Sullivan, *Urban Economics*, 333.

8. Olson, "The Principle of 'Fiscal Equivalence,'" 479; Boadway and Shah, *Fiscal Federalism*, 241; O'Sullivan, *Urban Economics*, 334.

9. Orfield, *American Metropolitics*, 132.

How does this model look in Texas? First, Texas clearly passes the fragmentation test. This provides a nice segue to the second point that while Texas is the second most populous state in the union, it also covers the largest land mass in the continental United States. Indeed, the state is very spread out and possesses a low population density which renders the fragmentation ratio that much more remarkable. Finally, the more fragmented states include much smaller populations overall with New York being the next largest, but still nearly six million behind. There is really only one state that compares population-wise. California has a comparable population, but is less fragmented.

Table 2–1:

Fragmentation Comparison for Largest American States

State	Population	Municipalities	Ratio	Per 100k
USA	321,418,820	90,107	3,567	28.03
California	37,253,956	4,426	8,417	11.88
Florida	18,801,310	1,651	11,388	8.78
Illinois	12,830,632	6,954	1,845	54.20
New York	19,378,102	3,454	5,610	17.82
Ohio	11,536,504	3,843	3,002	33.31
Pennsylvania	12,702,379	4,898	2,593	38.56
Texas	25,145,561	5,148	4,885	20.47

Source: U.S. Census Bureau. "American Community Survey";
U.S. Census Bureau. *Government Organization.*

This static data proves interesting but perhaps misses an important point: the Sunbelt examples are growing in population while the fragmented, rust-belt examples are facing declining population numbers. How do state and local leaders manage these challenges? This book obviously examines Texas as a case study but it will be interesting to see whether heavily fragmented states can continue funding municipalities as the population (and tax base) continues to decrease, while also monitoring how states such as Florida and Texas manage the "blessing" of increased populations.

How does the United States fragmentation picture compare to other federations? Table 2–2 provides the "application ratio" for five large federations. While Germany (15.6) and Spain (17.4) practice a high level of fragmentation (especially compared to American states), the ratios pale in comparison to the US (28.3).

Table 2–2

Comparing Fragmentation among Large Federations

Country	Population	Municipalities	Ratio	Per 100k
USA	321,418,820	90,107	3,567	28.0
Canada	3,200,000	3,700	865	116
Germany	81,800,000.00	12,749	6,416	15.6
Spain	46,500,000	8,118	5,728	17.46

Source: Forum of Federations, "Partnering Countries."

Suburb Spotting

The modern American, middle-class experience is suburban. This residential area/district/city/town/state-of-mind category enjoys a large, checkered public relations portfolio. Suburbs have been the primary subject of books (both scholarly and trade), movies, comics, cartoons, and songs. With that said, the PR effort is only successful if you subscribe to the "no coverage is bad coverage" ethos. As mentioned earlier, critics savage these simple outlying units as bland, homogenized, over-manicured, inefficient, tax revenue hoarding, and white. So very white. According to critics, suburbs are soul-sucking, racist (yes), mall magnets destroying America.[10]

This is not *another* book about the suburbs (and a text analyzing municipal government innovation hardly screams screenplay worthy). However, one cannot tell the American municipal story without addressing the impact suburban sprawl has had on local governance. Indeed, the suburban reality yielded our fragmented world.

10. Brooks, "Patio Man and Sprawl People;" Kuntsler, *The Geography of Nowhere*.

So, how do we define or identify suburbs? Reputable urban affairs scholar Kenneth Jackson focuses on 4 characteristics:[11]

1. Population density

While people move to the suburbs for a variety of reasons, space is clearly a significant factor. The suburban vision (or critique of said vision) is unrecognizable absent large, half acre plus lots with large front yards and spacious backyards housing swing sets, or forts hidden from the HOA.

What is population density, you may ask? The better question is how one calculates population density. The formula is incredibly simple: Total population divided by livable square miles (we exclude bodies of water, for instance). For example, my current town of residence has a population of 32,344 living on 47.6 incorporated miles which equals a population density of 679.49.[12] This is a pretty typical suburban number.

2. Homeownership/Owner Occupied Dwellings

Suburban dwellings are more likely to be unattached single family homes owned by the occupants, according to Jackson. For example, 54 percent of all residential units in urban Dallas county are classified as detached single units while 70 percent of all residential dwellings in suburban Collin County fit into that category.[13]

3. Middle-Class Socioeconomic Status

Young, college-educated parents with mid-to-high income earnings comprise the traditional suburban population. In fact, critics argue that suburbs are havens for these families from crime-riddled central cities. However, the family still benefits from the economic core of the large city without contributing to its tax base.[14]

---

11. Jackson, *Crabgrass Frontier,* 4–11.
12. U.S. Census Bureau. "American Community Survey."
13. U.S. Census Bureau. "2010 Census."
14. Rusk, *Cities Without Suburbs,* 23–25.

4. Commuting Distance

Most people equate suburbs with the distance from the region's major city or largest city. However, the most important geographic measure would be the average distance residents travel in their daily commute to work. You may ask what it means if most of the residents work in the same city they live in, or if people from smaller towns actually commute to a suburb. Well, that suburb may no longer be a suburb.

My Two Cents (Or Two Additional Characteristics)

Jackson's methodology remains an excellent tool for identifying suburbs and this author would never quibble with these criteria. With that said, there are additional characteristics that could aid our suburban spotting efforts. In fact, my suburban identification model would also include two additional criteria flowing from these characteristics.

First, ethnic statistics (or homogeneity) essentially pairs with socio-economic status. My big picture argument holds that the model should examine all forms of diversity including economic, racial/ethnic, age, and income. After all, critics historically slam suburbs as repositories for "white flight" where middle class folks escape from inner city evils and danger.[15] We need to broaden this category.

Finally, while total commuting distance certainly has my respect, "net commuters" might serve our purpose. What is "net commuters," you ask, and how do we calculate such a number? The objective would be determining whether a city has as many workers who commute to an employer within city limits as it has citizens commuting to a larger city. Suburbs should not have more workers commuting to it than from it on a daily basis.

These categories develop a substantive profile of suburban units. We can (and will) compare suburbs to other cities or towns based on these criteria. Also, we can (and will) compare a suburb historically to determine whether it has become more or less suburban in nature. For example, does historical census data indicate that Plano, Texas, a massive "suburb" outside Dallas, has become more diverse or experienced reduced homeownership?

While this approach is sound, one major caveat is in order. Scholars have identified the characteristics that make a suburb a suburb. However, they have accomplished this feat without actually developing quantitative

15. Rusk, *Cities Without Suburbs*, 23–25.

standards. For example, how many miles must citizens commute on a weekly basis? What percentage of residents must be homeowners? Research is strangely silent on the numbers. Chapter 4 analyzes the profile categories in greater detail.

Fragmentation and its Challenges

Our charge remains determining how might sprawl-driven fragmentation compromise the quality (and perhaps the very delivery) of these government functions we have come to expect and take for granted, and what cities should do about it? The performance issues include weak service quality, town's failure to provide services, and ignoring regional issues. The first two concerns describe challenges facing jurisdictions struggling with revenue issues due to a small, lower income tax base, while regional issues receive scant attention from city managers concerned about their own employers (the town's residents).[16] The excess cost issues stem from multiple jurisdictions providing the same service. These standard critiques revolve around the old economic standards of efficiency and effectiveness. People frequently confuse these two standards but we define and distinguish these and other criteria in chapter 6.

Budget Woes

Whether driven by fragmentation or fiscal reality, American municipalities are currently facing unprecedented fiscal challenges as these units grapple with reduced federal and state support as well as an increasingly globalized economy that breeds fiscal uncertainty. The National League of Cities determined via a survey of city finance officers that the municipal sector experienced a shortfall between $56 billion and $83 billion during the fiscal years of 2010–2012. Likewise, the National Association of Counties found that 86 percent of all counties experienced a shortfall during the fiscal year of 2010. Additionally, fiscal challenges obviously impact municipal operations. A recent survey of local officials found that 57.7 percent of surveyed cities were planning reductions in staff benefits with 60.3 percent intending

---

16. See Part III, 100.

to freeze wages.[17] In fact, 43.6 percent indicated staffing reductions "were almost certainly or likely" during that fiscal year.[18]

Decreased Revenue Combines with Increased Demand: The Population Conundrum

Granted, these associations conducted surveys right after (or during according to which economist you are listening to) the "Great Recession" which yielded higher unemployment, foreclosures, and bankruptcies that sapped tax revenue and lightened public coffers. The economic condition has improved since that calamity and could at least be described as stable, if not growing. Granted, economic cycles remain a permanent fixture of the American experience and smart public executives plan for the inevitable recession during the inevitable growth spurt. However, 2008–2009 represented the economic trough for the last twenty-five years which exacerbated fears and budgetary woes.

However, those same executives are facing unprecedented challenges. These emerging realities challenge the traditional modes of public service delivery while requiring local governments to discover innovative solutions that yield more effective and efficient service provisions and support services that reduce budgetary costs. For example, population trends forecast that the total population will increase to 438 million by 2050.[19] Demographers believe immigration will account for 82 percent of the population increase which leads to an increasingly diverse citizen base. Additionally, the population will be considerably older which increases the population dependent on social services.[20]

Essentially, booming populations tax government resources. Local schools must adapt which typically means more teachers and administrators working in new buildings and campuses. This is merely the tip of the infrastructure iceberg as cities and regions must address transportation networks to manage congestion and commuting time. Some metropolitan regions will respond more slowly as their public transportation may be small or non-existent. Building or adding to a massive highway network

---

17. National League of Cities, "City Fiscal Issues for 2010."
18. BakerTilly, *Local Governments Scramble*.
19. U.S. Census Bureau, "American Community Survey." This would result in a 48 percent increase for the half century from 2000–2050.
20. Potter, *Population Projections*, 6.

could take years, increase congestion during the development phase, and might prove archaic upon completion. Finally, how will local jurisdictions address rising demand for utilities?

The easy answer to such concerns is raising taxes. Meet increased costs with increased revenue. However, what if tax rates are already at a maximum? New or increased taxes might weaken economic growth. Additionally, elected officials are loath to introduce the topic lest they emerge unemployed. Therefore, metropolitan regions or municipalities could lose citizens who seek a cheaper tax base or a city with higher quality services.

Most readers have yet to envision a metropolitan region as a marketplace where consumers choose where to live based on the basket of public goods and services. However, public choice theory posits such a market driven by rational citizens pursuing the optimal results for their families. This brings us to a discussion of Charles Tiebout.

In his classic public choice theory article, "A Pure Theory of Local Expenditures," Tiebout put forth a model for determining the optimum expenditure level for public goods.[21] The model rests on two assumptions. First, an individual is a self-interested utility maximizer who knows his or her goals, can rank them, and will choose the option (or options) expected to maximize individual benefits and minimize individual costs when faced with an opportunity to choose among preferences. Additionally, public choice rests on methodological individualism which posits that only individuals, not collectives, make choices. Therefore, public choice rejects public interest since collective decisions are merely an aggregation of individual choices. The Tiebout hypothesis suggests that fragmentation stimulates competition, creates incentives for efficiency and responsiveness, and should lower spending.

According to Tiebout, mobility provides "the local public goods counterpart to the private market's shopping trip," in that citizen-consumers shop around for preferred tax-service packages, competitive pressures force producers (local governments and public agencies) to respond to citizen preferences.[22] He argues there is a market of local governments where mobile consumer citizens shop around for the communities that best fit their preferences. The competition among communities forces jurisdictions to provide public goods at the most efficient level. Tiebout hypothesizes that many agencies competing horizontally (across jurisdictions) and vertically

---

21. Tiebout, "A Pure Theory of Local Expenditures," 416–24.
22. Tiebout, "A Pure Theory of Local Expenditures," 422.

(within jurisdictions) will provide a higher-quality service at a lower price, and be more attuned to citizens' preferences than large bureaucracies in centralized jurisdictions.[23]

Tiebout made several assumptions regarding individual actors in developing his model. According to the model, citizens are perfectly mobile and able to move from community to community. They are also highly informed about tax service packages across jurisdictions. While he did not seriously propose that these conditions existed in reality, they were nonetheless integrated as necessary simplifying assumptions to make the model tractable. These assumptions and the model support the fragmented structure. Citizens in fragmented government settings will be more informed about public services than those in centralized government settings. They are also more likely to exit if they are dissatisfied with the services. Finally, since citizens can make choices about tax-service packages, they will be more satisfied with the services they do receive. This market knowledge and mobility allows citizens to act on that knowledge and creates a competitive market which requires local jurisdictions to provide higher quality services with greater efficiency and at a competitive price.[24]

Tiebout's model has both enjoyed praise and received criticism since he originally published it in 1956. Again, the concept of a municipal market is difficult for most readers to grasp. However, the model implications prove very instructive regarding the future challenges facing city manager, city councils, county commissioners, etc. Suburbia exists because people are escaping from something whether it be poor services, taxes, crime, squalor, or even diversity. The bottom line for local governments is those who leave take their (often middle class) tax dollars with them leaving, in some cases, citizens who need more from the system of services than they can contribute. They cost more than their ability to pay, in other words.

Summary: Consequences for Twenty-First Century Texas

This chapter explored the traditional American municipal structure in urban metropolitan regions. The primary characteristic is fragmentation with 90,000 local jurisdictions or one unit for every 3,419 citizens. Additionally, most of the jurisdictions are suburbs based on the accepted criteria of the suburban model. While fragmentation refers narrowly to polycentric

---

23. Frederickson, et al., *Public Administration Theory Primer*, 205.
24. Tiebout, "A Pure Theory of Local Expenditures," 418.

government and suburbanization (to a broader analysis including residential trends and cultural impact), both exist due to sprawl and migration by hub city residents looking to escape urban blight and rural populations seeking access to the urban economic engine. While this author appreciates the robust topic that is suburbia, the primary focus of this work is local government which directs our focus to fragmentation, or polycentrism.

With that said, the dynamic remains forever controversial. Polycentrism champions have long espoused the market-driven Tiebout model where residents can "vote with their feet," as they seek the ideal residential location based on their optimal basket of public goods and services they have rationally determined to be most important to them. Conversely, the critiques are numerous. Fragmentation critics charge the structure with facilitating racial segregation (and possibly racism itself), sapping large cities of tax dollars where they are most needed, and reducing focus on emerging regional concerns. Overall, fragmentation fosters ineffective government performance among smaller, poorer communities and inefficiency among suburbs.

While the theoretical battle wages on, the structure and the local units comprising it face threats on several fronts. A rapidly increasing, diverse population will increase demand for infrastructure and social services; at the same time, local governments can no longer count on traditional revenue sources to increase commensurate with said demand. Local jurisdictions are already feeling the pain as several indicated budget shortfalls, cutbacks, and layoffs were pending.

Additionally, Texas remains highly fragmented and suburbanized. Measurements indicate that Texas maintains a highly fragmented municipal structure compared to states of similar size. Granted, no other state truly combines the population size and land mass of Texas save perhaps California.

It is also important to note that the polycentrism could well be even more pronounced when focused on the urban regions. The next chapter examines this possibility while explaining how the Texas population grew in the post-World War II world. The chapter will illustrate that Texas political and municipal historically have addressed urban development and possess a long tradition of managing explosive urban growth and sprawl. With that said, this chapter clearly illustrates that the future presents challenges without precedent.

3

Why Texas?

WHY DISCUSS TEXAS AND the local governments serving Texans? Texas history is so compelling that it has achieved a status akin to mythology. However, does the Texas Revolution and the wildcatting, rugged individualistic image Texans have embraced truly impact the 5,167 local jurisdictions serving those Texans? Does a connection exist between the Texas culture and the forces shaping the population and economic climate?

This chapter identifies the challenges facing local governments by tracing the burgeoning Texas population explosion that has marched unabated since the 1940s. This exploration mandates an examination of the factors driving explosive population growth and economic development, with the spotlight hitting Daniel Elazar's lauded political culture research. The cultural and economic findings support his thesis that Texans prioritize high performing, limited government that is local, decentralized, and inexpensive. While the state benefitted from dynamic growth, demographic projections suggest alarming concerns requiring creative solutions. However, Texas' political culture stifles needed reform and innovation.

Explosive Population Growth

The Texas population is growing at a much faster rate than the rest of the country and that trend is expected to continue. Granted, explosive population growth is hardly a recent Texas trend. Table 3–1 summarizes the population growth from 1950–2010 compared to overall population growth for the entire nation. The sixty-year period saw Texas population increase from 7.7 million people to over 25 million. The growth was also consistent as the population grew by over 15 percent every decade. The data leads to several observations. First, the source of the growth has changed over the decades. The early (pre-1980) driving force was natural growth (simply, birth rate minus death rate). Texans, on average, were starting families at younger ages. The entire country, flush from World War II and a recovering economy, experienced this growth during these postwar years.

However, "net migration," especially the activity since the 1980s, sets Texas apart from the rest of the country. A simple equation that subtracts people leaving the state from those moving to it measures net migration. Overall, 55 percent of the Texas population growth since 1950 is attributable to migration. This is especially true since 1980, where migration accounts for over 65 percent of the population growth. The warm climate and job market combination set Texas on a pattern of growth unmatched by other states during this period. Basically, people never stopped moving to Texas.[1]

Table 3–1

Population Growth for Texas and United States

1950–2010

Year	Texas Population	Change Numerical	%	United States Population	Change Numerical	%	Year
1940	6,414,824			131,669,275			1940
1950	7,711,194	1,296,370	20.21%	150,697,361	19,028,086	14.45%	1950
1960	9,579,677	1,868,483	24.23%	179,323,175	28,625,814	19.00%	1960
1970	11,196,730	1,617,053	16.88%	203,302,031	23,978,856	13.37%	1970
1980	14,229,191	3,032,461	27.08%	226,545,805	23,243,774	11.43%	1980
1990	16,986,510	2,757,319	19.38%	248,709,873	22,164,068	9.78%	1990
2000	20,851,820	3,865,310	22.76%	281,421,906	32,712,033	13.15%	2000
2010	25,145,561	4,293,741	20.59%	308,745,538	27,323,632	9.71%	2010
		18,730,737	392%		177,076,263	10.6%	
						234%	

Source: Texas State Data Center and Office of the State Demographer.

1. Potter, *Population Projections for Texas*, 2.

Amazingly, various projections of Texas population trends identify an emerging explosion similar to the 1950s and 1960s that could last for decades. The U.S. Census Bureau projects the statewide population to increase from the 2010 level of 25.6 million to thirty-three million by 2030, an increase of 28.9 percent.[2] Likewise, the Texas state demographer projects a population increase ranging between nine and eighteen million with the variance dependent upon the rate of immigration. The report identified several target points for 2030 based on previous immigration trends.[3] These projections easily outpace projected growth patterns for the country as a whole with most analysts arguing that the population increase will deliver increases in both employment and household income.[4]

In fact, the explosive growth has already started. Table 3–2 compares the population growth for the ten largest states (and the entire country) from 2010–2015. While five years is a very small sample size for population analysis, the Texas population has already grown by 2.3 million residents since the last official census which yields a 9 percent increase. This more than doubles the nationwide growth rate of 4 percent, and Florida is the only state experiencing a similar growth rate at 8 percent.[5] This recent growth phase includes the additional source of immigration which creates additional challenges which we discuss toward the end of this chapter.

---

2. Gaines, "Looming Boom," 3–4; U.S. Census Bureau. "2010 Census."

3. Gaines, "Looming Boom," 3. Texas State Data Center, *Population Projections for Texas*.

4. Gaines, "Looming Boom," 6.

5. U.S. Census Bureau, *Interim State Population Projections*.

Table 3–2

Population Growth for the Ten Largest American States From 2010–2015

State	2010	2015	Growth	%
USA	308,000,000	321,418,820	13,418,820	4%
California	37253956	39,144,818	1,890,862	5%
Florida	18801310	20,271,272	1,469,962	8%
Illinois	12830632	12859995	29363	0%
New York	19,378,102	19,795,791	417,689	2%
Ohio	11,536,504	11,613,423	76,919	1%
Pennsylvania	12,702,379	12,802,503	100,124	1%
Texas	25,145,801	27,469,114	2,323,313	9%

Sources: U.S. Census Bureau, Population Projections for 2010–2015

Where is the growth occurring? The earlier population increases in central cities and urban areas easily outpaced statewide population growth in Texas. While growth is widespread, the urban areas will experience more growth, particularly the Central Texas Triangle that includes the Dallas/Fort Worth/Arlington Metropolitan Statistical Area (MSA), the Houston MSA, and the San Antonio MSA. Therefore, urban spatial design and the provision of public goods and services will remain vital to urbanized regions.[6] Table 3–3 compares the population increase of three major Texas cities (Dallas, Houston, and Austin) to the entire state for the same sixty-year period. As the table summarizes, the growth rate for these three municipalities far outpaces the robust statewide rate. Also, readers should note that the cities comprise 20 percent of the total statewide growth.

The growth rate is astounding but what is the cause? The Sunbelt region as a whole experienced massive migration for a variety of reasons. While newly transplanted Midwesterners found the sunny warm weather attractive, economic history found that families migrate toward jobs and career opportunities. Therefore, growing regions historically enjoy vibrant, growing economies. Of course, economic history also reminds us that

---

6. Gaines, "Looming Boom," 2.

vibrant economic regions enjoy certain advantages built into the people, culture, and resources within the region.[7] How does the Texas socioeconomic profile speak to the state's economic potential?

Table 3–3

Population Growth for Dallas, Houston, and Austin from 1940–2010

| Dallas | | | Houston | | | Austin | | |
Population	Numerical Increase	%	Population	Numerical Increase	%	Population	Numerical Increase	%
294,734			384,514			87,930		
434,462	139,728	47%	596,163	211,649	55%	132,459	44,529	51%
679,684	245,222	56%	938,219	342,056	57%	186,545	54,086	41%
844,401	164,717	24%	1,232,802	294,583	31%	253,539	66,994	36%
904,078	59,677	7%	1,595,138	362,336	29%	345,890	92,351	36%
1,006,977	102,899	11%	1,630,553	35,415	2%	465,622	119,732	35%
1,188,580	181,603	18%	1,953,631	323,078	20%	656,562	190,940	41%
1,197,816	9,236	1%	2,100,263	146,632	8%	790,390	133,828	20%
	903,082	5%		1,715,749	9%		702,460	4%
		406%			546%			899%

Source: Texas State Data Center.

Political Culture

The second most populous American city, Houston, has positioned itself as the corporate epicenter of the American (perhaps global) energy industry. Oil and gas hardly tells the Houston economic story. For example, The Port of Houston and the Houston Ship Channel serves an ever-growing maritime industry. In fact, the Port of Houston ranks first in foreign tonnage received and third in domestic tonnage which solidifies its status as a major destination in the global economy.

7. Levy, *Contemporary Urban Planning*, 9–12.

The Houston Channel sits adjacent to critical locations in Texas lore. Specifically, The San Jacinto Battleground location and its monument honors the sight where Texas won its independence from Mexico. Friends and acquaintances hailing from other states (or countries) often marvel (complain might be a more accurate verb) over the arrogance and prides native Texans clearly possess related to their home state. The events honored on the battle site perhaps serve as the genesis of said arrogance.

The San Jacinto Battleground symbolizes how Texas history is so very unique. The American origin story reveals a revolutionary streak that resulted in a successful fight for freedom from a tyrannical nation. This origin serves not merely as a source of pride and patriotism for Americans but impacts their very psyche.

Texans experience a dual independence psych boost. This is thanks to the Texas Revolution, which freed the state from the shackles of Mexican oppression to brief sovereign republic status for one decade. While one decade is a brief period of sovereignty, it is ten years more than any other state. This history is well known to anyone recognizing the existence of the Alamo.

Texas independence, and the fight to enjoy and preserve liberty, shapes the traditions, culture, and political norms the state carries today. The Lone Star State possesses unique economic, cultural, and political characteristics which set it apart from the rest of the country. Additionally, the population and demographic changes impacting the state merely contribute to the differences. Chapter 3 embraces these differences by initially examining the cultural and economic characteristics of Texas. The chapter proceeds to identify the population and diversity trends that may eventually challenge these norms.

One of the deep reservoirs of policy analysis involves identifying distinctive beliefs between regions or subnational units and how these differences translate into policy. State and local taxation provide one example, as citizens in the Atlantic and West Coast regions carry high state income burdens while several southern states (including Texas) have no income tax at all.[8] Criminal punishment provides another strong example as roughly twenty states no longer utilize the death penalty while Texas has carried out over 40 percent of all American executions since 1976. Different cultures yield distinct ideologies driving policy results and priorities.[9]

---

8. According to the Tax Foundation, The other states are Alaska, Florida, Nevada, South Dakota, Washington, and Wyoming.

9. Death Penalty Information Center, Executions State by State, https://

Noted federal scholar Daniel Elazar examined these distinctive policy approaches and determined something more permanent drove these results. He termed this permanent belief pattern: political culture. Political culture is like the climate—fixed and unchanging—while ideology is more akin to fickle weather. Like many government concepts, political culture is hard to define in a succinct, clear manner absent providing examples, graphs, etc. With that said, it is probably best defined as a framework of deeply rooted values and beliefs held by a society regarding the role, obligations, and limits on government, as well as its relationship between the people served and their rights, role, and responsibility.[10] That is as succinct as we can get for now.

In addition to developing political culture analysis, Elazar identified three distinct culture categories: moralistic, individualists, and traditional. The moralistic culture views government as a force for good that can erase inequality, inequity, and economic injustice. This is what I refer to as the bureaucratic superhero model fighting a utilitarian battle, with good society as the key objective. Public service is a civic duty and should be conducted as such. Policy decisions should benefit the community, as opposed to the cronyistic model that rewards friends and family. Finally, this culture eschews a top-down structure in favor of a democratic participation and decision-making approach that prioritizes inclusion and empowering voices that rarely enjoy a place at the table. Portland, Oregon is the optimal example of a region built on this idealistic belief system.[11]

The individualistic culture is perhaps the least idealistic culture. This belief system espouses minimal government interference in the economic or social lives of individuals. Private concerns trump public or community concerns which renders the good society an impractical waste of resources. This culture is perhaps the most pragmatic and cynical in accepting corruption or dirty politics as not only a reality but a preference. Do you have a friend who drolly laments that all politicians are corrupt and society just needs to deal with it? Your friend fits best in this culture. Illinois is the perfect case study for the individual culture.[12]

While these cultures speak to either nurturing or at least managing for social change, the traditional culture advocates for the status quo.

---

deathpenaltyinfo.org/state_by_state, reviewed on January 13, 2018.

10. Elazar, *American Federalism*, 81.
11. Elazar, *American Federalism*, 89–91.
12. Elazar, *American Federalism*, 86–88.

Political leaders and structures play a more custodial role in achieving maintenance of the existing hierarchy. Government is limited and small since its purpose rarely deviates beyond keeping the power base intact. The role of citizens is incredibly limited and superfluous and there is really no place for innovation. According to Elazar, this culture dominates the south and your parents.[13]

Which culture describes Texas? According to Elazar, Texas is a hybrid caught between individualistic and traditionalistic norms.[14] Granted, he produced these labels over forty years ago. Is this description still accurate? Texas has remained a one-party state for well over a century, even though the majority party status changed hands from Democrat to Republican in 1994.[15] Additionally, the majority party (whether Democrat or GOP) was always the safe, conservative party comprised of economic and electoral elites fighting to maintain the status quo.[16] Additionally, political intrigue is typically reserved for primary season which clearly limits voter influence, as the general election is typically insignificant. Voter turnout numbers historically confirm the irrelevance of general elections.

The cultural combination is hardly conducive to transformative governance structure or municipal innovation. The citizen base historically mistrusts government activity beyond basic transactional activities and calls for a focus on essential government functions. This conservative attitude prefers decentralized government structure where power is diluted among smaller entities. Therefore, the response chosen by state and local leaders to address the mid-century population explosion was consistent with the cultural framework.

The state's history is steeped in rugged individualist mythology as well as the traditional preference for transactional leadership that maintains the status quo power structure. This mythology flowed from the historical development of the Lone Star State. A brief analysis of this history is beneficial for two reasons (although the second reason is more vital for the purposes of this book). First, we gain a deeper understanding of Elazar's cultural diagnosis for Texas as we examine it within the historical context during the "framing era" of Texas. In other words, we view traditionalism and individualism in action as the structure for government at all levels, which is

13. Elazar, *American Federalism*, 92–93.
14. Elazar, *American Federalism*, 96.
15. Tannahill, *Texas Governmen*, 32.
16. Tannahill, *Texas Government*, 133–34.

codified via the framers of the Texas Constitution. More importantly, again for this book, the context provides historical analysis of how these cultures influenced the original development of municipal Texas.

Political Culture and the Texas Economy

How does culture impact the economic fortunes of the state? State taxation policy limits government influence as the state and local tax burden for Texans is very low, including no income tax and low business or corporate taxes.[17] Table 3–3 compares the state and local tax burden facing Texans with residents of Illinois and the District of Columbia. The state budget and bureaucracy is relatively sparse. The corporate worlds and potential residents alike find low tax, minimal regulatory environments attractive and Texas certainly fits that expectation. Finally, laws such as employment or landlord-tenant statutes are business friendly.[18] Therefore, Elazar's description remains accurate.

Table 3–4

State and Local Tax Burden Comparison between DC, Illinois, and Texas

Category	Washington, DC	Illinois	Texas
State Income Tax Rate	8.95%	4.5%	0
State and Local Burden	10.6%	11%	7.6%
Rank	10	5	46

Source: Tax Foundation. "Center for State Tax Policy."

Cost of Living

Low tax rates also contribute to a comparatively low cost of living. Table 3–5 compares the costs of a basket of typical living expenses between three cities for a family of four. The first is the nation's capital, Washington

17. Tax Foundation, "Center for State Tax Policy."
18. Tannahill, *Texas Government*, 27–29.

DC. Families living in the DC area need $106,493 annually to pay for basic expenses which is the highest rate in the country. The second city, Chicago, Illinois, is the second largest city in the country. The average basket cost for a Chicago family is much less at $71,995 per annum. However, a similar sized family living in Houston, the nation's fourth largest city and the most populous city in Texas, would only need $60,608 to fund the same living expenses.[19]

Table 3–5

Cost of Living Comparison between DC, Chicago, and Houston

Expenses	Washington DC	Chicago	Houston
Housing	$1,469	$979	$926
Food	$782	$789	$782
Child Care	$2,597	$1,294	$835
Transportation	$620	$583	$583
Health Care	$747	$702	$694
Other	$1,087	$851	$825
Taxes	$1,572	$809	$407
Total	$106,493	$71,995	$60,608

Source: "Family Budget Calculator." Economic Policy Institute.

The living cost impact is profound. This is especially true in a globalized economy. Large corporations and firms in a globalized context enjoy flexibility in operation location. This affords Texas a competitive advantage as workers can produce the same output and perform the same job, yet their needs are satisfied with a smaller salary. This contributes to the population explosion as families pursue career opportunities in a state with a burgeoning economic growth.[20]

19. Economic Policy Institute. "Family Budget Calculator." *Resources, Economic Policy Institute*, November 15, 2017, http://www.epi.org/resources/budget/.
20. Bluestone, Stevenson, and Williams, *The Urban Experience*, 50–51.

Several family expense items deserve special mention. For example, child care costs in Houston are far cheaper than the other two cities. The relatively young Texas population may partially explain this discrepancy. The state population includes as a far higher percentage of residents within traditional child bearing age range.[21] The large concentration can support numerous child care companies and services. Additionally, Texans pay considerably less in state and local taxes as discussed in the culture section.

Otherwise, future studies may well focus on health care and housing. Of course, family health care costs continue to increase and remains on the forefront of political debate. With that said, the policy argument is more national and carries less interest as a comparison among states. However, analysts will monitor the Texas housing market closely as population growth could easily challenge supply levels and construction pace, thereby increasing housing costs. This is especially true regarding urban regions.[22]

Education

While low taxes coupled with limited government drives business growth, education provides the tools of opportunity. Education and training simply increases individual marketability and access to high-paying jobs. Firms considering relocation will also prioritize locations with well-trained workforces.[23] This typically equates to advanced degrees from selective universities, although human capital accrues in various shapes and forms.[24]

Frankly, the Texas academic picture is a bit muddled. Merely 81.9 percent of all Texans over the age of twenty-five received their high school diploma, which ranks forty-ninth nationally.[25] The percentage of citizens completing bachelor's degrees is less onerous and still somewhat unimpressive. Overall, 18 percent of Texans over the age of twenty-five graduated from college which ranks twenty-ninth nationally. The table also compares results for the top seven Texas counties and includes the major city from each county, along with the five largest American cities outside of Texas and

---

21. Tannahill, *Texas Government*, 17–20.
22. Gaines, "Looming Boom," 4.
23. Bluestone, Stevenson, and Williams, 53–56.
24. Bluestone, Stevenson, and Williams, 250-53.
25. Fiftieth? California with 81.8 percent. A demographic trend connects these results which we address shortly.

their counties. Three Texas cities (Houston, Dallas, and San Antonio) are among the ten largest American cities based on population.

How might the Texas political culture influence academic attainment? The individualistic culture influences government spending levels including education spending. Texas ranks thirty-sixth in the nation in elementary-secondary spending per capita. Additionally, the federal government and local school districts provide the balance of education funding as the state of Texas ranks forty-seventh in per capita spending among the states.[26] Granted, spending does not guarantee quality but these figures shine a light on state priorities

Changes that Demand Attention

The Texas political culture and the policy evidences of said culture have remained relatively static for decades even through explosive population growth and economic development. However, recent population trends threaten that consistency as well as exert a new burden on public services. The current growth pattern is re-shaping the Texas population. In 2000, 53 percent of all Texans identified as white or Anglo. The percentage dropped to 45 percent by 2010 and the demographer's analysis projects a continued decrease to 32 percent by 2030. Conversely, the Hispanic population has experienced and will continue to experience massive growth. The ethnic group comprised 32 percentof the 2000 population which increased to 38 percent by 2010. By 2030, over 50 percent of the Texas population will be Hispanic.[27]

The demographic trends forebode significant consequences for the state economy and, by extension, local government if the education disparity between whites and Hispanics persists. If the trend continues, the State Data Center calculated that 30 percent of the Texas labor force will not have a high school diploma by 2040 (compared to 19 percent in 2000). Additionally, 38 percent of all Texas households will live on incomes of $25,000 or less by 2040 while families earning in excess of $100,000 will decrease by one-fourth from 12 percent to 9 percent (noteinflation impact).[28] Overall, studies find a direct connection between

---

26. Tannahill, *Texas Government*.
27. Potter, *Population Projections*, 2–3.
28. Potter, *Population Projections*, 16–20.

education levels and earnings which spells peril for the Texas economy.[29] More to the point, Texas municipalities face a future of meeting heightened expectations with fewer resources.[30]

Exactly how will these trends impact Texas local governments? A population increase naturally escalates demand for public goods and services. Transportation networks should experience increased congestion, school districts which rely heavily on local tax revenues will become increasingly overburdened, and local planning will become more critical and perhaps more politically charged. Additionally, several regions within the state could suffer from an inadequate water supply as well as experiencing increased costs for the provision of other utilities such as sewage service, natural gas, and electricity. These issues could adversely impact economic growth and quality of life for Texas residents.[31]

Summary

Chapter 3 identified the Texas population and cultural characteristics impacting local governance. Specifically, the analysis addresses the multi-decade population explosion while explaining the factors driving population growth. These factors are tied to prevailing traditionalistic and individualistic political cultures that question government efficacy while seeking to minimize its influence. The culture also rejects innovation.

The Texas political culture is a working hybrid of the traditional structure combined with the individualistic approach. The Texas one-party political system coupled with low overall civic participation and economic conservatism maintains government status quo. Additionally, Texans idolize the rugged individual who succeeds unimpeded by excess government intervention. This historical development yielded an electoral reality that prioritizes minimal government spending, influence, or innovation that deviates from the accepted norm. This culture also prefers the local, decentralized decision-making model. The prevailing culture shaped the Texas municipal culture as the population grew and middle-class families exercised their Tiebout predicted options to move farther away from the urban hub.

29. Bluestone, Stevenson, and Williams, *The Urban Experience*, 53.
30. Potter, *Population Projections*.
31. Gaines, "Looming Boom," 4.

WHY TEXAS?

The history of Texas is fascinating, as is the development of decentralized policymaking among state and local entities. However, we need to review contemporary conditions and future consequences which naturally invite new questions. What does the modern urban Texas look like? What is the level of fragmentation? Most importantly, what emerging challenges face local leadership?

Future projections portend a coming storm that several municipalities cannot weather utilizing business as usual strategies. The combination of domestic migration, immigration, and natural population activities should yield a population increase between 30 and 50 percent. Additionally, the coming population boom promises greater diversity. The seismic shift could alter Texas political culture as well as the socioeconomic profile. Larger populations with less capacity to fund public services creates operational risks for many municipalities.

Which cities carry a heavier probability of financial catastrophe? Can we develop a risk profile which identifies these jurisdictions? The next chapter attempts that very exercise with an examination of the socioeconomic and human capital profiles of the municipalities comprising urban Texas. The risk profiles become readily apparent and alarming in some cases. Chapter 4 segues into Part II where we ask the most pressing question of how to save at-risk communities.

4

Profiles of Urban Texas

WHICH CITIES CAN FUNCTION independently and which need help to survive? Does Texas have entire counties or regions with at-risk socioeconomic profiles? Chapter 4 addresses these questions by developing and examining the population, economic, and academic profiles of the ten most populous urban Texas counties. As I stressed earlier, my objective is to prescribe a remedy for a festering illness facing municipal Texas. This chapter describes what ails many Texas cities or towns. Part II explains the cure.

Characteristics

Suppose you were tasked with determining the fiscal health of a local jurisdiction. How would one determine the fiscal fitness level? This chapter creates a profile for each of 236 cities comprising the chosen counties. The author utilized cluster analysis to divide the cities in each county into four groups. Cluster analysis allows researchers to divide data or entities into homogenous groups based on chosen characteristics.[1] This chapter is dividing cities (entities) by socioeconomic and human capital data. First, Table 4–1 identifies the ten largest counties with population totals according to the 2010 census, as well as the total population for the country and Texas for the sake of comparison.

---

1. Creswell, *Research Design*, 148.

Table 4-1

Ten Largest Texas Counties' Population Increase

	2000	2015	Increase	Raw Increase	Total Increase
USA	281,421,906	321,428,820	4%	40,006,914	14%
Texas	20,851,820	27,469,114	9%	6,617,294	32%
Harris	3,400,578	4,538,028	11%	1,137,450	33%
Dallas	2,218,899	2,553,385	8%	334,486	15%
Tarrant	1,446,219	1,982,498	10%	536,279	37%
Bexar	1,392,931	1,897,753	11%	504,822	36%
Travis	812,280	1,176,558	15%	364,278	45%
Collin	491,675	914,127	17%	422,452	86%
El Paso	679,622	835,593.0	4%	155,971	23%
Hidalgo	569,463	842304	9%	272,841	48%
Denton	432,976	780,612	18%	347,636	80%
Fort Bend	354,452	716,087	22%	361,635	102%
Total	11,799,095			4,437,850	
State %				67%	
USA %				17%	

Source: U.S. Census Bureau, "2010 Census."

As Table 4-1 indicates, 58 percent of all Texans call one of these counties home. The five most populous counties each serve populations in excess of 1,000,000. Overall, Texas grew by 32 percent from 2000–2015 which more than doubled the rate of the country as a whole. In fact, Texas is responsible for almost 17 percent of United States population growth for a decade and a half. The growth rate for the entire nation falls to 11 percent if one were to subtract Texas.[2]

---

2. U.S. Census Bureau. "2010 Census"; Steele, "Boom!"

PART I: THE CURRENT TEXAS MUNICIPAL STRUCTURE

The population explosion is narrowly focused. 67 percent of the increase occurred with the ten most populous counties. Each of the counties grew at faster rates than the entire state as a whole. Urban economists describe a high growth city as one experiencing a population increase exceeding 10 percent over a two decade period.[3] The growth for each county eclipsed that pace. Indeed, some of the results are staggering. For example, Collin County grew by 86 percent over the fifteen year cycle. Fort Bend, the fastest growing, increased by 102 percent. Counties harboring large principle cities such as Denton, Tarrant (36 percent), and Harris (33 percent) still grew at a rapid clip. Four of the counties are part of the Dallas/Fort Worth/Arlington Metropolitan Statistical Area (MSA), which remains home to the case studies in Part III. One final note: population growth often indicates positive economic growth.

Characteristics Creating Profiles

While population growth remains a significant concern for public service provision, this project must measure the ability of these city populations to fund needed government functions. Therefore, we are examining two characteristic categories—economic characteristics and human capital characteristics—to divide our 236 municipalities into clusters. We will then examine the cluster breakdown of each county. One of the challenges in ranking or clustering cities is determining which characteristics to include and which get discarded. For example, the crime rate of a city sounds like a great characteristic for inclusion. Indeed, high crime rates increase demand for public good including law enforcement (obviously), but also potentially fire/EMS. However, the author chose the six characteristics for the following reasons: 1. The chosen categories are standards macro determinants of living standard quality and 2. The group includes independent variables that yield other characteristics. For example, a city with a high poverty rate typically deals with high crime rates and EMS costs.[4]

Table 4–2 summarizes the results for each county. This is a good time to define each characteristic, explains its value to our profile, and present results for our ten counties.

---

3. Bluestone, Stevenson, and Williams, *The Urban Experience*, 32.
4. Bluestone, Stevenson, and Williams, *The Urban Experience*, 41–55.

PROFILES OF URBAN TEXAS

Table 4–2

Socioeconomic Characteristics for Ten Largest Texas Counties

County	Population		MHHI	Poverty	Health Care	HS	Bachelors
USA	308,745,538		$53,482	16%	86%	86%	18%
Texas	25,145,561		$52,576	18%	78%	82%	18%
Harris	4,092,459	Urban	$53,822	18%	75%	79%	19%
Dallas	2,368,139	Urban	$49,925	19%	74%	78%	19%
Tarrant	1,809,034	Urban	$57,727	15%	80%	85%	20%
Bexar	1,714,773	Urban	$50,867	18%	81%	83%	17%
Travis	1,024,266	Urban	$59,620	18%	81%	87%	29%
Collin	782,341	Suburban	$84,233	8%	86%	93%	32%
El Paso	800,647	Urban	$40,783	23%	73%	75%	14%
Hidalgo	774,769	Urban	$34,952	35%	64%	62%	12%
Denton	662,614	Suburban	$74,662	9%	85%	92%	28%
Fort Bend	585,375	Suburban	$86,407	9%	84%	89%	28%
Total	14,614,417						
State %	58%						

Sources: U.S. Census Bureau, "American Community Survey."

Economic Characteristics

Median Household Income (MHHI)

How do we measure the fiscal fitness of municipalities and their citizens? Why is that important to our objective? Median household income serves as a useful tool for several reasons. First, it remains perhaps the most macro of measures and allows us to make assumptions about cities or towns by comparing the MHHI to other jurisdictions. Cities with low MHHI often face several struggles such as high poverty, high crime rates, lower education levels, and low health care coverage which leads to an increased use of emergency medical services.[5]

Poverty Rate

There are actually two important terms related to poverty—the poverty threshold and the poverty rate. The poverty threshold is the total household annual income a family must fall below to be considered impoverished. For example, the 2010 poverty threshold for a family of four was $22,475.[6] We will examine the poverty rate, which is the percentage of citizens in every city that falls below the poverty threshold.

Table 4-2 also provides the poverty rate for the targeted counties. 16 percent of American families lived under the poverty line in 2010. The Texas rate is 18 percent. Merely four of our counties serve citizens with a poverty rate lower than both of these standards with three possessing single digit poverty rates. Collin County in North Texas has the lowest poverty rate at 8 percent with Denton and Fort Bend close behind at 9 percent. Conversely, the south Texas counties of Hidalgo and El Paso have the highest poverty rates at 35 percent and 23 percent respectively. The former figure is perilously close to the 40 percent rate that economists refer to as concentrated poverty regions.

Low socioeconomic families are particularly problematic for efficient and effective provision of public services. As mentioned in chapter 1, families falling below the poverty line contribute to inefficiencies in several ways. For example, they have a greater likelihood of using emergency medical services even in non-emergency medical situation as these families struggle to afford a general physician and preventative care.[7] Additionally, a positive relationship and correlation exists between poverty and high crime rates.[8] Basically, low economic populations increase the cost of government without the capacity to contribute to the burden of supporting these agencies.

Concentrated poverty regions create an even more daunting challenge. Regional solutions, whether cooperative or structural, depend on the ability

---

5. Bluestone, Stevenson, and Williams, *The Urban Experience*, 41.
6. U.S. Census Bureau, *2010 Census*.
7. Dallas County Health, "Horizons," 3-4.
8. Bluestone, Stevenson, and Williams, *The Urban Experience*, 54-55.

to leverage high and middle income communities and cities in order to balance those revenue streams and provide affordable, quality services to low income communities. This might best be described as a regional balancing act (or possibly re-distribution), if you will. However, what if the entire region suffers from concentrated poverty and the high/middle income communities simply do not exist, or are overwhelmed by low income communities? The case study in chapter 9 addresses such a situation.[9]

Health Care Coverage

The profile also includes the percentage of the population covered by some form of health insurance. The Affordable Healthcare Act passed in 2012 obviously complicated this statistic as the legislation presumably opened the healthcare insurance market to a larger population especially for low income families.[10] However, the legislation is clearly controversial and the results are mixed and complex which is another reason for utilizing data from the 2010 census.

Why include health care? First, the health care industry represents 18 percent of American economic activity while also providing an essential service.[11] Also, individuals or families without health care insurance (or even those who have insurance with poor coverage) struggle with merely accessing these services.[12] The coverage rate speaks to both the fiscal and physical wellness of a city population. Fiscal wellness impacts the ability to fund and support public agencies while physical wellness impacts the burden on several services such as EMS and public hospitals.[13] Finally, health insurance actually provides revenue for some of the public services we are examining including EMS agencies, which remain a significant part of the Medstar case study in chapter 10.

Additionally, Texas and several Texas counties possess coverage rates that lag behind the other regions. 86 percent of all Americans received some

---

9. Bluestone, Stevenson, and Williams, *The Urban Experience*, 41–45.

10. Patient Protection and Affordable Care Act; HHS Notice of Benefit and Payment Parameters for 2012, 78 Fed. Reg. 15410 (March 11, 2013) (to be codified at 45 C.F.R. pts. 153, 155, 156, 157, & 158).

11. U.S. Department of Health, "Effects of Health Care," 3.

12. Dallas-Fire Rescue, *The Future of EMS Service Delivery*, 8.

13. Bluestone, Stevenson, and Williams, *The Urban Experience*, 374–78.

form of health care coverage in 2010 compared to merely 78 percent of all Texans. Collin County is the only jurisdiction meeting the national average with 86 percent of the population holding coverage. Several of the larger counties such as Harris (74 percent) and Dallas (73 percent) have relatively low coverage rates as well as the South Texas counties.

Human Capital Characteristics

Human capital is an economic school of thought that is defined as any tool that enhances worker productivity such as training, education, good health, flexibility, and soft skills. While these are all vital traits, education is easiest and most accurate metric to measure on a macro level.[14] Therefore, the profile also includes the high school and college graduation rate for the city population. To clarify, the college graduate variable measures the percentage of residents over the age of twenty-five who completed their bachelor's degree.

Both characteristics are beneficial to our mission as they help determine a population's ability to financially support government services. Educational attainment clearly impacts the economic status and earning capacity of individuals and families. With that said, urban economists also found that high college graduation rates benefit metro areas and cities. Cities with high college graduation rates among the population enjoy significantly higher median household income rates than cities with low graduation rates.[15] Like health care coverage, Texas (82 percent) lags behind the rest of the nation (86 percent) in high school graduation rates while equaling the college graduation rate of 18 percent. Additionally, the variation among our targeted counties as vast as some counties (Collin, Denton, Fort Bend, and Travis) have college rates approaching or exceeding 30 percent while counties such as El Paso and Hidalgo remain well below state and national averages.

Statewide Results

The author ran a four cluster model and created the following cluster labels: affluent, upper middle class, middle class, and lower socioeconomic.

---

14. Bluestone, Stevenson, and Williams, *The Urban Experience*, 219–20.
15. Bluestone, Stevenson, and Williams, *The Urban Experience*, 53.

Affluent Cluster

Of the 235 cities or towns, only seven fall under the affluent cluster with three existing in Harris County, two in Dallas County, and one in Bexar and Tarrant respectively. Given the state's manageable cost of living, the residents of these jurisdictions fit the affluent profile. The average MHHI exceeds $210,000 with 96 percent receiving some form of health insurance coverage pre-ACA. Impressive human capital numbers drive the fiscal levels as 99 percent of the residents graduated from high school and nearly 40 percent from college. Obviously, these cities and towns enjoy solid fiscal support for public services and budgetary needs. However, the financial elite are elite for a reason as their numbers are scarce. Merely 57,086 residents call these affluent enclaves home which converts to far less than 1 percent of the urban Texas population. Like any state or region, the urban Texas regions must rely upon a solid collection of middle class and upper middle class families for fiscal support.

Upper Middle Class Cluster

The upper middle class cluster includes thirty-nine well-funded cities with a MHHI exceeding $133,000 or nearly three times the national MHHI. While this cluster earns less than the affluent category, they match that group overall with a similar poverty rate (4 percent) and health care coverage rate (94 percent). The human capital metrics are also essentially the same. Overall, 547,662 residents, or 3.7 percent, of the urban Texas population calls these comfortable suburbs or cities home

Middle Class Cluster

Of course, the middle class cluster predictably includes the largest number of municipalities with ninety-seven. While representing a clear middle, the standard of living remains well above national and state standards based on several metrics including MHHI ($76,728 compared to $53,000) and the poverty rate (8 percent) which is half the national rate. 1,780,307, or 12 percent, of urban Texas residents occupy these cities.

Lower Socioeconomic Cluster

With that said, the lower income cluster includes ninety-two cities. These municipalities serve populations with increased dependence on public service coupled with a decreased ability to fund said services. The MHHI for these jurisdictions is $42,530 which falls well below state and national averages. Additionally, over one in five citizens live under the poverty line and the health care coverage rate falls well below national averages. Finally, the human capital metrics fall well below both state and national averages.

These are the "dependent" jurisdictions requiring needed innovation. Regional advocates point to such low income concentrations when prescribing regional governing structures that deliver public services. To be honest, the population simply cannot afford needed services. This is the crux of the equity or service equalization argument. The gravest concern perhaps is that these municipalities serve the largest concentration of the urban Texas population which actually makes sense, as this cluster includes almost all of the principal or hub cities (note Plano is the only outlier). Overall, 12,229,362 Texans live in these cities which comprises 83.6 percent of the urban population and almost half of the entire state population according to the 2010 census. Additionally, 62 percent of all Texans living under the poverty rate call one of these 92 cities home.

County Profiles

Harris County

Table 4–3

Harris County Socioeconomic Profile

Profile	Number	Population	Population %	MHHI	Poverty	Health Care	High School	Bachelors
Affluent	3	22,787	1%	$ 231,189	2%	98%	98%	36%
Upper Middle	5	26,575	1%	$ 156,502	3%	95%	98%	40%
Middle	9	98,629	4%	$ 75,861	9%	83%	88%	16%
Lower socio-economic	10	2,397,331	94%	$ 42,763	23%	71%	75%	17%
Total	27	2,545,322						

Source: U.S. Census Bureau, "2010 Census."

The largest Texas county is also concentrated with poverty. The low socioeconomic cluster includes 94 percent of the county population among ten of the twenty-seven incorporated cities. Houston, the most populous city in the state, represents 82 percent of the county population and is part of this cluster. The MHHI ($42,763) falls well below national averages as nearly one out of every four residents falls under the poverty line.

Table 4–3 summarizes the county data. Interestingly, several cities are either affluent or upper middle class, thanks largely to the energy sector. In fact, seventeen cities or towns are at least categorized as middle class while eight are upper middle to affluent. With that said, the middle class is the second highest cluster with nine jurisdictions and 4 percent of the population. The MHHI is comparatively high ($75,000) and the poverty rate is low (9 percent).

PART I: THE CURRENT TEXAS MUNICIPAL STRUCTURE

Dallas County

Table 4–4

Dallas County Socioeconomic Profile

Profile	Number	Population	Population %	MHHI	Poverty	Health Care	High School	Bachelors
Affluent	2	31,632	1%	$ 184,891	5%	97%	99%	43%
Upper Middle	1	38,659	1%	$ 111,325	4%	91%	97%	39%
Middle	10	412,709	16%	$ 75,726	9%	82%	90%	26%
Lower socio-economic	14	2,160,526	82%	$ 47,797	20%	73%	77%	18%
Total	27	2,643,526						

Source: U.S. Census Bureau, "2010 Census."

Dallas County is the second most populous county in Texas and part of the most fragmented metropolitan area in the state along with Tarrant County. The region simply presents the most prescient case study of fragmentation. This is problematic as the county includes a wide variation of fiscal viability among its twenty-seven municipalities.

Table 4–4 presents the county breakdown. Dallas County serves fourteen cities in the low socioeconomic cluster which comprises 82 percent of county population. This obviously includes the hub city of Dallas itself which comprises 50 percent of the county population. One in five residents live under the poverty line with the median income falling slightly below $48,000. The health care coverage (73 percent) and high school graduation (77 percent) rates fall well below national and state averages.

The middle class cluster includes ten cities and 16 percent of the county population. The median income exceeds $75,000 and the poverty rate (9 percent) is in single digits. The health care coverage rate is well above the state average while educational achievement rates are well above national averages. Merely three towns comprise the two wealthiest clusters—Coppell is the only occupant in the upper middle cluster while the twin cities of University and Highland Park, near downtown Dallas, fall under the affluent cluster.

Tarrant County

Table 4–5

Tarrant County Socioeconomic Profile

Profile	Number	Pop.	Pop. %	MHHI	Poverty	Health Care	High School	Bachelors
Affluent	1	682	0%	$196,250	9%	96%	100%	20%
Upper Middle	5	99,292	6%	$135,875	3%	95%	98%	39%
Middle	14	341,846	19%	$71,904	8%	85%	92%	22%
Lower socio-economic	17	1,315,109	75%	$47,287	18%	77%	82%	12%
Total	37	1,756,929						

Source: U.S. Census Bureau, "2010 Census."

Tarrant County, home to 700,000 plus, hub Fort Worth, and suburb Arlington, typically play the little brother role to sprawling Dallas County. However, Tarrant has experienced the second most growth (36 percent) among the top five counties since 2000 and remains the third most populous county among the 254 total. While it carries somewhat less cache than its larger neighbor, Tarrant serves thirty-seven incorporated cities and seventy-one governments total which also makes it one of the most fragmented among the five largest counties.

Table 4–5 summarizes the county breakdown. 75 percent of the county population resides in cities falling in the low socioeconomic cluster, which of course includes Fort Worth and Arlington. The two hubs serve 63 percent of the county population. While the MHHI for this cluster ($47,000) falls below the state and national standards, the remaining metrics for this cluster indicate that a higher standard of living persists in Tarrant County compared to the rest of urban Texas. For example, the poverty rate for the poorest cities matches the state average and the health care coverage rate is only slightly below state standards.

This trend continues for the remaining clusters. The poverty rate is single digits and the health care exceeds state levels. The human capital benchmarks also exceed national levels for all three clusters. The county overall looks less stratified than other counties as the affluence is limited but the upper middle class and middle class cities are numerous and well-populated.

Bexar County

Table 4–6

Bexar County Socioeconomic Profile

Profile	Number	Pop.	Pop. %	MHHI	Poverty	Health Care	High School	Bachelors
Affluent	1	985	0%	$212,917	2%	91%	100%	31%
Upper Middle	5	28,271	2%	$127,356	3%	94%	97%	33%
Middle	11	100,182	7%	$74,466	8%	87%	91%	19%
Lower socio-economic	6	1,354,195	91%	$44,768	20%	79%	81%	16%
Total	23	1,483,633						

Source: U.S. Census Bureau, "2010 Census."

Bexar County is an urban jurisdiction with the fourth largest population among the 254 Texas counties. It is the second fastest growing counties among those with a population in excess of 1,000,000. The county is relatively non-fragmented as the per capita average per 100,000 (3.67) is second lowest among the top urban counties. Overall, the county serves twenty-three cities and sixty-three local governments.

Table 4–6 summarizes the breakdown of the twenty-three cities. Merely six occupy the low socioeconomic cluster although 91 percent of the county population calls one of these units home. This cluster of course includes San Antonio, the county seat and second most populous city in Texas. One in five residents of these cities lives under the poverty line. With that said, this cluster eclipses the statewide low socioeconomic cluster in every profile category.

Conversely, the middle class cluster for Bexar County falls slightly below statewide benchmarks in certain categories. The seven cities in this cluster serve 7 percent of the county population. The MHHI is $74,466 which is slightly below the statewide MHHI. The remaining metrics mimic the statewide results save health care and college graduation rates.

Five cities are categorized as upper middle class and serve 2 percent of the county population. The MHHI is $127,000 which is below the cluster average although the poverty rate (3 percent) is a bit lower than the state wide average. Bexar County does include one of the affluent cities as Hill Country Village carries a population of 985 and an MHHI of $212,917.

Travis County

Table 4–7

Travis County Socioeconomic Profile

Profile	Number	Pop.	Pop. %	MHHI	Poverty	Health Care	High School	Bach-elors
Affluent	—		0	0	0	0	0	0
Upper Middle	6	19,607	2%	$143,065	4%	96%	99%	44%
Middle	8	65,535	7%	$77,777	10%	86%	93%	25%
Lower socio-economic	4	792,818	90%	$47,846	19%	80%	87%	29%
Total	18	877,960						

Source: U.S. Census Bureau, "2010 Census."

The fifth most populous county and home to the state capital, Travis County, has experienced the fastest growth among the five largest counties and is also the fastest growing urban county. While the county only serves eighteen cities, it is highly fragmented with 11.3 governments per 100,000 and 116 local units overall.

Table 4–7 provides the county data which does not include an affluent cluster. The lower socioeconomic cluster includes merely four of the eighteen cities within county limits. However, one of these four is Austin, the Texas capital and the state's fourth largest city. The inclusion of the state capital brings the population share of these four units to 90 percent.

Granted, this story applies to most of the counties which is discussed later in the chapter. With that said, the cluster profile is far more robust than the state cluster as every metric easily eclipses state standards.

The middle class cluster includes eight cities serving merely 7 percent of the population. Most of the metrics are slightly higher than the states averages although the poverty rate (10 percent) is fairly high for the middle class. Finally, six cities serving 2 percent of the population fall under the upper middle cluster. The cluster profile is far more robust than the state profile. For example, the MHHI ($143,000) is well above state average as is every benchmark.

Collin County

Table 4–8

Collin County Socioeconomic Profile

Profile	Number	Pop.	Pop. %	MHHI	Poverty	Health Care	High School	Bach- elors
Affluent								
Upper Middle	5	153,097	21%	$123,309	5%	91%	96%	39%
Middle	16	560,007	77%	$80,318	6%	86%	93%	32%
Lower socio- economic	3	10,930	2%	$43,301	22%	70%	86%	14%
Total	24	724,034						

Source: U.S. Census Bureau, "2010 Census."

Our story thus far has yielded two large takeaways:

1. The majority of the urban Texas population lives in incorporated cities comprising the lowest socioeconomic cluster.
2. The principal/central cities are always part of the lowest cluster and remain the primary reason for takeaway number one.

Collin County serves as a glaring outlier to these trends. Collin is the largest suburban county in Texas and continues to grow at a furious clip (86 percent population increase since 2000). The county experiences the least fragmentation among the large suburban counties (7.29 units per 100,000) with fifty-seven local jurisdictions and twenty-four cities. Table 4–8 summarizes the population stratification.

Overall, merely three of the cities which serve only 3 percent of the county population fall under the low socioeconomic cluster. The vast majority of the population (77 percent) lives in one of the sixteen cities in the middle class cluster which includes the county seat (Plano) and two large, growing suburbs (Allen and McKinney). Furthermore, this cluster easily eclipses the statewide middle class cluster in all categories. For example, the MHHI ($80,318) surpasses the statewide middle class MHHI by $4,000. The human capital metrics are also impressive as 32 percent of residents graduated from college. Also, 21 percent of the population lives in five upper middle class cities. Interestingly, Collin County does not contribute to the affluent cluster.

El Paso County

Table 4–9

El Paso County Socioeconomic Profile

El Paso County	Population	MHHI	Poverty	Health Care	HS	Bachelors	Cluster
County	800,647	$40,783	0.23	0.73	0.75	0.14	
Anthony	5,011	$30,541	0.28	0.656	0.77	0.072	2
Clint	926	$38,125	0.28	0.754	0.741	0.159	2
El Paso	649,121	$42,037	0.215	0.745	0.772	0.154	2
Horizon City	16,735	$52,030	0.208	0.754	0.821	0.158	2
Socorro	32,013	$30,416	0.35	0.632	0.565	0.051	2
Vinton	1,971	$32,935	0	0.672	0.96	0.401	2

PART I: THE CURRENT TEXAS MUNICIPAL STRUCTURE

Table 4–10

Hidalgo County Socioeconomic Profile

Profile	Number	Pop.	Pop. %	MHHI
Affluent				
Upper Middle	0	0	0	0
Middle	2	2,847	1%	$74,283
Lower socioeconomic	20	531,649	99%	$34,247
Total	22	534496		

	Poverty	Health Care	High School	Bachelors
Affluent				
Upper Middle	0	0	0	0
Middle	13%	75%	75%	20%
Lower socioeconomic	30%	67%	78%	14%

Source: U.S. Census Bureau, "2010 Census."

Why are we reviewing these two counties together? Well, this is a good time to remind everyone of the contrast between regionalism arguments and the thesis of this book. Essentially, regionalism condemns social stratification among cities within a region as caused by the racism that drives middle class and upper middle class families out of the inner cities (and poor suburbs) along with their tax dollars. Of course, the flight leaves central cities and lower income suburbs without the means to provide essential public services. According to regionalism advocates, the proper solution involves regional or consolidated (where the county is a regional unit possessing the legal authority and responsibility of cities) local jurisdictions that tip the economic scale by capturing all tax revenue from all socioeconomic levels and thus guaranteeing that everyone receives equalized levels of service quality regardless their level of affluence or poverty.

However, what happens if a county or region does not include an affluent or even middle class cluster of communities to balance the fiscal scales? The counties El Paso and Hidalgo present such a quandary (or nightmare if you have a flair for the dramatic). Table 4–9 presents the El Paso county breakdown which includes six cities or towns that are in the low socioeconomic cluster. The MHHI falls well below the national average at $40,783 as nearly one out of every four residents live under the poverty rate. Health care coverage rates and human capital metrics also fall well below the average.

Hidalgo County perhaps fares even worse as Table 4–10 attests. Twenty of the twenty-two incorporated units are part of the low socioeconomic cluster which also captures 99 percent of the county population. Overall, the citizens of this county endure a worse standard of living than their El Paso county counterparts. The MHHI is merely $34,247 or 65 percent of the national average. Over one-third (35 percent) of all county residents live under the poverty rate with merely 67 percent of all cluster residents possessing some form of health care coverage. The county does include two cities in the middle class cluster but both the economic and human capital measures fall well below the statewide averages.

Denton County

Table 4–11

Denton County Socioeconomic Profile

Profile	Number	Pop.	Pop. %	MHHI	Poverty	Health Care	High School	Bachelors
Affluent								
Upper Middle	9	99,728	22%	$119,894	3%	94%	97%	39%
Middle	18	125,017	28%	$79,944	4%	85%	93%	24%
Lower socio-economic	6	219,780	49%	$47,091	16%	76%	89%	18%
Total	33	444,525						

Source: U.S. Census Bureau, "2010 Census."

PART I: THE CURRENT TEXAS MUNICIPAL STRUCTURE

The ninth most populous Texas County, Denton County, has grown by 80 percent since 2000. A suburban jurisdiction just north of Dallas County and adjacent to Collin, remains strongly middle to upper middle class as 50 percent of the population living in cities meeting those standards and almost 73 percent (twenty-four) of all incorporated municipalities fitting within one of clusters. With that said, roughly half the population lives in cities falling in the lower socioeconomic cluster including the two largest cities Denton and Lewisville.

Fort Bend County

Table 4–12

Fort Bend County Socioeconomic Profile

Profile	Number	Pop.	Pop. %	MHHI	Poverty	Health Care	High School	Bachelors
Affluent								
Upper Middle	3	82,433	37%	$142,092	5%	88%	93%	6%
Middle	4	73,595	33%	$74,591	12%	85%	92%	28%
Lower socio-economic	10	67,118	30%	$44,126	18%	73%	77%	14%
Total	17	223,146						

Source: U.S. Census Bureau, "2010 Census."

The tenth most populous Texas County, Fort Bend County, has experienced the largest population explosion (102 percent) since 2000 with most of that growth occurring in the first decade. Additionally, Fort Bend is easily the most fragmented county with a unit ration of 30.74 per 100,000 which more than doubles the closest county. This is an interesting figure as merely seventeen incorporated municipalities call Fort Bend County home. What is the fragmentation source? The county is home to 158 such districts which or 18 percent of all special districts in urban Texas were formed in Fort Bend County. Chapter 5 expounds this development more deeply.

Fort Bend County has perhaps the most socioeconomically balanced population in urban Texas as summarized by Table 4-12. None of the affluent communities are incorporated within the county which seems appropriate given the lack of stratification. The low socioeconomic cluster includes ten municipalities which serve a mere 30 percent of the county population. The middle class cluster includes four cities and 33 percent of the population, the upper middle cluster has the fewest number of incorporated municipalities with three but this includes Sugarland which is the largest city in the county. This raises the population share for this cluster to 37 percent.

Summary

What lessons can we extract from this data and how does it shape our examination going forward? The data actually informs and supplements our analysis thus far while also setting the table for the rest of the book. Overall, the county profiles illuminate the impact of fragmentation. The uneven distribution of wealth and income evolves as families express their preferences in the municipal market. Granted, a variety of factors and options explain their decisions. The cause is hardly clear cut. Some families relocate based on perceived (or measured) school quality while others simply chase the newest, largest home either to accommodate a growing family or start one. Some scholars think the cause is racially motivated or driven by personal safety concerns.[16] However, this work examines the provision of public services which means we are less concerned with the question of why and instead focused on reality. Revenue displacing fragmentation is very much an urban Texas reality.

With that said, we remain very concerned about the consequences. The vast majority of the urban Texas population occupies lower socioeconomic cities or towns. Predictably, a stark dichotomy exists between the urban and suburban counties. For example, Harris County possesses the highest percentage at 94 percent while merely 2 percent of all Collin county jurisdictions fall under the lowest cluster. Additionally, the MHHI gap between cities and countries is vast.

The balance and wealth distribution hammers home the need for some level of regionalism. However, which approach (structural or functional) provides the optimal benefits? What do we want municipal

16. Wilson, *When Work Disappears*, 111.

innovation to achieve? Additionally, which option provides the best fit culturally? Part II addresses these questions by introducing the policy criteria driving this analysis as well as the various options experts have extolled over the years.

Part II: Candidates & Criteria

WHAT ARE THE VARIOUS reform options available to Texas and its local officials? How do we determine the optimal structure or mode for Texas municipalities? What objectives should leaders and the populations they serve prioritize? These are the questions that ultimately develop an evaluation model with selected criteria for municipal reform.

Part I described the challenges normally facing municipal American and profiled the state of Texas based on those characteristics. We now understand the challenges facing the over 1,200 Texas cities and their ability to respond. Specifically, Part I identified challenges facing cities or towns serving populations that struggle with funding local services at a high quality level, whether these jurisdictions are central cities, suburbs with high poverty rates, or remote towns serving smaller, blue collar populations. This also includes better understanding of how they can respond based on political and social limitations.

Part II delivers prescriptive solutions to the jurisdictions facing the barriers of funding the provision of high quality government services. Indeed, this section essentially follows a policy evaluation structure. Chapter five identifies the regional options available to municipalities that could potentially yield the benefits of a regional structure. The list includes permanent approaches that alter the regional structure (structural consolidation) such as consolidation or regional governments as well as voluntary, potentially temporary relationships such as special districts or interlocal agreements (functional consolidation). This chapter also includes Councils of Governments (COGs) among the voluntary structures, although COGs will ultimately play a supporting role in our examination. Additionally, we also consider the impact of innovative planning approaches and technology including data analytics and Six Sigma.

Chapter 6 identifies the priorities prescriptive options should achieve, which emerge as our policy criteria for measuring and comparing the various regional solutions. The criteria package includes both pragmatic standards such as effectiveness, efficiency, and political feasibility that are vital to practitioners as well as more scholarly (less concerned with the real world and more idealistic, if you will) concerns such as equity, service equalization, accountability, and transparency. Chapter 6 concludes with our first "regional score card" that utilizes a rubric to measure and compare the options based on chapter 4 criteria. This chapter includes a review of current existing governments and relationships based on research of the outcomes each structure tends to produce based on the policy priorities.

5

Candidates for Selection

PART I INTRODUCED THE concept of fragmentation and the 90,000 plus local American governments fighting for citizens and tax dollars. We also examined the development of Texas style polycentrism including a case study of the ten largest counties. The findings echo the gravest fragmentation fears as socioeconomic stratification colors each region. Middle class and affluent families move away from perceived issues such as crime and poor schools to suburbs that are increasingly on the outer fringe of the urban region. They take income, jobs, and tax revenue with them leaving central cities (and several older suburbs or towns) struggling to make ends meet and provide needed services to the remaining citizens. Many critics believe a better way exists: regionalism.

Regionalism clearly has benefits. The regional profiles presented in chapter 4 illustrate that fragmented metropolitan regions include pockets of low income communities that could experience service gaps or poor service quality. Regionalism in both structural and cooperative forms can remedy these disparities. Given these concerns regarding polycentric regions, regional advocates argue that local governments should share the burden of regional responsibilities. Local governments should exist in a structure that nurtures cooperation as opposed to competition.[1] According to regional advocates, regional structures equalize the quality of public services while reducing the cost of government, enhances economic development and regional marketing efforts, and promotes spatial equity.[2]

---

1. Orfield, *American Metropolitics*, 55; Rusk, *Cities Without Suburbs*, 9; Soja, *Seeking Spatial Justice*, 21.
2. Carr and Feiock, *City-County Consolidation*, 3–7.

Texas city managers certainly find regional cooperation attractive. The author's 2013 survey asked respondents which jurisdiction types were their most frequent contracting partner as well as their preferred partner. Overall, 62 percent identified a regional jurisdiction (county, COG, special district) as the most frequent partner type. Most cities (47 percent) partnered with counties. Additionally, a majority (54 percent) preferred contracting with regional units as opposed to other cities.[3]

While such scholarly analysis is valuable, we can simply separate the options into two categories: structural consolidation and functional consolidation. Structural consolidation or regionalism includes permanent, general purpose governments that either governs over smaller jurisdictions or replaces/absorbs said jurisdictions into one regional mothership. Structural examples include true regional governments such as Portland and actual city-county consolidated governments such as Indianapolis and Louisville.[4] Functional consolidation typically includes temporary (or at least voluntary) structures created for a limited, specific purpose or to fill a certain void. The most prominent examples include special districts, privatization of public services, and intergovernmental contracts.[5]

Regional and Consolidated Structures

Regional Governments: The Case of Portland

Metropolitan governments such as Portland, Oregon[6] and Toronto/Vancouver[7] provide established, functioning examples of structured regional government. Metropolitan or regional governments are general purpose governments possessing all municipal powers codified by state law. While some regional or county governments enjoy limited powers, regionalism advocates argue that metropolitan jurisdictions should wield "exclusive" powers within the designated areas of responsibility. The power would

---

3. See Chapter 12.
4. Rusk, *Cities Without Suburbs*, 89–107.
5. Texas Urban Development Commission. *Urban Growth in Texas.*
6. Abbott, Carl and Margery Post. *Historical Development of the Metropolitan Service District.* Report prepared for the Portland Metro Home Rule Charter Committee, 1991.
7. Fox "Halting Urban Sprawl," 43–59; Rose, *Governing Metropolitan Toronto*, 224.

include controlling planning and zoning powers as well as developing and implement housing policy.[8]

Metro, the elected regional government for Portland, Oregon, is currently the only elected regional government in the United States. The regional government provides the structure for integrating Oregon's urban growth management laws in the region. Metro serves an area that includes the counties of Multnomah, Clackamas, and Washington, as well as encompassing twenty-five municipalities, including the city of Portland. Of course, Portland enjoys a well-deserved reputation as an enclave for "enlightened" progressives and hipsters who yearn for organic coffee, brunch, artisan farming, and urban chicken ranches. However, the proponents of metro-regional land control initially pursue more conventional objectives.[9]

The Oregon State Legislature originally passed Senate Bill 100 creating the Land Conservation and Development Commission in 1973 to curb urban sprawl and manage urban land use with a primary focus of protecting agricultural land from sprawl. The law enumerated fourteen goals and objectives including the pivotal goal fourteen which required metropolitan regions to establish and maintain an urban growth boundary that limited residential and commercial development. The policy authorized Oregon counties to implement the coordination effort for most regions within the state. However, elected officials and public administrators in the Portland metropolitan area coordinate their land use plans with Metro. The Oregon Land Conservation Development Commission still possesses the authority to review all local land use plans for compliance with Senate Bill 100.[10]

While the Oregon land use legislation originally targeted the preservation of rural land for agricultural purposes, the states (and specifically Portland's) moralist political culture[11] transformed rural agrarian policy into a living, breathing urban progressive ecosystem. The modern Metro essentially addresses environmental, economic, and equity concerns via its land use authority.[12] This includes transportation, housing affordability, urban density, and socioeconomic diversity issues. The region's "New Urbanist"[13] approach pursues spatial equity benchmarks such as public

---

8. Orfield, *American Metropolitics*, 37.
9. Rusk, *Inside Game/Outside Game*, 157–58.
10. Rusk, *Inside Game/Outside Game*, 155; Statewide Land-Use Planning Act of 1973.
11. Elazar, *American Federalism*, 89–91.
12. Wheeler, "Planning for Metropolitan Sustainability," 133–45.
13. Duany, Plater-Zyberk, and Speck, *Suburban Nation*, 186–96.

transportation, walkability, and urban compactness which reduce automotive dependency. Indeed, Metro prioritizes and quantifies walkability as part of its economic development strategy which has driven several transit oriented development projects.[14]

Overall, the Portland ideal involves equitable transportation solutions within a framework of spatial equity and democratic equality that dilutes elite regimes. Translated, the Metro governance model prioritizes multi-modal commuting that limits reliance on the automobile. Encouraging residents to walk, bike, and utilize public transportation planning whether falling under the categories of transportation or economic development targets these priorities by maintaining a compact urban core that avoids urban sprawl.

While the Portland regional model remains unique among American local governments, our neighbor to the north has a very different story. For example, Vancouver pursues the same goals by utilizing a structure and approach consistent with Canadian political culture and policy. In fact, Canadian provinces and local government, in general, enjoy significant property and land use zoning powers compared to American municipalities.[15] For example, The "Takings" clause of the Fifth Amendment to the United States Constitution prohibits the government taking property from private ownership absent just compensation.[16] This is the controversial practice known as eminent domain, where governments take privately owned real estate in furtherance of a public project. Interestingly, Canadian property owners do not possess such constitutional protections.[17]

The role of Canadian provinces and local governments in land use planning are also very distinct from American state and local jurisdictions. Provinces enjoy police power requiring municipalities to enforce comprehensive plans. Comprehensive plans are binding law unlike American municipal plans which carry no weight absent voluntary cooperation from regional jurisdictions and private sector partners.[18] The greater Vancouver Regional District has coordinated planning among local units since 1967, while the Greater Vancouver government developed the Livable Region

14. Dill, "Final Technical Report, 49; Metro Regional Government, *Portland*, 63.
15. Fox, "Halting Urban Sprawl," 43–59; Frierson, "How Are Local Governments Responding?," 497.
16. United States Constitution, Article V.
17. Fox, "Halting Urban Sprawl," 45–47.
18. Fox, "Halting Urban Sprawl," 50–51.

Strategic Plan in 1972 which implemented Smart growth policies similar to the Portland model based on four guiding components: mass transit, compact, dense housing development, complete, multi-use communities, and an urban growth boundary.[19] These components are obviously designed to attack and eliminate urban sprawl.[20]

City-County Consolidation

While the Portland model provides a regional structure with the authority over smaller jurisdictions in key policy areas, city-county consolidation absorbs smaller entities into one large countywide unit. I always ask my undergraduate students what image best represent the American federal structure. They typically envision a layer cake with three completely separate layers. (Flavor is optional but I always think chocolate—with vanilla ice cream works, too.) However, the American federal map looks like a matrix with thousands of governing layers possessing overlapping responsibilities and authority. To be honest, this confuses my students and most Americans. Basic civic activities like voting in local elections can prove exhausting. For example, urban Texas voters frequently "pull the lever" for candidates in 100 plus races that elect representatives, senators, state representation, judges, etc. Consolidation presumably remedies this confusion.

Otherwise, consolidation remains an urban reality few citizens experience. Since 1947, merely thirteen American cities with populations exceeding 100,000 have "successfully" consolidated with their counties since 1947.[21] Table 5–1 identifies each consolidated government fitting this profile. Success in this context merely refers to merging the largest city in a county with the regional jurisdiction (aka county). This does not in any way refer to city-county consolidation actually achieving the goals or benchmarks such as reduced tax burdens or higher quality service, that leaders no doubt promised voters approving the consolidation. Of course, it is difficult to possibly justify such a massive undertaking unless it saves money or improves service quality. This remains the rub with regional consolidation.

---

19. Young, "Vancouver," 1109.
20. Kushner, *Healthy Cities,* 55–57.
21. Hardy, *The Consolidation of City,* 2–4.

PART II: CANDIDATES & CRITERIA

Table 5-1

Urban Region Consolidations Since 1947

City	County	State	Consolidation year	Population (as of 2010)
Baton Rouge	East Baton Rouge Parish	Louisiana	1947	229,493
Hampton City	Elizabeth City	Virginia	1952	137,436
Newport News	Warwick	Virginia	1957	180,719
Chesapeake-South Norfolk	North Norfolk	Virginia	1962	222,209
Virginia Beach	Princess Anne	Virginia	1962	437,994
Nashville	Davidson	Tennessee	1962	601,222
Jacksonville	Duval	Florida	1967	821,784
Indianapolis	Marion	Indiana	1969	820,445
Anchorage	Greater Anchorage	Alaska	1975	291,826
Athens	Clarke	Georgia	1990	115,452
Lafayette	Lafayette Parish	Louisiana	1992	120,623
Kansas City	Wyandotte	Kansas	1997	145,786
Louisville	Jefferson	Kentucky	2000	597,337

Sources: Hardy, *The Consolidation of City*, 3-5; U.S Census Bureau, "2010 Census."

Several heavily populated urban regions such as Unigov in Indianapolis, Indian, Nashville-Davidson, Tennessee, Jacksonville, Florida, and Kansas City, Missouri have consolidated.[22] The process itself is simple to explain. City-county consolidations merge the functions and structure of a city or numerous cities with the county-level government into one mega-regional governing behemoth.[23] As mentioned earlier, this process initially requires legislation that grants local jurisdictions the authority to consolidate as well as voter approval via an election that includes all voters who would

22. Hardy, *The Consolidation of City*, 2-3.
23. Carr and Feiock, *City-County Consolidation*, 3-5.

become citizens of the consolidated jurisdiction in many cases (this refers to suburbs). Unigov remains the only successful, large-scale consolidation that did not require voter approval.[24] Once created, the new governing entity replaces the existing city and county as well as suburbs and smaller towns that opted in the consolidated government. Suburbs and municipalities on the fringe of the region are not required to join the consolidated unit and can choose to remain independent. This option can weaken the ability of consolidated units to provide expected benefits since it compromises the provision of uniform service quality and scale.[25] Also, residents can obviously opt to move to suburbs outside the consolidated boundaries which undermine the point of consolidation in the first place.

What do consolidated jurisdictions look like and how do they govern? An elected mayor and council lead the five major consolidations.[26] Additionally, the new entities refer to themselves as "cities" while providing both city and county level services. Typically, the consolidated jurisdictions provide two-tiers of service. General Service Districts (GSD) include the entire consolidated region. Citizens pay the same tax base rate for the same public goods and services. Conversely, the Urban Service District (USD) includes the old central city. Citizens living in the USD receive a different basket of goods but also pay a higher tax rate. The process eliminates duplication of public goods and services as the new entity provides most of the services that individual jurisdictions previously offered separately. However, case studies of the thirteen successful consolidations determined that outlying suburbs could decide not to avoid consolidation. Schools districts and volunteer fire departments also avoided consolidation.[27]

Benefits of Regionalism and Consolidation

What are the perceived benefits of converting to the regional or consolidated structure? Four very distinct schools of thought emerge including: (a) the classical or reform school argument that consolidation yields greater government efficiency, (b) the metropolitan renewal/social equity

24. Staley, et al., "The Effect of City-County Consolidation," 1–2; Hardy, *The Consolidation of City*, 3–4.

25. Carr and Feiock, *City-County Consolidation*, 7–8.

26. Pennsylvania Economy League of Southwestern Pennsylvania. *A Comparative Analysis*.

27. Carr and Feiock, *City-County Consolidation* 55.

advocates (neo-progressives) who envision city-county consolidation as the solution to inner city decay by controlling urban sprawl, (c) regional scholarship that argues consolidated governments provide a better structure for regional governance that can address regional issues, and (d) economic arguments that consolidation provides a stronger approach for promoting local business development and employment growth.[28] Chapter 6 measures the veracity of these claims against the criteria rubric.

Interlocal Contracts & Other Examples of Functional Regionalism

As chapter 6 (spoilers) will explain, the structural approach remains a daunting option with a mixed track record. Additionally, the merger process often provides a "policy window" for elites to pursue their narrow priorities. Still, local governments increasingly face multi-jurisdictional policy challenges and adapting to the globalized economy. Indeed, cities are struggling with managing complex social and economic policy problems unilaterally which possibly signals the declining importance of jurisdictions and borders.[29] This new paradigm forces city managers and administrators to pursue innovative solutions that include intergovernmental communication, coordination, and collaboration as opposed to competition. Are interlocal agreements or other forms of functional regionalism the solution? Now is a good time to consider functional regionalism or cooperative options available to municipal America.

Special Districts

Special districts have earned the derogatory nickname "shadow governments" for a viable reason. Many voters remain oblivious to the existence of these jurisdictions, much less have any clue regarding what special districts actually accomplish. While special district authority varies by state, the structure remains consistent. They are specific or limited purpose jurisdictions that nonetheless enjoy administrative and fiscal autonomy from other local governments. Elected or appointed special district boards provide governance that does not require approval from

---

28. Carr and Feiock, *City-County Consolidation*, 5–9.
29. Frederickson, et al., *The Public Administration Theory Primer*, 236–37.

other local jurisdictions in the region. (Texas law requires board members to win elections). Most importantly, special districts enjoy the authority to create multiple revenue options including taxes, fees, and debt without approval from other impacted cities or counties.[30] These entities actually possess greater administrative freedom in purchasing or personnel than most general purpose local governments.[31]

The number of special districts has increased more rapidly than any other American government jurisdiction type.[32] In fact, the number of special intergovernmental districts increased by 12 percent between 1987–1992 and are the most numerous jurisdictional type in Texas with 3,205 created as of 2015.[33] Additionally, local officials have formed special district for a large variety of purposes including service provisions normally carried out by local governments including water, river authorities, agriculture, health care, schools, and community colleges.[34] While several districts exist for these purposes, transportation and economic development districts remain prominent and controversial.

Special districts have received their fair share of criticism mostly from equity and accountability arguments. Critics argue that this lack of voter accountability and transparency among special districts threatens participative democracy. Bottom line: the reasons for special district proliferation concerns critics as much as the actual growth itself. The criticism typically revolves around the reasons legislative bodies choose to create special districts:

1. Special districts are a toll for skirting state constitutional limits on taxation, spending, and borrowing.
2. Special districts enable state and local governments to appear to be cutting their budgets while continuing to ensure service provision. For example, cities can "pass the buck" for supplying water to a special district. It looks like officials saved taxpayers money but the provision of water and wastewater is merely removed from the city coffers to the new district.

---

30. McCabe, "Special-District Formation," 121–31.
31. Foster, "*The Political Economy of Special Purpose Governments*," 101.
32. U.S. Census Bureau. *Government Organization: 1992 Census of Governments*.
33. Perlman, "Going It Alone," 5S-16S.
34. McCabe, "Special-District Formation," 124.

3. Special districts tools for intergovernmental collaboration cutting across political boundaries to meet regional needs. However, due to the lack of direct public accountability, there is a high possibility of abuse such as nepotism, overpricing, and mismanagement. Therefore, special districts contribute to secretive governance, allows special interests to subvert state or constitutional law, and provide a structure for corruption.[35]

Conversely, there are less nefarious explanations for special districts proliferation. For example, a special district sometimes provides the most effective or efficient service delivery option. The practice sometimes actually receives public support and provides a multijurisdictional structure when it is most needed and effective.[36]

Privatization/Outsourcing

One of the primary alternative arrangements to interlocal contracting employed by local governments is outsourcing to a private contractor as opposed to another public entity. The practice is widespread and involves a broad scope of government functions much like interlocal contracting. For example, Baker Tilly (2010) surveyed local government leaders from Midwestern states regarding budgetary issues. A significant majority of respondents (86.4 percent) indicated their government utilized private contractors at for at least one function. The municipal leaders identified twenty-seven outsourced functions.[37]

Also called outsourcing, privatization transfers government responsibilities to the private sector.[38] While the vast majority of privatization activity involves local jurisdictions outsourcing functions to private contractors or "contracting out," municipalities also transfer assets or develop managed competition. The best candidates among the array of government functions are those services which are private in nature such as debt collection or child support collection. Governments have contracted out certain tasks as well as entire services. However, the client government cannot escape

---

35. Foster, 101–102.
36. Ibid.
37. Baker Tilly, "Local Governments Scramble for Budget Solutions," 4.
38. Featherstun, Thornton, and Correnti, "State and Local Privatization," 643–75.

accountability via privatization as it retains responsibility to the public for providing the service effectively.[39]

Interlocal Contracting

Definition

Interlocal contracts are agreements between two or more municipalities, or local jurisdictions, to provide a good or service, manage support services, or integrate technologies. The practice actually goes by several additional terms such as shared services or intergovernmental agreements. Granted, a distinction exists between these terms since interlocal agreements (ILA), or shared servicing, can occur via formal or informal arrangements, while an interlocal contract is a formal, legally binding agreement between jurisdictions.[40] While this project evaluates interlocal contracting activity among Texas cities and towns, a significant theoretical thread connects these practices whether municipalities partner formally or informally, since research[41] argues that interlocal agreements encourage cooperation among jurisdictions as well as provide similar benefits—whether they include a legally binding contract or remains an informal agreement.

The agreement or contracting process typically involves negotiations and agreements at the administrative/bureaucratic level followed by ratification from elected officials, although some states merely require the latter step.[42] In fact, state legislation is typically required to both authorize and provide structure to the practice.[43] For example, the Texas Interlocal Cooperation Act [44] requires formal approval from authorized elected officials.[45] The formal, contractual agreements establish three types of relationships among governing units: (1) Services of a jurisdiction provided for a fee, (2) Joint enterprise agreements where jurisdictions share resources, or (3) Conditional stand-by arrangements where one jurisdiction pays a retainer to another

---

39. Auger, "Privatization, Contracting, and the States," 435–54.
40. Tees, Cole, and Searcy, *Durable Partnerships in Texas*, 2.
41. Thurmaier and Wood, "Interlocal Agreements," 113.
42. Tees and Stanford, *Handbook for Interlocal Contracting*, 13–15.
43. Thurmaier and Wood, 113–16.
44. Texas Govt. Code, chapter 791, Vernons 1994.
45. Tees and Stanford, *Handbook for Interlocal Contracting*, 14.

jurisdiction.[46] This final arrangement type is appropriate for emergency services such as police, fire, or disaster relief.[47] Fee-based or retainer services would involve interlocal collaboration as described while joint agreements involve their definition of coordination. The proliferation of this tool reflects the inter-jurisdictional nature of problems local governments face. Issues such as crime, pollution, transportation as well as economic development often require a regional response and these issues are proliferating. These contracts create niche opportunities for local officials to address these issues without sacrificing the benefits of fragmentation.[48]

Benefits

Studies indicate that these cooperative opportunities yield several benefits. Given that interlocal cooperation involves a transaction as opposed to wide-scale reform, greater efficiency and effectiveness in service provision, as well as increasing the quality of products and services, remains the primary objective for most municipalities. The results of a survey of Texas local jurisdictions at the city, county, and voluntary regional council levels by Tees, Cole, and Searcy (1995) found that a majority of jurisdictions identified economic or regional factors when agreeing to an interlocal contract. For example, 52 percent identified reducing the unit cost for services as a significant factor while nearly 57 percent identified avoiding costly service duplication, and 58 percent also cited the need for additional personnel. Additionally, a positive correlation existed between the population size and the percentage of municipalities that considered efficiency factors. Conversely smaller jurisdictions were more likely to contract for needed additional personnel.[49] Likewise, a case study including interviews with municipal administrators in the Kansas City, Missouri region showed that "providing the public with better service and reducing the uncertainty of service delivery" remained higher priorities than even generating savings.[50]

Since interlocal agreements are transactions negotiated by administrators, social equity issues typically fail to appear as priorities in the literature. Consolidation advocates fear that interlocal cooperation actually

46. Tees, Cole, and Searcy, *Durable Partnerships in Texas*, 5–6.
47. Tees, Cole, and Searcy, *Durable Partnerships in Texas*.
48. Thurmaier and Wood, "Interlocal Agreements," 114–23.
49. Tees, Cole, and Searcy, *Durable Partnerships in Texas*, 7–9.
50. Thurmaier and Wood, "Interlocal Agreements," 123.

discourages needed consideration of underprivileged areas as mentioned earlier in this paper. For example, some argue that intergovernmental agreements fail to address social and economic divisions within metropolitan areas such as housing, schools, and fiscal disparities.[51] This remains a significant critique of fragmentation. However, contracts do frequently provide needed services, equipment, personnel, or expertise to jurisdictions that cannot afford them from their own operating budget. These include services that most citizens would consider basic or even vital including safety, emergency services, utilities, hospitals, and sanitation.[52]

Therefore, while contracting parties typically focus on efficiency and effectiveness, it also provides badly needed services to areas that cannot afford them as well as reducing uncertainty of service delivery.[53] While this approach may not address social and economic disparity, it does provide a practical, politically viable tool for addressing service equity issues.

Disadvantages/Critique

The primary critique of interlocal agreement falls under the democratic ideal itself, as transacting with a different entity potentially compromises government accountability and transparency. This argument has both practical and theoretical implications. Specifically, the democratic process provides a forum for citizens to express grievances over inadequate government service. Voters typically hold elected officials responsible for addressing and fixing such concerns who can either initiate inquiries to identify who or what caused the problem or face electoral backlash. However, citizens subject to service provision from a different jurisdiction, thanks to an interlocal contract, cannot register a complaint or seek new representation.[54] The response is left to elected officials or administrators who can terminate the relationship, or perhaps pursue a higher level of consolidation.[55]

Additionally, advocates for pure, structural regionalism argue that interlocal cooperation prevents true needed reform. These groups view intergovernmental cooperation or functional consolidation as little more

---

51. Rusk, *Cities Without Suburbs*, 23–25.
52. Tees, Cole, and Searcy, *Durable Partnerships in Texas*, 13.
53. Thurmaier and Wood, "Interlocal Agreements," 113–30.
54. Tees, Cole, and Searcy, *Durable Partnerships in Texas*, 8; Thurmaier and Wood, "Interlocal Agreements," 116–18.
55. Thurmaier and Wood, "Interlocal Agreements," 120.

than piecemeal transactional agreements that blind leaders and citizens alike to problems facing fragmented local regions. The only solution remains structural reform that replaces competition with regional leadership, develops solutions to regional issues, provides equitable public goods and services, and most importantly spreads tax revenue evenly across metropolitan regions.[56]

Summary

Chapter 5 introduced readers to the various regional models. While the optimal model remains subject to debate, Part I presented clear evidence that local leaders must embrace innovative solutions that alter the service provision process. This question remains highly complex. A minuscule dose of critical thinking would lead anyone reading this study to surmise that the author possesses a bias toward voluntary cooperation. That is correct.

However, Part I also stressed the crucial cultural variable which directs not only policy decisions, but general public sentiment toward elected officials, government, and the public sector in general. The government elite laden contracting approach probably fits the traditional/individual Texas culture but possibly falls short of the moralistic ideal which explains why regions such as Portland embrace structural regional jurisdictions.

Finally, how can public officials and the public identify optimal innovative tools without first determining what said changes should accomplish? What do we want from altering the provision process in other words? This comprises the subject matter for chapter 6.

---

56. Orfield, *American Metropolitics*, 148–50.

6

What Do We Want From Our Local Governments?

As mentioned in chapter 5, two questions drive this and ultimately our entire evaluation:

1. How do we determine the optimal structure or mode for Texas municipalities?
2. What objectives should leaders and the populations they serve prioritize?

Chapter 6 introduces readers to the prevailing policy evaluation model the author utilizes in Part III to measure whether chosen cooperative governments achieve said desired objectives. This involves developing and explaining the policy analysis steps, identifying and describing the chosen criteria, and explaining how the author assessed or measured evidence from each study against the prescribed criteria. This chapter then prescribes remedies for the alleged fragmentation ills based on said criteria. In fact, this process ultimately yields a "Municipal Cooperation Checklist" to help compare the various innovation tools and each structure in Part III. The chapter concludes with a report card for structural regionalism.

Methodology

How can we determine whether innovations achieve our chosen criteria? Additionally, how can we compare the options? Answering these questions requires a process, criteria, and an outcome illustrating results. This section develops all three requirements.

First, the policy analysis process satisfies requirement number one. Figure 6–1 summarizes the steps in the policy process, explains each step, and adapts each step for our study. This model is hardly unique as it simply utilizes a rational-comprehensive approach to social issues.[1] While the process probably strikes some readers as complex and erudite, you actually utilize this process frequently (perhaps daily) in a variety of arenas. You "rationally" decide what to eat for lunch, what to wear, when to study, and which entertainment option (TV? Games? Movies?) is preferable based on your mood. Higher level decisions such as buying a car also illustrates the mental process:

1. You have a problem (or opportunity) which necessitates your purchasing new transportation. The unreliability of your current mode might be the cause as would getting a new job.
2. You have several options: compact, sedan, SUV, truck. Some readers will argue that public transportation should be included as well.
3. Criteria: What are your transportation priorities? Do you need speed, reliability, efficiency, cost, or space?
4. The conclusion involves driving away with the shiny new vehicle of your choosing. Enjoy that new payment! Granted, you could decide a new car is cost prohibitive and stick with your reliable, older transportation mode.[2]

---

1. Kraft and Furlong, *Public Policy*, 115.
2. The cynics in the audience (including the author) will argue that deciding to not spend money is an unrealistic conclusion for both the government agencies and American consumers.

Figure 6–1

Stages of the Policy Process

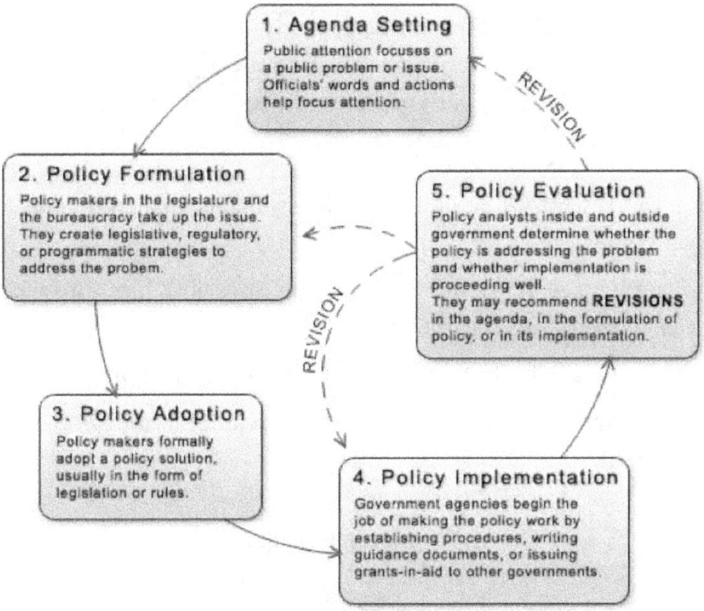

```
1. Agenda Setting
Public attention focuses on
a public problem or issue.
Officials' words and actions
help focus attention.

2. Policy Formulation
Policy makers in the legislature and
the bureaucracy take up the issue.
They create legislative, regulatory,
or programmatic strategies to
address the probem.

3. Policy Adoption
Policy makers formally
adopt a policy solution,
usually in the form of
legislation or rules.

4. Policy Implementation
Government agencies begin the
job of making the policy work by
establishing procedures, writing
guidance documents, or issuing
grants-in-aid to other governments.

5. Policy Evaluation
Policy analysts inside and outside
government determine whether the
policy is addressing the problem
and whether implementation is
proceeding well.
They may recommend REVISIONS
in the agenda, in the formulation of
policy, or in its implementation.
```

Source: Brewer 1972, Lasswell 1958

Indeed, the process is hardly complex. The complexity flows from the subject matter. First, the criteria for optimal government services typically varies based on your socioeconomic status or role. Additionally, the data or evidence examined during the assessment phase remains more difficult to find and dissect.

Might you grant me the indulgence to spend another paragraph discussing the assessment phase? Recent studies examining cooperation and innovation (including mine) relied primarily on surveys of city managers or local leaders.[3] Some surveys probe policy criteria such as effectiveness or efficiency while others focus on networking and cooperative impact. Interestingly, few studies examine empirical data such as budgetary data, industry benchmarks, eliminative duplicate steps, jurisdictions, or agencies (horn tooting). Most importantly, studies consistently fail to address the causation question. For example, is a contract or consolidation responsible

3. Tees, Cole, and Searcy, *Durable Partnerships*; Carr and Feiock, *City-County Consolidation*.

for cost reductions within a police department? A simple before and after picture never emerged. Conversely, the author's assessment process involved digging through budgets, meeting minutes, annual reports, etc. to provide hard, factual data for each case study.

However, we need a tool for evaluating the data. Therefore, this study adopts a very basic report card based on the following method:

1. Develop list of binary questions
2. Answer yes/no. One point for each yes. Each explanation lists the relevant questions.
3. Create average for each criterion. So, five possible questions with three "yes" answers equates to 60 percent.
4. Create average for both policy and democracy sections.
5. Each study receives a report card with a letter grade and average for all criteria.

Policy Criteria

Efficiency & Effectiveness

It is truly in our best interest to discuss these standards in tandem because everyone confuses the two. Effectiveness is really pretty easy to understand once you separate it from efficiency. Effective organizations simply achieve their objectives. Effective sports teams win championships or at least have winning seasons. Effective campaigns consultants win elections. Effective corporations make a profit. Effective organizations are essentially successful organizations. It is a results-driven or outcomes driven standard.

How do experts measure effectiveness? Why benchmarks, of course. The non-governmental examples include some fairly obvious benchmarks—win/loss record or championships won for sports teams; number and types of elections won for political consultants; earnings, sales volume, or market share for businesses. So which benchmarks measure government effectiveness? Like private industries, public industries identify and (hopefully) measure benchmarks. The EMS industry identifies several operational standards with response time perhaps being the easiest to comprehend. We will measure and discuss applicable benchmarks in the case studies chapters comprising part three.[4]

4. Kraft and Furlong, *Public Policy*, 153–54.

Conversely, efficiency considers the process or how things are done and is therefore a little more complex. Basically, pursuing efficiency requires discovering ways to do more (or even the same) with less. Less what? Specifically, less money, people, steps, or resources. Efficiency experts are typically called management consultants who are tasked with identifying and eliminating superfluous activities (or people) resulting in a leaner and meaner organization.

Therefore, government efficiency refers to the process for providing government services as opposed to the outcome or product citizens receive. Will innovations reduce waste, reduce service delivery cost, enhanced operational use of resources, or achieve the same quality of service with reduced personnel or units? Measuring efficiency actually results in creating what one might refer to as "micro-criteria," or sub-criteria standards such as service or duplication or scale.[5]

While the concept of efficiency is more difficult to describe than effectiveness, it remains a fairly easy criterion to measure. Efficiency at its most basic should reduce the cost of doing business. Therefore, budgetary data proves instructive. Several studies reviewed in this chapter compared budget results prior to a specific innovation or agreement to the results once the program was fully implemented. For example, consolidation studies might compare the last five pre-consolidation budget cycles to the first five years after the consolidated government becomes fully operational.[6] Additionally, studies can also compare innovative results with similar municipalities or agencies. For example, chapter 10 compares the Medstar regional EMS budget to EMS agencies serving larger cites.[7]

The efficiency analysis also considers process management and waste reduction. Several industries (including EMS) developed metrics for measuring whether organizations or agencies were wasting or underutilizing resources. Finally, cost-per-unit provides a simple efficiency analytical tool. For example, cities could measure the cost-per-fire response (or first responder) and maintain annual or monthly results.

---

5. Kraft and Furlong, *Public Policy*.
6. Campbell and Selden, *Does City-County Consolidation Save Money?*, 2.
7. Whether the innovation caused the efficiency remains a more elusive question.

PART II: CANDIDATES & CRITERIA

Duplication of Service

Duplication of service refers to two units providing the same service that one could provide at a reduced cost for both. The author defines elimination of service duplication based on whether contracting or a specific contract eliminated redundant agency or bureaus that provided the same service as the contracted partner.[8]

Economies of Scale

We just exhumed another difficult standard. Economies of scale exist when per unit cost to produce a good or services decreases as volume increases. Do you ever watch "Shark Tank"? The sharks frequently ask hopeful entrepreneurs whether their product and operations are scalable. Scalable operations possess greater growth potential since costs actually decrease as the number of units produced increases (at least per unit). This is a benefit regional government enjoys as they could potentially serve a larger population than one city.[9]

A few thoughts are in order before continuing the criteria identification. It is very important to understand that an organization can easily be effective without being efficient. The opposite is also true. You may (logically) ask why an organization would possibly sacrifice or comprise its standard of excellence to save money. Readers should understand that not only does this occur but industries typically focus on saving money. This remains a common critique of private contractors providing public goods. However, recall the axiom from chapter 1 that service quality cannot be sacrificed.

Table 6–1
Policy Checklist

Policy
Efficiency
The Innovation/New Structure:
–Saved money/reduced operational costs

---

8. Tees, Cole, and Searcy, *Durable Partnerships*, 5.
9. O'Sullivan, *Urban Economics*, 10–11.

Policy

- Achieved scalability
- Eliminated duplication
- Created revenue streams
- Eliminated process steps/standardized operations

Effectiveness

The Innovation/New Structure:

- Increased performance quality
- Provided service to citizens they could not otherwise afford
- Decreased uncertainty of service delivery
- Provided service quality cities could not afford otherwise

Democratic Criteria

Accountability

Accountability asks whether citizens receiving public goods or services from an agency can express their grievances or concerns regarding said agency performance to the officials they elected. Accountability remains a major concern with interlocal contracts or shared services. For example, say SmallVillage cannot afford its own police force and contracts with the Megaplex police chief who proceeds to utilize excess capacity to provide law enforcement for Smallvillage. What if some SmallVillage citizens are frustrated that the contracting police force does a poor job monitoring school zones? Technically, the force and its chief do not report to the mayor and city council of SmallVillage. Compromising democratic accountability remains a concern with intergovernmental transactions.[10] For example, accountability in the Medstar case study (chapter nine) is determined by whether the regional EMS authority and its board remain subject to public scrutiny and accountable to citizens of the fifteen partnering cities.

---

10. Tees, Cole, and Searcy, *Durable Partnerships*, 10–11.

PART II: CANDIDATES & CRITERIA

Transparency

Popular sovereignty structures democracy. Likewise, transparency is a non-negotiable democratic pillar. In fact, it is a distinctive that separates democracy from more authoritative forms of government. While accountability is critical, it is easier to hold leaders and officials accountable if citizens know what they are doing. Indeed, transparency enables accountability.

How can we determine what leaders are doing? What do we monitor? A good start involves access to budgetary data or spending, operational results, and policymaking or decisions. This book measures transparency by accessibility to these data categories. How easy is it for the average citizen to access the budgetary data, decision-making, and operation benchmarks of a specific agency or entity? A transparent jurisdiction makes such data readily available.

How can democratic scholarship examine and measure government transparency? The Office for the Texas State Comptroller of Public Accounts prioritized public transparency to the point that it created a "Transparency Stars" program honoring local governments that intentionally pursue public fiscal disclosure, or "go above and beyond in their transparency efforts," as stated on the website.[11]

As the comptroller's office stresses, transparency mandates that governments and agencies shed light on traditional finances such as the budgetary process and expenses as well as contracts, procurement, economic developments (if appropriate), public pensions, and debt obligations. Additionally, leaders pursuing successful transparency consider clear and concise communication efforts that extend beyond merely posting financial documents, and incorporate "jargon-free summaries, visualizations, downloadable data, and other relevant information" vital to voters.[12] Staffing and turnover data such as hires and salaries would definitely fall under the other relevant information category. Accessibility should also be added to the list, as interested citizens are able to locate the data with minimal difficulty or searching.

The agency identified criteria for recognizing local jurisdictions that practiced transparency. Therefore, it presents a model for determining the existence of transparency in the options and cooperative agreements

---

11. Comptroller.Texas.Gov, "Transparency Stars," https://comptroller.texas.gov/transparency/local/stars/general-criteria.php.

12. Comptroller.Texas.Gov, "Transparency Stars," https://comptroller.texas.gov/transparency/local/stars/general-criteria.php.

covered in this book. Table 6–2 presents said transparency model. The author simply grants one point upon identifying a transparency or clarity standard. For example, any government posting its budget online receives one point for "Finances" under the first category.

Table 6–2

Transparency Criteria

Transparency Available Data	Clarity
Finances	Summaries
Contracts	Visualizations
Procurement	Downloads
Economic Development	Other
Pensions	Staffing
Debt	
Total	

Source: Texas Comptroller of Public Accounts

Political Feasibility

Glenn Heights, then a miniscule community of 4,500 citizens, faced a budget crisis in the early 1990s. Rising service costs and debt servicing coupled with an eroding tax base left the town in the same condition many Texas cities face. The toxic brew of providing suboptimal services without the revenue and capital to improve service quality absent unpopular tax and utility cost increases. Everyone suffered including city staff, employees, and citizens as the infrastructure decayed and crucial personnel positions remained unfilled.

Desperate, the city manager and mayor met with Dallas County to discuss solutions. Together they identified the magic bullet: contract with the Dallas County sheriff's department for police services. The feasibility study determined that funding police services sapped 75 percent of the city budget. This idea worked for both parties as it saved Glenn Heights $175,000 annually and would potentially improve police services while also providing additional revenue to the county as it leveraged excess capacity. The classic win-win. Most importantly, city officials suddenly had additional revenue for improving other services for grateful citizens.

Unfortunately, the citizens never fully expressed their gratitude. In fact, residents emerged vocally against the very concept. The staff underestimated public appreciation for the Glenn Heights police force and the officers serving the city. Citizens were proud of the low crime rate and quick officer response to calls as it turned out. Additionally, the contract faced internal resistance as city staffers questioned outsourcing in general. The city council, itself divided on the idea, placed the agreement on the council agenda. 1,000 citizens appeared to oppose the idea. The police service interlocal contract died on the vine.[13]

The lesson? The ultimate democratic barometer of great ideas and innovations falls to public support. Granted, the ILC Act does not require placing every contract on a ballot for public approval. Indeed, the only true nod to public support flows from the requirement that elected officials approve all agreements. However, local public officials answer to the people either directly or indirectly. This says nothing of keeping the peace among insiders. The most important task city managers face is "keeping all the BB's in the box" to avoid friction among the city council and staff. Calamities like the kind Glenn Heights experienced are avoidable if everyone is aligned in serving citizens as well as preserving community distinctive.

Political feasibility addresses one question. Would the population impacted approve an innovation or structural reform? Many good ideas fail because voters or citizens refuse to accept the concept for a variety of reasons. Examining feasibility involves reviewing previous efforts such as consolidation elections. Additionally, studies should examine the state's political culture, dominant ideology, and partisan election results.

Equity/Equality of Service

This study evaluates the ability of interlocal contracts and the other options to provide governing equity or service equalization.[14] In fact, one of the primary critiques of cooperative structures is the inability to provide government functions on an equal level of quality to all jurisdictions regardless of the tax capacity of municipalities participating in such agreements.

---

13. Tees, Cole, and Searcy, *Durable Partnerships*, 9–10.
14. Orfield, *American Metropolitics*, 55.

To be honest, the critique is not entirely fair. A more accurate critique would be that municipal management and public officials develop shared service or interlocal contracting relationships to save their jurisdiction's (and by extension taxpayers') money. Indeed, my 2013 survey determined cost reduction is far and away the top contracting priority as 79 percent of responding city managers chose it as a reason. However, 57 percent also chose "improving service quality" while another 45 percent contract so their citizens could receive services the city could not otherwise afford. Further, the mere provision of basic functions becomes a greater priority when available funds become part of the discussion.[15]

Overall, determining whether city, agency, or innovation provides or enhances equity remains a tricky proposition. The first question addresses motive. Are the parties concerned about equalizing service quality? Again, the Texas culture hardly prioritizes this criterion. Additionally, most equity arguments target systemic approaches which typically mandate full scale re-structuring. However, this author remains satisfied that equity exists if lower socioeconomic communities or towns receive higher quality or more effective services than could be afforded absent innovation. Still, that remains a "passing" standard as opposed to an A for equity.[16]

Table 6–3 Democracy Questions

Democracy
Feasibility
The Innovation/New Structure:
–Enjoys sustainable public support
–Fits the political culture of the state/region
–Has low political capital cost
Accountability
The Innovation/New Structure:
–Does not shift accountability away from officials serving recipients
–Accountability shifts but voters enjoy recourse for poor service or general concerns

15. Sullivan, *Urban Economics*.
16. Kraft and Furlong, *Public Policy*, 157.

PART II: CANDIDATES & CRITERIA

Democracy

Transparency

The Innovation/New Structure (provides easy access to):

–Meeting minutes

–Performance results

–Budget data

–Policy decisions

–Data presented in easily understood format

Equity/Equalization

The Innovation/New Structure:

–Leaders prioritized and achieved systemic equity

–Innovation improved service quality for low income communities

---

Report Results

Thus far, this section explained the process, introduced the criteria, and described how we will assess said criteria. This leaves the outcome. What will the process produce? The author decided that a regional/cooperative checklist provided the optimal combination of accuracy and simplicity in communication. The checklist includes binary questions addressing the selected criteria. This methodology molds a complex assessment approach into a visual designed with clarity in mind.

The final phase develops the scoring and reporting tools. The scoring is very basic. A "yes" response earns the innovation 1 point. For example, the checklist includes five efficiency questions. Say the examination of data indicates a structure earns a yes to three questions. The grade for that criterion would be 60 percent. Indeed, the report card for each case study includes a grade for every criteria. However, the aggregate average for both major categories retains our focus.

Regional/Consolidated Results

How would the profiled innovations measure up based on our chosen criteria? This helps compare the structural and functional options. The remainder of this chapter is devoted to examining the regional/consolidated results while cooperation and other innovations are reserved for Part III.

Efficiency

Like most innovative efforts, consolidating governments is really about saving money. Everyone from voters to city managers are satisfied if the change shrinks the budget. Logic would indicate that merging two jurisdiction levels into one accomplishes cost reduction by eliminating service duplication, leveraging scalable economies by increasing the population served (and reducing providers), and eliminating externalities. Consolidation advocates note that jurisdictions engage in costly service duplication when providing services that one countywide entity could provide.[17] Additionally, advocates extol the virtues of scale which exist when the unit cost or average cost of a good or service decreases as production increases. Regional experts argue that spreading the cost over a larger population arguably creates scalable efficiencies.[18] For example, case studies indicate that consolidation reduces the cost for providing utilities.[19]

However, the world of providing local government service is hardly that simple. In fact, little real world evidence exists supporting the money saving claims. The nature of public goods complicates the picture. Most local services such as law enforcement or fire safety are labor intensive where consolidating into larger departments yields an increase in compensation. Several studies have found this result. For example, a consolidation[20] of fourteen suburban police forces in the Los Angeles area actually resulted in an increased cost of production, while a study of consolidating fire departments had the same results.[21] Additionally, smaller towns pay less than large central cities. Consolidating into one massive urban core creates an "average up" scenario for both wages and material

17. Staley, et al., "The Effect of City-County Consolidation."
18. O'Sullivan, *Urban Economics*, 333–35.
19. Carr and Feiock, *City-County Consolidation*, 125.
20. Finney, "Scale Economies," 121–26.
21. Duncombe and Yinger, "An Analysis of Returns to Scale," 49–72.

costs. Now, this may ultimately yield higher performing service which is the topic of the next section.[22]

Bottom line, the most optimistic studies produce results that are best described as mixed. Some researchers identified long-term savings or at least budgets that rose more slowly than similar jurisdictions that never consolidated. However, the upfront capital cost was typically significant and it took several years to justify the investment.

Effectiveness

Again, little research considers whether the chosen innovation improved service performance. Conversely, full scale consolidation does invariably set the table for higher performance. First, smaller or low income towns benefit from skilled professionals rendered beyond affordability within their budgets. (A word of caution: this statement does not indict the many mangers and agency leaders who zealously serve smaller and poorer jurisdictions. However, larger municipalities and units enjoy the luxury of expertise and specialization in narrow functions such as procurement.) Conversely, the local fire or police chief probably carries the responsibility of purchasing equipment, fire trucks, squad cars, etc., whereas their central city counterparts can focus on agency performance. The procurement officer can then negotiates the best deal while the budget and finance officers maximize tax revenue. Consolidation feeds such opportunities to smaller units. However, citizen response typically supports smaller jurisdictions. For example, residents living in small jurisdictions indicated a higher level of satisfaction with public services rendered than residents of consolidated cities. The small town residents also found elected officials to be more responsive. These results require several warnings starting with the nature of survey data. This author does not intend to demean survey data as much as stress that readers should not treat opinions as empirical fact. Additionally, the nature of small town governance builds more personal relationships which is significant in labor intensive services or elected officials.[23]

---

22. Hardy, *The Consolidation of City*, 8–11.
23. Hardy, *The Consolidation of City*.

Equity

Consolidation or regional government advocates also argue that regional government structures stimulate social and spatial equity arguments that spur city revitalization. Equity cannot occur absent expansion of the tax base to include wealthy suburbs.[24] Social equity supporters also note the fairness of taxing suburban dwellers since they currently enjoy the cultural and economic benefits of a central city without providing financial support to the central city. Additionally, one of the primary equity reasons used to justify merger is the elimination of fragmentation so the reformed government can equalize the quality of municipal services such as streets, safety, and sanitation across the newly consolidated territory.[25] Of course, this goal directly counters the rational argument for competition.[26] However, please recall axiom/truth number one from the first chapter that public services are considered essential for most citizens who have the right to expect the responsible municipality to provide at a reasonable level of quality. Therefore, a regional, consolidated entity represents the best option for ensuring a minimum level of quality for all citizens regardless of their income status.[27]

However, studies often find that structural government reform fails to yield spatially equitable results or equalized service provision. In fact, one study found that the thirteen major consolidations included separate service provision districts for the central city and the outlying suburbs. These districts provided different services as well as a higher level of quality for certain servicers at a higher cost.[28] Additionally, an examination of the Louisville-Jefferson county merger in 2003 found that the new government failed to provide equalized municipal services. Subsequent revisions to the original merger bill established "special taxing service districts." The new legislation allowed the metro council to create separate service districts within the newly consolidated area to be managed by appointed boards. These districts would permit different levels of service within the county and were coupled to different taxation rates. Under this legislation, the former city of Louisville could be established as an "urban service district"

---

24. Cisneros, *Interwoven Destinies*, 147–66.
25. Downs, *New Visions for Metropolitan America*, 8–11.
26. Tiebout, "Pure Theory of Local Expenditures," 416–24.
27. Orfield, *American Metropolitics*, 155–172.
28. Leland and Thurmaier, "Lessons from 35 Years," 3–10.

whereas other areas of the county could petition their voters to establish "taxing districts," also to be managed by appointed boards. The merger may have actually increased service disparities by legitimizing differences in levels of service and taxation.[29] Finally, most consolidation agreements do not mandate participation from suburbs since consolidated city government often cannot control land use and continued outward migration of middle class taxpayers seeking asylum from the central city.[30]

Accountability

Again, empirical data is minimal. However, the Tennessee surveys from the 1990s capture the citizen perspective as mentioned in the effectiveness section. Overall, smaller town citizens are more likely to agree that their local government is responsive to their needs and their neighbor's needs more than their counterparts who resided in a consolidated district.

With that said, the consolidated structure does afford citizens the opportunity to directly choose elected officials and communicate (see complain) with these same officials. Therefore, consolidation wins the structural arguments for this criterion at least.[31]

Transparency

Consolidation advocates also note that a larger structure provides greater transparency with less opportunity for engaging in covert dealmaking or corruption. For example, a study of the consolidation of Kansas City and Wyandotte County found the development of a professional bureaucratic structure that highlighted accountability and efficiency. This presumably shifted the personnel process from patronage to merit, thus reducing corruption.[32]

Feasibility

Political feasibility remains a remains weakness for the consolidation movement on several logical fronts. First, consolidation elections are rarely

29. Savitch and Vogel, "Suburbs Without a City Power," 758–90.
30. Staley and Cato Institute, *Bigger is Not Better*, 18.
31. Hardy, *The Consolidation of City*, 3–4.
32. Leland and Thurmaier, *Lessons from 35 Years*, 3–10.

successful. Merely twenty-two out of 132 twentieth century consolidation elections (16 percent) were successful.[33] Additionally, the transition as mentioned previously often dilutes the new government's capacity to achieve the objectives driving structural reform.[34] Finally, culture is crucial to widespread reform. The Texas tradition/individual dominated political culture, coupled with the reigning conservative ideology, hardly yields an optimistic environment for creating massive regional governments.[35]

Results

Table 6–4

Regionalism Report Card

Criteria	Structural Regionalism
Efficiency	50%
Effectiveness	75%
Feasibility	0
Policy Average	41.6%
Transparency	66%
Accountability	100%
Equity	0
Democracy Average	55.3%
Overall Average	48.45%

Table 6–3 summarizes the results. The functional options scored higher in the policy/performance categories while the structural approach proved more transparent according to research findings. The results lead to two questions:

33. Hardy, *The Consolidation of City*, 2–4.
34. Campbell and Selden, "Does City-County Consilidation?," 2.
35. Elazar, *American Federalism*, 80–120.

1. Why would a region pursue a costly structural consolidation given the mixed results? (Yes, I already asked this question but it bears repeating.)
2. How might interlocal cooperation/agreements surpass these results across the board?

The case studies in Part III address question two.

Part III: Policy Prescriptions

Case Studies Incorporating the Best Practices Involving Cooperative Regionalism and Innovation in Texas

MUNICIPAL REFORM EFFORTS ENJOY a long and storied history thanks to the historic proliferation of corruption and incompetence within local government since its earliest incarnation. Indeed, Industrial Revolution era urban squalor spurred earnest movements focused on improving the plight of the working class. Granted, the combination of unprecedented migration and immigration driven by job seekers to the manufacturing hubs along the Atlantic seaboard taxed public services such as public safety and utilities.[1] It is perhaps unfair to blame local officials for failing to keep pace with millions of new residents huddling in crowded tenements adjacent to billowing factories.

However, early reform efforts paint a bleak governance picture from this era. The forthrightly named Bureau of City Betterment illuminated the ills of turn of the century public service via a timely tome addressing the unprofessional and corrupt nature of local leadership. The bureau staffed and deployed a cadre of newly minted high-thinking researchers and muckrakers that examined the political machines "serving" the five New York boroughs.[2] Its most famous publication, "How Manhattan is Governed," developed a template for identifying when public agencies struggle with transparency, efficacy, and performance issues.[3]

1. Levy, *Contemporary Urban Planning*, 30–35.
2. Caro, *The Power Broker*, 102–15.
3. The Bureau for Public Betterment, "How Manhattan is Governed."

PART III: POLICY PRESCRIPTIONS

The work examined the operations of the Manhattan borough president, William A. Ahearn, and his staff in carrying out (funding) local government functions from 1904–1905. Borough presidents had served as the chief executive officer of their respective jurisdiction since 1897. While most people identify "New York, New York" as a Broadway tune, it also serves as the official name for the municipality serving the city.[4] In fact, New York, New York serves as an early example of city-county consolidation where the central city of an urban region merges with the county to create a municipal monolith serving all citizens. The New York boroughs are essentially extensions or subdivisions of this governing behemoth.[5]

With that said, the behemoth must serve its population. Prior to 1900, the Board of Public Improvement served as the policymaking arm by making decisions in creating and funding public works that the borough leadership simply implemented. However, borough infighting emerged when some boroughs alleged that the board played favorites in funding public works projects. This ultimately led to the 1900 charter decentralizing the public works process which granted the borough presidents unprecedented authority. According to the City Betterment analysts, how the boroughs exercised said authority proved troubling.[6]

The problems started at the top. President Ahearn and his cadre of cronies ascended to their lofty positions via their many years spent toiling in the arena of "practical politics" which the bureau authors used as a euphemism for "served as a loyal soldier in the corrupt Tammany political machine." In other words, Ahearn and his five agency heads had no business managing any aspect of local government. Indeed, their professional backgrounds included carpentry, butcher, dry goods, and elected office along with the "practical" role of mid-level political operative/thug.[7]

The results brought these fears to reality. The bureau found the following issues:

1. Manhattan roads/highways were not properly maintained even though the borough had paid millions to private companies. By improperly maintained the author means the roads were marked by holes with pipes sticking out.

---

4. Hardy, *The Consolidation of City*, 2.
5. Hardy, *The Consolidation of City*.
6. Bureau for City Betterment, *How Manhattan is Governed*, 12–15.
7. Bureau for City Betterment, *How Manhattan is Governed*.

PART III: POLICY PRESCRIPTIONS

2. The protruding pipes were leftover from half completed sewage projects where constructions crews utilized the holes to access the sewage system.
3. About the sewage system: the system was well over fifty years old, as of 1904, and woefully out-of-date.
4. The concrete used for road repairs was substandard even though contracts specified certain materials.
5. No method existed for managing street signs and traffic.
6. The railroad system was in need of repairs.
7. The borough managed public baths by the lakes, which the bureau found excess spending.
8. Sidewalks were defective.

However, the public works issues paled in comparison to the incompetence/corruption displayed by borough leadership:

1. The borough hired inspectors responsible for reviewing the work of private contractors who were simply political hires with no audit or quality control capacity.
2. This meant many public contracts made were never fully enforced as leadership failed to follow up on project progress and results.
3. Even more damaging, Ahearn made over $1 million in public purchases of materials and services without going through the formal contracting process. This meant the public had no idea how the money was spent.
4. The bureau analysts also noted the lack of oversight. The report clearly included the 1904–1905 bureau budget and noted several examples of excess spending. The authors were careful to note that this was the first time Ahearn and his team had ever seen the figures or even a budget.[8]

The dearth of professional expertise doomed any attempts at effective governance. Granted, good government was hardly the goal. Ahearn and his lackeys "ascended" to their positions via a cronyistic system regarding loyalty and reciprocity (kickbacks) that kept the machine humming. The reformers haunting the halls of the Bureau of City Betterment endeavored

8. Bureau for City Betterment.

PART III: POLICY PRESCRIPTIONS

to change the system forever in the name of the good folks of New York. Their idealistic efforts reversed the course of local government and swept the corrupt Tammany political machine from its lofty perch.

Actually, that did not happen at all. The report successfully removed Ahearn from office.[9] Most history students delegated the enviable task of researching Tammany Hall focus on the industrial revolution era and Boss Tweed. However, the machine kept humming along well into the 1960s. Many a fastidious reformer vainly watch as their efforts soaked in idealism amounted to little.[10]

Why? How did corruption prevail over doing the right thing? Three words immediately come to mind: politics, power, and prescriptions. Regarding politics, the bureau continued the full scale battle with local corruption and incompetence as the battle actually afforded a young Robert Moses his first taste of power as an aide to reform minded New York mayor John Mitchel. With the young mayor's blessing, Moses crafted a dissertation length efficiency analysis of municipal government and agencies.[11] The solution was simple-all agencies and government contractors eliminate the bloat weighing down the budget.

Of course, the "bloat" had names, faces, and families. The seemingly endless stream of Tammany loyalists received compensation for said loyalty via plush government appointments. Moses called for mass expulsion in the name of efficiency and reform. It was the right thing to do for the citizens of New York.

One problem emerged. The citizens of New York apparently took issue with the idea, according to the results of the 1920 election. Voters ushered Mitchell, Moses, and the roster of reformers to the unemployment line. What happened? The "bloat" population voted as well (several times in one election, typically). Indeed, the Tammany loyalists possessed vested interests that motivated a trip (or two or three) to the polls. Bottom line, jobs are real while vague calls for reform and efficiency merely confuse most citizens.[12]

---

9. Ahearn resigned two years later. Also, the borough president would have most likely survived the report but he could not survive an ongoing conflict with the Tammany backed mayor.

10. Caro, *The Power Broker*, 115.

11. Moses' actual dissertation examining the British bureaucratic personnel process inspired the manifesto.

12. Caro, *The Power Broker*, 115–20.

PART III: POLICY PRESCRIPTIONS

Tammany Hall and other reservoirs of corruption or special influence thrive because patronage typically annihilates principle. The lesson is instructive for purveyors of big ideas. The very people you are trying to help may not want your help or may seek a different type of help. Most cannot afford the long-term vision innovation and reform requires. However, ignore their desires and needs at your own peril. Their preferences are the fuel to the democratic engine.

The Glenn Heights police department example from chapter 6 offers a perfect case study. Every expert pointed to the blatantly obvious benefits contracting with another city afforded the citizens. A small exurb with dwindling resources and public safety needs is better served by a modern, professional department. However, the people who elected city leadership vehemently opposed the concept. They had their own priorities as did the officers and staff of the Glenn Heights Police Department that enjoyed popular support.[13]

The message: big dreams are great but will remain glorious thoughts in one's cranium unless one tempers them with political reality. This involves working within the prevailing political "regime" framework, as well as crafting plans that receive popular support.[14] Granted, such compromise creates a sobering effect as some truly earth shattering concepts and plans experience dilution, thanks to the machine and politics as usual. Make no mistake, this author champions innovation and ideas that change the world. An analogy with high technology seems appropriate. Brilliant minds develop technological innovations. However, the market decides which innovation is most successful and useful. Government innovation faces the same "market" challenge as voters and vested interests determine whether new ideas have value.

Furthermore, authority and power explains problem number two as the fine folks at the bureau had no authority to remove Ahearn from office or mandate the reforms. Of course, mayors, city council members, and city managers possess significant levels of public authority. However, local political authority in the American context pales in comparison to local power in countries such as Canada or France. Regional and local jurisdictions in these and other sovereign states enjoy greater land control authority as well as greater economic control and taxing authority in general. Conversely, their American counter parts persist in a stronger free market

---

13. Tees, Cole, and Searcy, *Durable Partnerships*, 8.
14. Stone, *Regime Politics Governing Atlanta*, 3–12.

environment where re-purposing private property for public use remains verboten.[15] Additionally, the political culture of most regions and states staunchly question government authority and any means for increasing the revenue needed to impose policy initiatives. Elected officials obviously remain directly accountable to the public but even appointed public officials such as city managers struggle in long-term plan creation when democracy often calls for the here and now.

Finally, a major problem with the bureau's manifesto and the calls for reform is that while the authors aptly described the corruption and incompetence, they failed to prescribe a cure. *How Manhattan is Governed* details in precise fashion the many ethical and performance ills corroding borough public services. However, each of the eight chapters (the final chapter dealing with sewage, which I like to think was planned) merely describes the many problems flowing from borough offices. Like many reformers of that era, the bureau researchers decided that telling everyone what was wrong was enough to spark change. True reform starts with prescribing a remedy.[16]

Given these limitations, most policy analysts describe (and prescribe) successful policy reform efforts as incremental.[17] Indeed, scholars identify strains of incrementalism from a cursory examination of the great American social movements. For example, visitors to the civil rights museum in Memphis should note the slow and steady flow of legal decisions and legislation that built a wall of protection for individuals against discrimination based on racial or ethnic preferences. The penultimate events were over a century in the making. Reformers should prepare for the experience of small victories that hopefully build to a crescendo.

How does the experience of past reformers speak to our examination of innovation and cooperation? How do these lessons drive our analysis, or at least influence it?

First, city managers must put politics first even though they are not elected officials. In fact, the council-manager structure emerged in response to political abuse and the spoils system.

However, city managers and all city employees work for elected officials who can end their tenure quickly if things go south. One manager stressed

---

15. Fox, "Halting Urban Sprawl," 44–46.

16. Caro, *The Power Broker*, 115; Bureau for City Betterment, *How Manhattan is Governed*.

17. Lindblom and Woodhouse, *The Policy-Making Process*, 32.

how much time he spent keeping city council members from hating each other. This leader and his staff meets with new council members in the name of relationship building but also stresses accepted protocol. Yet another city sponsors leadership weekends where citizens wanting to get involved can meet with staff and learn more about the city and its culture. Bottom line, even term limited councils can foster continuity of culture and priorities when the leadership pool is deep and connected to city staff already.

While this work heralds innovation and cooperation, the process and achievements cannot exist in a vacuum. Perhaps the most applause worthy element of such innovation is that the ideas survive the political cauldron rife with public impatience, special interests, and the politics of urgency. Successful public innovators must leverage their persuasive skills to sell ideas in addition to crafting them.

Speaking of special interests, American municipalities work within capitalist framework and leadership must leverage relationships with stakeholders. The staid profile of button down administrator supervising public service providers no longer seems apt. City managers currently lead economic development initiatives which mandates leveraging city assets such as land, zoning, and planning in an effort to attract development capital, new businesses, and existing corporation considering re-location. The climate is competitive.

Finally, the case studies prescribe actual cures to waste/inefficiency/poor performance that cities or local governments created. This is the part of the book where we examine problem solving emerging from innovative ideas and cooperation. Overall, the Manhattan experience illuminates what we need from our cities, counties, or special districts. City leadership or management must be experienced public executives possessing the requisite skills and expertise. The city needs lawyers and accountants, for example. Additionally, leadership must monitor service effectiveness and efficiency. Most importantly, leadership must remain accountable to the people they serve who should enjoy access to budgetary data, policy decisions, and performance results.

Which local services are subject to interlocal agreements? Specifically, which function is part of a regional cooperative structure? How successful are these structures when measured based on the criteria from Part II?

The chapters in Part III illuminate how voluntary regional structures achieve the identified policy criteria or objectives. Each chapter in this section includes the following structure:

PART III: POLICY PRESCRIPTIONS

- A brief history of the development of the service
- A summary of the traditional service provision approach
- The history of the innovative regional structure with a summary of its inception
- An examination of the new jurisdiction's performance based on the evaluation criteria
- An analysis of how cooperative regionalism fosters innovation

Chapter 7 discusses the Panhandle Plains Regional Planning Commission's city manager contract. Smaller towns remotely located in west Texas simply struggle with affording professional management and administration within their strict budgets. This case study focuses on the effectiveness criteria as towns receive a service they could not afford on their own due to the scalability of regional innovation.

Chapter 8 examines the Terrell/Kaufman County Economic Development district. The leadership team of Terrell has partnered with various jurisdictional types (including the state of Texas, county, and even MUD special districts) to create an attractive incentive for big box retailers to locate a store in a medium sized town (population 16,000) on the tipping point between urban and rural that is the fringe of the DFW region. The contract has increased property values as well as the economic outlook for the entire county.

Chapter 10 covers Medstar, the emergency service district in Tarrant County. Medstar is a regional agreement between sixteen towns (including Fort Worth) of varying wealth levels which leverage all forms of innovation to provide service exceeding industry benchmarks at no cost to taxpayers.

While my research focuses on regional cooperation, municipal innovation in all forms merits discussion. The public sector is slowly integrating private sector methods and process analysis tools spurred by budget concerns. Corporations have leveraged the lessons of Lean Six Sigma (LSS) to remove waste and improve produce quality for decades. Recently, some Texas cities followed suit included the north Texas town of Gainesville which utilized LSS for numerous projects. Chapter 9 examines one of the larger projects as Gainesville leadership followed the method in replacing its aging wastewater treatment plant.

With that said, we begin the case studies with a city management history lesson.

7

Cooperative City Management

When Justin Kimball authored "Our City Dallas" in 1925, the council-manager form of government was very much in its infancy. The first city to authorize the hiring of a full time manager was Ukiah, California in 1904. Dayton, Ohio (population 125,000 at the time) became the first major city to include a manager in its charter. The city appointed five commissioners after the Miami River flooded the city, which was eerily similar to the formation of the Galveston commission after the 1900 hurricane.[1] By 1925, several Texas cities adopted the form with the Fort Worth and Waco serving as the largest.[2]

Still, the structure was young and unproven, which is clear when perusing Kimball's thoughts. It is a fascinating window into the history of a movement or paradigmatic shift right before the shift occurs. Kimball begins his discussion of the city management model by summarizing the growing popularity of the commissioner model that was created post-hurricane Galveston to rebuild after the tragedy of 1900. Interestingly, over 300 American cities adopted the commission model by 1925. This tidbit is interesting because the model no longer exists in any city or town.[3]

Conversely, the city manager/council-manager structure was slowly emerging. City managers were but new tools local leaders were considering to fix their broken down municipal machines. The structure eventually becomes dominant in urban America due to the following reasons or movements:

---

1. Kimball, *Our City—Dallas*, 240.
2. Blodgett, *City Government That Works*, 5.
3. Kimball, *Our City—Dallas*, 245.

1. The actual growth of urban America
2. The American love affair with business leadership, strategy, and tactics
3. The scientification of knowledge, specifically public administration
4. The public reform movement

Essentially, the call for effective management, based on best practices as opposed to politics, emerges from a combination of fighting corruption and keeping up with the industrial machine driving explosive economic population growth that increased the demand for quality public services.[4]

The Scope of City Managers

Today, the vast majority of large American cities utilize the council-manager form of government as opposed to the other option, mayor-council. The key distinction (especially for the purposes of this chapter) is the council-manager requires the inclusion of a city manager who serves as the city CEO tasked with executive leadership for all of the government services. The agency chiefs (i.e. fire, police) refer to the city manager as their boss. The council-manager structure is the most utilized form for cities with populations over 5,000 and is actually a true American export to several European and Latin American nations.[5]

Every major metropolitan city save Houston employs a council-manager structure. In fact, most municipalities exceeding 100,000 in the state chose the council-manager structure as seventy-eight of the 100 largest cities in the state employ a city manager. This makes sense both operationally and culturally.[6] Larger cities obviously require larger operations with more agencies and greater complexity. Therefore, this introductory section provides a two-fold purpose-explaining the typical city manager responsibilities and structure as comparison to this chapter's innovative case study. However, this profile essentially connects every case study in Part III as they all address the many challenges facing city managers tasked with maintaining high service quality despite dwindling resources. Given this dual purpose, this section provides the "textbook" city manager job description with the thornier reality.

4. Kimball, *Our City—Dallas*, 245-46.
5. Blodgett, *City Government That Works*, 13
6. Tannahill, *Texas Government*, 231.

City managers and their operational staff offer professionalism and a singular focus on city services and economic growth. This also helps facilitate networking among professionals in neighboring cities as regional issues emerge. Conversely, mayors and city council members cannot devote their entire attention to city operations given the political demands. Additionally, city councilors typically represent a district which could yield a territorial battle based on political expediency. Efficiency is often the victim of political expediency. For example, a finance manager for a major city once told the author that the city had far more fire stations than the emergency volume required because every councilor wanted at least one in their district because their constituents wanted to feel safe.[7]

Political culture shapes city structure. Texans prefer limited government with limited pay for elected officials. The traditionalistic aspect holds politics to the public service standard rejecting career politicians whose livelihood flows from public coffers. The individualistic influence calls for limited government in general. The optimal model for both cultures is a part-time leadership that serves out of public duty and sacrifice. Indeed, many mayors and council members receive minimal compensation with some leaders receiving as little as fifty dollars per meeting.[8]

What City Managers Do

Council manager cities normally hire their own city managers and support staff. This includes specialists in budget, economic development, planning, zoning, legal, and data analytics, perhaps. The city manager's office provides the following services:[9]

1. Manages agencies and the city bureaucracy (public safety, parks, libraries, etc.)
2. Budgets management
3. Hires/manages chiefs
4. Office services including personnel management, legal, procurement, etc.

---

7. Richard Ngugi, interview with the author, July 7, 2014.
8. Tannahill, *Texas Government*, 292.
9. Tannahill, *Texas Government*.

PART III: POLICY PRESCRIPTIONS

5. City managers who lead the comprehensive planning efforts and are often the driving force
6. Maintains infrastructure and streets

However, while most residents envision their city manager as a staid bureaucrat tasked with ensuring responsive public services and maintaining public works, the truth is far more dynamic. The most vital role few people discuss is economic development and economic development support. Granted, that role might involve serving more as a facilitator than creator as many private and public actors engage in the process. Additionally, economic development tends to possess a regional quality. However, public services cost money which necessitates attracting employers and residents alike to a city. City managers are deeply rooted participants in the Tiebout competitive municipality model.

Probing the complexity of economics in general and the factors contributing to the economic development of a region or municipality is fascinating stuff. However, such theoretical and applied analysis falls way outside the scope (and preferred length) of this book. Finally, people usually define economic development as the process of job creation and supporting or luring new businesses that spend money, create infrastructure, and hire employees. The real process is more complex and nuanced. Leadership must consider how the community constructed an economic framework. The construct and culture varies within each community.

Finally, this brief examination of the city manager role remains incomplete without addressing the strategic aspects of the job. Private corporations never hire CEOs for their operational management skills. Great CEOs cast a vision and set a direction while keeping key stakeholders aligned with the mission. In other words, great leaders convince vested parties to subjugate their ego in order to best fulfill the organizational mission.

City managers carry out their role with the added complexity of answering to elected officials and citizens. Part III includes some inspiring innovations producing incredible outcomes. Innovation and strategic thinking cannot happen in a drama filled environment with leadership constantly putting out fires. Given these realities, the political requirements of the municipal CEO are vast and of the highest priority. Torry Edwards, Terrell city manager, notes that he spends most of his time keeping city council members happy by meeting their project needs.[10] Bottom line, great things can happen if the city staff keeps all of the BBs in a box.

Does a City Manager Provide Benefits for Citizens?

Most studies have indicated that a city manager reduces the cost of service delivery and all costs associated with governance. Specifically, city managers make local government more efficient, more productive, increase performance, leverage technology more effectively, and are more aggressive in revenue collection. These studies also do not consider the impact on economic development, infrastructure, and preparations for regional issues.[11]

Challenges to the Traditional Model

City managers clearly handle issues vital to cities, and data indicates the position yields value for council-manager municipalities. However, what if a town could not afford to hire a manager much less an administrative/professional staff?

How much do city managers make? Several variables answer that question: city population, MHHI, and location. Obviously, large hub cities pay their managers well to navigate a difficult work environment. Additionally, wealthy towns or upper middle class suburbs rank high in average compensation studies.

These examples are either large cities or suburbs serving relatively prosperous citizens in an urban setting. In fact, the location for each example falls within an urban enclave boasting significant population density (by Texas standards) that afford close proximity to other cities, an educated population, and economic development opportunities they can either participate in or possibly experience as externalities. The location provides revenue opportunities, economic development projects, and partners to share the cost of expensive services via a contract.

However, consider smaller towns existing in a remote region like Western Texas. These jurisdictions cannot leverage population growth or an increased tax base. Additionally, no hub city dealing with excess capacity exists to contract with the small villages to guarantee quality public services.

---

10. Torry Edwards, phone interview by author, September 13, 2017.
11. Blodgett, *Current City-County Consolidation Attempts,* 14–16.

PART III: POLICY PRESCRIPTIONS

These units need professional management but cannot afford the personnel costs. The remote locations also render many of these jobs unattractive.

The Panhandle Regional Planning Commission (PRPC) developed a regional contract program to fill this void. The Panhandle Regional Planning Commission is a "Council of Governments" (COGs) under Chapter 391 of the Texas Local Government Code.[12] COGs are voluntary regional jurisdictions promoting collaboration, coordination, and cooperation among local units within the region.[13] They are also the service provider for many interlocal agreements as the 2013 survey found.[14]

The PRPC serves sixty-three towns in the most remote region in the state with the least population density. The commission serves the towns and counties like any COG based on the unique needs and opportunities facing the jurisdictions in the region. Since the location is West Texas, the best description for the PRPC's approach might be as "gap-filler" that provides badly services smaller units cannot afford on their own or provide effectively on their own.[15]

One of the essential needed services is city management. The PRPC staff led by Executive Director Ken Jones determined through conversations with mayors and city councils that a need for competent, professional public administration and the skill set it provided was great. Several meetings convinced the staff many smaller communities could not muster the budget revenue needed to hire competent, full-time management. Some potential clients had $10 million budgets, but many struggled with annual budgets below $100,000. Upon reviewing the managerial salary scale, the staff found that fitting the role was impossible for most of the towns they visited.[16] Managers serving cities in the west Texas region typically make in excess of $120,000 in total compensation while the average for smaller towns (2,000–10,000) still averaged over $50,000, peaking at $100,000. The PRPC clients simply could not afford to pay a manager at these levels.[17]

---

12. Regional Planning Commissions, Texas Local Government Code.

13. Orfield, *American Metropolitics*, 142–43.

14. Sullivan found "that city managers of any type or size were more likely to contract with a regional partner and also preferred such arrangements." Sullivan, *Valuable Partnerships*, 188–90.

15. Kyle Ingham, interview by author, February 13, 2017.

16. Kyle Ingham, interview by author, February 13, 2017.

17. Kyle Ingham, interview by author, February 13, 2017.

Innovative Structure

Therefore, the commission leveraged the Local Government Services staff which included several graduate degrees in political science and public administration as well as city management certificates to fill this specific gap. These credentials, along with extensive staff networking and training with the Texas City Managers Association and the Texas Municipal League, empowered the creation of the Contract Management Program (CMP) in 2000.

The CMP, led by current local service director Kyle Ingham, provides short-term or long-term leadership based on the needs of individual city-clients. The commission structures each contract based on service needs, PRPC staffing capacity, and the overall situation requiring expertise. With that said, the CMP services typically fall under four categories:

1. Long-Term Contractual City Management
2. Interim City Management
3. City Manager/Department Head Searches
4. Strategic Planning Services

Each contract is different based on local need and demand. Long-term and short-term contracts also differ significantly. Search and strategic planning contracts also have very different components.

1. Managing the bureaucracy: This is present in both long and short-term contracts.
2. Hiring/managing chiefs: Long-term contracts are in communities so small there aren't really department heads. In interim work, this is a major area of focus since the staff must often fill a power void due to a termination.
3. Developing comprehensive plans: Strategic planning is a category in its own realm and the CMP handles most of these via long-term contracts. Interim, short-term contracts fail to meet this demand.
4. Economic development/working with developers: The PRPC/CMP program serves communities that are typically too small for economic development programs. Minimal development occurs in remote, rural communities. These towns must take care of basic needs met before addressing growth.

PART III: POLICY PRESCRIPTIONS

5. Maintaining Infrastructure: The CMP does help manage infrastructure. The infrastructure levels vary greatly from community to community.

6. Budgeting: This is often a major area of focus in both long-term and interim work. Walking communities through how to legally develop, post, and adopt tax rates and budgets in the state of Texas is a major component of the staff's effort.

7. Smaller towns also need extensive help in meeting the Texas Open Meetings Act, Truth in Taxation, and Open Records Act in both interim and long-term contracts. This is an area where many communities need assistance

8. Meeting and agenda package development are also time consuming areas.

9. Communicating with a community's legal counsel to address issues is another major area of focus. Small communities try to save money by avoiding legal consultation on important issues often, so reopening those lines of communication and beginning to right any poor practices is crucial.

Table 7–1 provides the list of clients and also summarizes the same socioeconomic data from chapter 3 to quantify the challenges facing these communities.

Table 7–1

PRPC Contract Management Program Client List

Town	Term	Population 2010	Population 2015	MHHI	Poverty?	HS	College
Lake Tanglewood	2000	796	694	$104,750	8%	98%	28%
Timbercreek Canyon	2001	418	408	$88,542	2%	97%	32%
Bovina	2000	1,868	1,825	$34,792	24%	53%	2%
Clarendon	2002	2,062	1,993	$34,063	21%	83%	9%
Fritch	2006	2,117	2,982	$57,880	9%	94%	14%

COOPERATIVE CITY MANAGEMENT

Town	Term	Population 2010	Population 2015	MHHI	Poverty?	HS	College
Cactus	2009	3,179	3,210	$40,825	19%	34%	4%
Stratford	2009	2,017	2,145	$48,889	11%	73%	13%
Dimmitt	2010	4,393	4,354	$36,038	18%	72%	10%
Tulia	2010-2012	4,967	4,872	$31,530	27%	75%	8%
Silverton	2013	731	722	$36,458	16%	72%	8%
Sunray	2015	1,926	2,071	$49,716	15%	73%	8%
Dumas	2017	14,691	14,997	$49,798	22%	68%	10%
Borger	2016	13,251	13,041	$49,918	22%	81%	10%
Lockney	2016	1,842	1,835	$38,750	25%	72%	9%
		54,258	55,149				
		3,876	(891)				

Source: U.S. Census 2015 and Kyle Ingham interview.

The average client city population (3,876) falls well below the home rule threshold of 5,000. Overall, the communities have experienced modest growth from 2010–2015 (2 percent) while the rest of Texas has grown by 5 percent and at a 32 percent clip since 2000. Nine towns or villages serve populations under 2,000.

The socioeconomic figures paint a bleak picture. The MHHI for eleven communities falls below the state average with six jurisdictions serving a citizen base with median household incomes under $40,000. Seven units serve a population with a higher poverty rate than the state average with six populations facing a poverty rate exceeding 20 percent. Finally, the high school graduation rate for nine communities is below the state average.

The West Texas population comprises a large chunk of the 13 percent that the Census Bureau designates as rural/nonurban. The remoteness factor presents perhaps the greatest challenge to service provision for those towns or villages struggling to find funds for essential services. The larger (or wealthier) municipal partners that low income urban cities lean on are not an option for a Bovina or Tulia. This highlights the void filled by the PRPC.

PART III: POLICY PRESCRIPTIONS

Results

Cost/Efficiency

Obviously, the CMP client cities are less concerned about creating a more efficient operation. However, the program does save money and yields some efficiency. Simply put, the commission can structure contracts based strictly on client needs as opposed to general services. Smaller towns might receive general managerial services such as strategic or comprehensive planning plus administering public services while larger communities such as Dumas or Borger might need help with zoning, budget, or a search for a zoning or finance director. The contract duration affords additional flexibility as the agreements can be long-term for towns or villages that do not generate sufficient tax revenue to hire a manager, or short-term for cities in transition after the city manager leaves.

The contractual rate is sixty dollars per hour plus travel with long-term contract including a twenty hour cap. The schedule also includes personnel searches and strategic plans rates. Overall, the program generates significant savings when comparing the hourly management rate to paying a full-time manager. The contract in many instances is simply filling "staff time" already budgeted for at a reduced rate. Additionally, the rate for personnel searches and strategic planning is roughly 33–50 percent less than comparable private sector services.[18]

Performance

Frankly, the CMP performance analysis deviates heavily from the other case studies. The partnering communities are often fighting to keep service running and actual, measured improvement remains a luxury. As Kyle Ingham so aptly stated during our interview, many villages or towns employ small staffs of less than ten people and are "barely keeping water running and toilets flushing" on a daily basis. So, the primary benefit provided by the CMP is filling a "provision absence" that would compromise public safety or continued utility service.[19]

---

18. Kyle Ingham, interview by author, February 13, 2017.
19. Kyle Ingham, interview by author, February 13, 2017.

Analysis/How

The feasibility study is fairly informal compared to other interlocal arrangements. The PRPC receives numerous calls from elected leaders in dire situations or a short-term bind. Local government service (LGS) staff members are well versed in examining community needs and problem solving. Both parties review the proposal and arrive at an agreement which is formalized via an interlocal contract between the city and PRPC. The city council and PRPC board approves each agreement per the ILA as discussed in chapter 2.

Summary

Table 7–2 presents the PRPC report card. At first glance, The CMP program clearly helps small remote communities achieve higher performance in a variety of strategic and administrative arenas. The program addresses high level services including legal, budget, strategy, comprehensive plans, and compliance with state regulations. The small towns emerge from the program with needed services they would otherwise struggle to afford. Therefore, this easily checks off the effectiveness box.

Table 7–2

PRPC Report Card

Efficiency	5	5	100%
Effectiveness	4	4	100%
Feasibility	3	2	67%
Accountability	2	2	100%
Transparency	6	6	100%
Equity/Equalization	2	1	50%
Total	22	20	91%
Policy	12	11	92%
Democracy	10	9	90%

Additionally, the program perhaps indirectly addresses equity and equalization of service issues to a certain extent. Twelve of the fourteen client towns fall into the low socioeconomic cluster. In fact, ten towns serve residents with poverty rate close to or eclipsing 20 percent. The CMP provides essential services these communities could not afford.

One might also argue that the program helps smaller communities address the challenge of gap filling. Specifically, the transition phase between the departure of a city manager and finding a permanent replacement. Larger urban jurisdictions frequently utilize the interim model buying time to conduct a search for a suitable replacement. Smaller remote towns in the PRPC portfolio simply function absent this luxury which carries two major risks. First, the manager's office could simply sit empty which creates a leadership void leaving the town in an inert state. Second, towns stymied by the lack of a town manager could make a rash decision leading to the wrong hire. Hiring a manager who does not fit the community culture leaves the town only further behind. The results could be disastrous for struggling communities. The CMP allows the dust to settle and promotes a more deliberative hiring process.

Conversely, the program struggles in meeting the democratic standards. COGs exist through voluntary participation from communities within their region. Residents possess little control over COGs' activity other than voting out the mayor and city council that choose to contract with the regional entity. Transparency is another matter, as residents can access contract terms from the COGs or town. Overall, the program does not enhance democratic accountability but is clearly on a different level than say special districts that possess a secretive structure and develop outside of the public eye.

Of course, the primary objective driving most intergovernmental agreements is saving money. The CMP saves money compared to the typical market cost for such consulting services. Additionally, one could argue that the program allows towns to receive city management level expertise without actually paying for a full-time city manager. The contract management service is hardly an efficiency home run but it does produce savings for participating municipalities.

8

Terrell Economic Development and Water

TERRELL, TEXAS OCCUPIES AN interesting cultural spot on the map of Texas. Perched on the outskirts of Dallas/Fort Worth (DFW) metroplex a mere thirty-three miles from downtown Dallas, the home of Jamie Foxx could just as easily be considered the gateway to rural East Texas. This geographical juxtaposition creates many of the opportunities and challenges facing the community. The largest city in Kaufman County, Terrell leadership faced metro-level challenges in a rural area with rural resources. As city manager Torry Edwards notes, the town needed an "urban IQ" that could create complex solutions to complex challenges.[1]

Established in 1873 as a railroad town, Terrell has enjoyed steady population growth like the rest of the state since 2000. The official population currently exceeds 15,000 which is a 25 percent increase from 2000, although city studies determined the daytime population swells to approximately 40,000.[2] Additionally, smaller communities directly outside Terrell are experiencing explosive population growth rate eclipsing 102 percent during the same period.[3] The overall Terrell standard of living is slightly below statewide standards at least based on MHHI ($40,000) and poverty rate (19.7 percent) which typically creates barriers to both economic development and funding public services. However, city leadership leveraged innovation in the form of regional cooperation to potentially transform the economic future of the city and the surrounding region it serves.[4] Terrell

---

1. Torry Edwards, interview by author, September 14, 2017.
2. Torry Edwards, interview by author, September 14, 2017.
3. Torry Edwards, interview by author, September 14, 2017.
4. U.S. Census Bureau, "2010 Census."

and its municipal neighbors are now poised to reap the economic benefits of the unique combination of the following factors:

1. The historic core of a city founded in 1873, well-preserved with numerous opportunities for redevelopment
2. The largest TIF in a rural county in Texas, a 4,445 acre zone with a $158 million project plan
3. An approximately 4,100-acre master planned development of mixed-use community created through the state of Texas legislature, which is a quasi-city forming directly adjacent to Terrell under a development agreement with the city

All of these work together in complex fashion to create an environment which promotes private investment in public infrastructure, secures investment in historic properties, attracts big box retail, increases property values, and creates jobs.[5]

One final dynamic demands attention. While Terrell sits on edge of DFW, it actually falls under rural Texas category. As deputy city manager Mike Sims attested: "A new Terrell arrival comes for rural East Texas Living." That is the Terrell market and brand. And rural Texas population shrunk from 2011–2014 per chapter 3. Therefore, Terrell economic development projects and innovation probably achieves success by merely achieving a stable population for that period. For example, Mineral Wells, a municipality west of Fort Worth, experienced a net loss of 1,426 residents during that three year period. However, Terrell proactivity bucked this trend.[6]

This case study examines perhaps the most complex innovative structure in part. Our story begins in 2002 with water. Like all case studies, we examine the "normal" or traditional water delivery system approach. With that said, the "normal process" is anything but normal given the eventual expansion of the Terrell partnership from water to regional economic development. Therefore, the chapter will proceed in a two-prong fashion by discussing the innovative water delivery partnership and how it transformed into an engine for economic development. With that said, Figure 8–1 ably summarizes the typical water delivery process.

---

5. City of Terrell, *TIF Budget Overview*, 2007.
6. Mike Sims, interview by author, October 31, 2017.

Figure 8–1

Standard Water Delivery Process

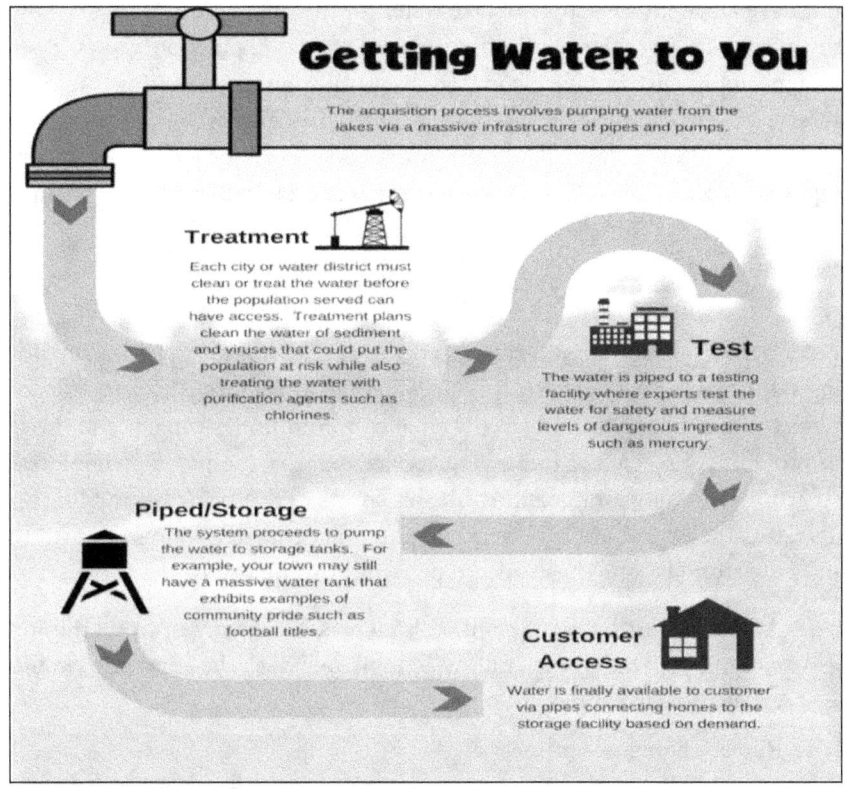

Source: North Texas Municipal Water System, "Our Water System."

The Typical Water Delivery Process

The provision of water remains an optimal cooperation candidate for several reasons:

1. Expensive infrastructure
2. Inefficient, multi-step process
3. Scalable structure and process

PART III: POLICY PRESCRIPTIONS

Water Source/Acquisition

Texans typically receive their water from local lakes. However, the state does not have an adequate supply of lake water for the population. Of course, the severity of this problem will only increase as the population grows. State Water Supply Districts have concocted several solutions including building reservoirs that capture rainwater (also, some cities may seek to obtain water from Lake Texoma which flanks the Texas/Oklahoma border), and purchasing water rights from lakes outside the jurisdictional boundaries.[7]

Not Enough Drops to Drink

Like many communities, Terrell faced the frightening prospect of providing safe drinking water from an aging water infrastructure. This conundrum reflects the challenges facing many smaller communities caught in the vice of providing a service or improving service delivery (and supporting infrastructure) it simply cannot afford. The prospects were especially troubling for Terrell as the urgent improvements would not adequately address long-term infrastructural issues. The needed repairs/improvements included:

1. A new water treatment plant with increased capacity from six million gallons per day to ten million gallons per day. The total cost would exceed $50 million
2. Replace aging water lines
3. Construct a new water tower and infrastructure facilities
4. Terrell needed to also address a decreasing water supply as the city owned lake needed replenishing. Previously, Terrell owned a lake that served as the water supply source from the 1950s through the early part of the next millennium.[8]

Bottom line, Terrell could not afford the price tag for solving the existing water issues but could also ill afford to ignore the problem for a variety of fiscal, legal, and moral reasons (in addition to state water regulatory mandates). However, Terrell and American towns with similar profiles and geographic locations face problems that are more fundamental, cyclical, cultural, and systemic. Rural towns typically struggle with modernizing an

---

7. North Texas Municipal Water District, "Our Water System."
8. City of Terrell, *2002 Comprehensive Plan.*

aging infrastructure due to limited capital reinvestment. Aging infrastructure leads to deferred maintenance costs and also yields lower quality goods and services. Rural regions also face economic upheaval as the agricultural staples fade, taking jobs and industry with them.[9]

Granted, Terrell sits on the outskirts of a large metropolitan region, which has proven beneficial over the years, yet creates a unique collection of challenges. Indeed, the city actually faced the prospect of explosive population growth and how to prepare for it in the same manner as the more urban regions of the state. Many towns struggle with long-term planning and nurturing cooperative partnerships that could solve major problems, such as water quality and availability due to the lack of proactive leadership.[10] Additionally, both the federal and state government provide little in the way of support, incentives, or expertise to struggling regions facing dwindling economic and service prospects.[11] This remains consistent with the individualist/traditionalistic Texas political culture steeped in limited public sector spending or planning. Overall, small towns in rural settings could fall into a downward spiral characterized by an eroding tax base, declining city revenues, nonexistent economic development, and the inability to compensate bright public administrators equipped with the ability to develop innovative solutions to systemic problems.[12]

9. Torry Edwards, interview by author, September 14, 2017.
10. City of Terrell, *2002 Comprehensive Plan*, 5–7.
11. Kyle Ingham, interview by author, February 13, 2017.
12. Kyle Ingham, interview by author, February 13, 2017.

PART III: POLICY PRESCRIPTIONS

Innovation

Faced with a growing array of challenges, the city leaders had three options:

Table 8–1

Terrell Water Source Options

Option 1	Option 2	Option 3
Stay with Lake Elmo and face a building moratorium due to lack of water supply.	Make a deal with the water supplier that has the closest water resources. North Texas Municipal Water District's Lake Tawakoni project would happen regardless and it is only eight miles from the city limits.	Make a deal with a water supplier located further from the City of Terrell. While this would be feasible, city leaders judged the water costs as similar and the infrastructure payments as greater.

While ultimately choosing option two, the staff developed a comprehensive plan in 2002 that dealt with these merging challenges head-on while prioritizing the water system as a critical component. This decision leveraged innovation while rejecting options that would have cost ten times as much as their final solution. Overall, the 2002 plan focused on six specific goals/objectives:

1. Preserving Terrell's small town character
2. Capital investment in the town Infrastructure
3. Wealth creation for both newly created private sector markets combined with tax base expansion and growth for public sector
4. Creating fiscal structures and systems to support a premier clean water drinking system
5. Design polices to encourage local economic development
6. Create a culture that encourages intergovernmental relations and public/private partnerships to stimulate private investment without fiscal risk to the local small municipal government.[13]

Eventually, Terrell successfully met each objective and incorporated all aspects of these approaches in the plan implementation. Based on the plan,

13. City of Terrell, *2002 Comprehensive Plan.*

TERRELL ECONOMIC DEVELOPMENT AND WATER

Terrell took the regional partnership route in developing a new water system. The result was groundbreaking as the city negotiated a partnership between five jurisdictions. The first partners were developer-created municipal utility districts (MUDs) which were designated to create infrastructure in anticipation of residential development. The MUDs, while technically outside the Terrell city limits and therefore separate jurisdictions, were situated within Terrell's extraterritorial jurisdiction (ETJ), state-mandated zone.[14] Texas law grants cities the authority to enforce ordinances within a 1.5 to five mile ring (depending on population) outside the city limits. Additionally, new cities cannot incorporate with the ETJ absent approval from the existing city.[15]

Terrell completed the multi-partner model by including the North Texas Municipal Water District (NTMWD) and the Sabine River Authority to secure additional water capacity and supply. This partnership produced scalable benefits as the unit cost for water and wastewater decreased while also providing a dependable revenue stream from the MUD jurisdictions.[16] For example, the agreement increased the city's water capacity, thanks to adding new water sources, while also providing new revenue streams. Most importantly, the agreement yielded a sustainable infrastructural creation model to manage economic development and growth. The relationship also provided the city access to a new water treatment plant that the NTMWD built at a budget of $200 million. This plant served as the distribution of clean, quality water for the next seventy years to North Central Texas, far beyond the small town of Terrell and into other larger cities around Dallas.[17]

The partnership clearly transformed the provision of water. Terrell currently receives water from a regional source with greater capacity. The regional model afforded greater efficiencies as Terrell's capital investment decreased from $35 million to just under $12 million. However, the cooperative agreement further transformed Terrell from a mere water consumer to an entrepreneurial role as wholesale provider to other cities and unincorporated MUD communities poised for further development. The agreement changed the water issue to an income stream.[18] Figure 8–2 illustrates the innovative Terrell water delivery system.

While the water partnership alone proved to be the most productive (and ultimately enterprising) approach, the utility infrastructure merely

14. Torry Edwards, phone interview by author, September 14, 2017.
15. Tannahill, *Texas Government*, 308.
16. City of Terrell, *TIF Budget Overview*.
17. Mike Sims, interview by author, October 31, 2017.
18. Torry Edwards, phone interview by author, September 14, 2017.

PART III: POLICY PRESCRIPTIONS

served as a foundational framework for a groundbreaking structure that ignited economic recovery for Terrell, Kaufman County, and the region. The city leveraged the water plan to establish a tax incremental financing zone in 2007 securing over 4,400 acres. According to the Texas State Comptroller's Office, the acreage size represented the largest rural Tax Incremental Funding (TIF) in the state.[19] Therefore, the specific objectives driving the Terrell TIF included not only motivating developers and corporations to conduct business in Kaufman County while receiving funding assistance, but also leveraging the tax revenue captured from the new developments to improve the public infrastructure with a particular focus on the water drainage system as well as the water and wastewater facilities.[20]

Figure 8–2

Terrell Water Delivery Process

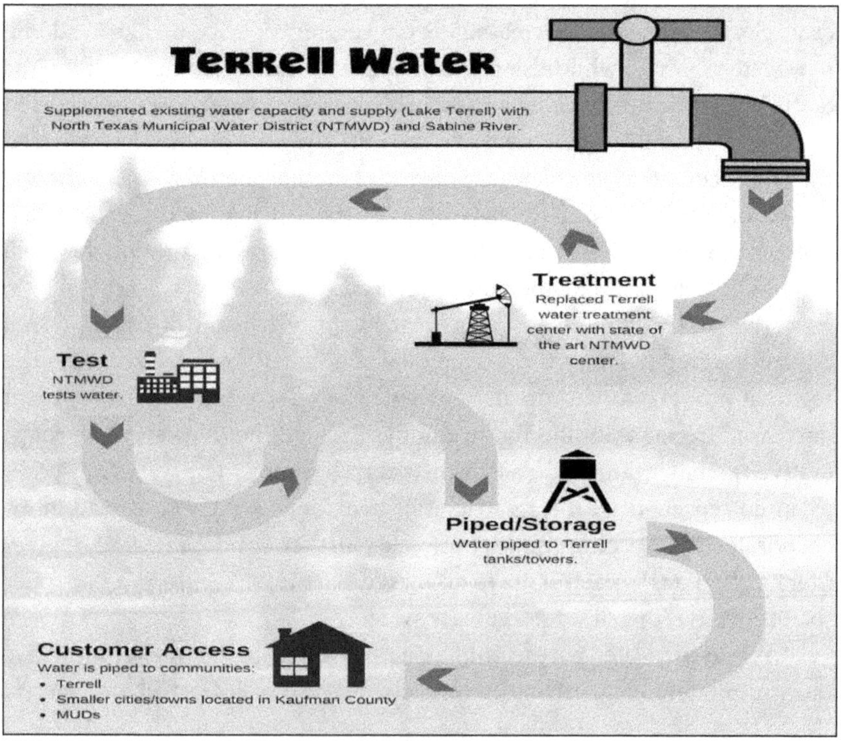

Terrell Water

Supplemented existing water capacity and supply (Lake Terrell) with North Texas Municipal Water District (NTMWD) and Sabine River.

Test
NTMWD tests water.

Treatment
Replaced Terrell water treatment center with state of the art NTMWD center.

Piped/Storage
Water piped to Terrell tanks/towers.

Customer Access
Water is piped to communities:
- Terrell
- Smaller cities/towns located in Kaufman County
- MUDs

Source: Infographic created by Erin Smith.

19. City of Terrell. *Building a Sustainable Community*.
20. City of Terrell, *TIF Budget Overview*, 2007.

A Brief Summary of the TIF Process

Figure 8–3 summarizes the typical TIF structure and process. TIF agreements create a tax increment reinvestment zone (TIRZ) which is a geographical designation chosen by local governments (usually cities but sometimes counties) based on the current development socioeconomic prospects. In other words, the neighborhood or area is trending downward and the city needs to attract developers with the goal of increasing future tax revenue streams from the zone by improving its economic fate. This situation is more accurate with pure urban municipalities trying to revive the inner city and perhaps less characteristic of a more rural community like Terrell. Still, it speaks volumes of the city leadership to leverage complex financial instruments utilized by larger central cities.

TIF programs incentivize developers to build quicker in the zone by pledging future revenue streams to reimburse upfront capital cost by the private developer for the delivery of public infrastructure or some aspect of the development. The classic TIF creates a "win-win" scenario as the incremental property valuation growth flows as passing through funds from the increased tax revenue the development created. To recap, the real estate value within the zone will no doubt increase, thanks to new development, whether it is residential or commercial. Higher property values increases tax revenues. The subsidy comes from that increase which means the city has already benefited from the TIF process. One complexity: the subsidy for early developments might be based on *projected* revenue increases with future construction subsidies receiving actual tax increases.[21]

Layering Statutes for Maximum Revenue

The typical TIF partner arrangement is a pretty straightforward agreement between two parties: the jurisdiction (usually a city) and the developer who will receive the subsidy from increased tax revenues. However, the Terrell Public-Private Partnership (PPP) legalized the initial partnership between Terrell, Kaufman County, and the MUDs via an interlocal contract. The partnership eventually included the power center special district and its elected board.[22]

---

21. Arvidson, Hissong, and Cole, "Tax Incremental Financing," 155–57.
22. City of Terrell, *Public-Private Project Overview*.

PART III: POLICY PRESCRIPTIONS

The Unique Terrell TIF

The Terrell TIF initially included three partner categories:

Governments

The city of Terrell and Kaufman County partnered in the TIF and both ultimately contributed tax revenue from the new development to the TIF fund. Terrell agreed to return 75 percent of revenues from the increase in values while the county retuned 50 percent. Additionally, several developers created MUDs partnered in the TIF agreement.

Developers

The TIF attracted the attention of both commercial and residential real estate developers scanning the state for opportunities partnered in the TIF. These entities created the infrastructure driving the economic development zones. Of course, these capital investments were targeted for TIF subsidies. The commercial developers included several respected names such as Oakridge Investments and General Growth Properties.

Businesses

The big box retailers, hotels, hospitals, and stores deciding to locate in Terrell, Texas. The commercial developers recruit business and retail. It is simply part of their job and business model. . The city sits on I-20 which delivers two types of enthusiasts to their favorite hobby: gamblers to Shreveport, Louisiana and antique lovers to Canton, Texas. The TIFs empowered the city to leverage Terrell's unique location as the largest municipality between the sprawling DFW region and these destinations. The agreement and participating businesses reflect this reality.

Goal/Objectives

The motivation to pursue large-scale economic development stemmed from a desire to keep people from leaving Terrell to work. Terrell was born with access to a major East West Rail Line and a series of state and federal highways. These combined to make Terrell a rural commercial hub supporting commerce and business throughout its history.

Unlike many suburban cities, Terrell has long been home to employment opportunities. Terrell features a major regional bank making its corporate headquarters downtown, a state hospital serving as the largest single employer in town, an industrial base bolstered by an airport with success dating back to WWII, and an economic development corporation founded in 1990. This has created a common vision of an "intact" community where families can both live and work. This shared vision is the basic political foundational idea that made these policy successes and technical innovations possible. It was never "new" to think of Terrell as a great place to live, work, learn, and raise a family. City leaders sought to further this vision to a region bursting at the seams with industrial, manufacturing, health science center jobs, and retail jobs. Additionally, the community needed a large medical center as well as other amenities attractive to current and future residents.[23]

The TIF emerged as the legal, financial, and ultimately physical foundation for these dreams. The TIF objective centered on encouraging developers to create the infrastructure (roadways, utilities, planning, and engineering) required for sustainable, large-scale development envisioned by city and county leaders. Of course, the city and its citizens would benefit from the economic activity as well as the improved public utilities, highways, and infrastructure.[24]

Terrell and it partners added a "secret ingredient" to its structure that expanded both investment capital and partnering incentives. Readers must understand that while this structure is very impressive, the relationships, capital flow, and reimbursements create a complex partnership. However, such complexity increased the project scope and thus the development opportunity.

While the TIF economic development agreement leverages complex public financing transactions, the "secret sauce" added the legal strategy of essentially layering various statutes granting economic development authority to local jurisdictions. The project became so vast in scope that this section focuses on the Farm to Market Road 148 expansion and the Film Alley development specifically.

---

23. Mike Sims, interview by author, October 31, 2017.
24. Torry Edwards, phone interview by author, September 14, 2017.

PART III: POLICY PRESCRIPTIONS

Figure 8–3

How a TIF works

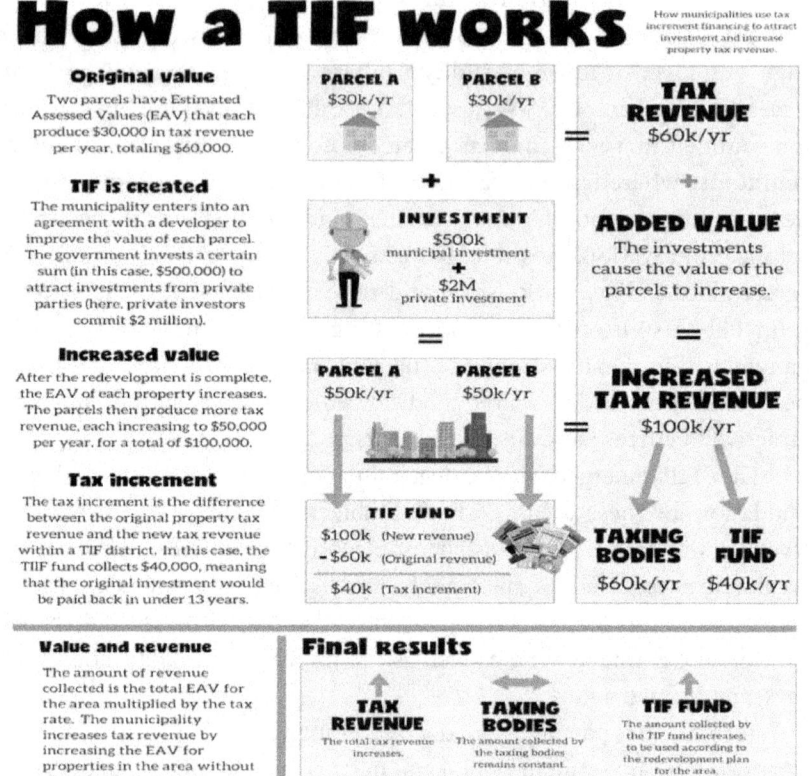

Source: City of Dallas Office of Economic Development

Private investors fronting Buc-ee's (a massive convience store) development initiated the TIF region by funding the FM 148 expansion which increased highway capacity from two to five lanes. The original TIF reimbursed these developers through city and county taxes. This remains the standard TIF process but the Terrell partnership created the Power Center as an added reimbursement piece. The center combines three state laws listed in Figure 8–4 to create a contract between Terrell and Kaufman County for additional reimbursement (and incentive) for developers. You may recall that the TIF creation phase includes both private and public investment yet the Power Center allowed this agreement to move forward absent public capital.

This innovation merely yielded additional revenue sources as the Texas Department of Transportation (TxDot) pass through finance agreement. The TxDot agreement will pay Terrell $11.6 million for the FM 148 construction over the course of fifteen years. This revenue funds yet another layer as Terrell will dedicate $4.5 million to road contraction and $7.1 million to a partnership with the North Texas Council of Governments. Terrell receives $8.6 million upfront to finish FM 148 in exchange for this deferred payment. Finally, the TIF/Power Center structure also birthed two public improvement districts which assess landowners for maintaining drainage facilities.

The original agreement occurred between Terrell and Kaufman County via an interlocal contract with expectation for additional partners. The residential and commercial developers later joined as did the MUD communities. Two agreements emerged: TIF zone #1 which included the cities, MUD communities along the FM 148/20 connection which became TIRZ #1, and the power center agreement along spur 557 which eventually included a large medical center and Buc-ee's. This also included an adjoining 250 acres for the construction of over 350,000 square feet of retail and commercial center economic development, hotels, and shopping. The power center included an appointed board with the objective of developing the massive Crossroads shopping center.[25]

Process

TIFs are essentially public/private business partnerships with the partners responsible for three tasks: the private partners (developers) develop (build) while the public partners (cities and counties) collect the additional tax revenue and reimburse the private partners based on performance agreements to build commercial centers. Both TIF arrangements followed this blueprint as the jurisdiction created a TIF fund account to deposit the tax revenue reimbursement monies. The developers received the deposited money as reimbursement for front end capital costs to build public infrastructure and will continue to receive payments over a fifteen year period or the life of the TIF.[26]

---

25. Mike Sims, interview by author, October 31, 2017.
26. Terrell TIF Budget Overview, 2007.

PART III: POLICY PRESCRIPTIONS

Outcomes Benefits/Economic Development Indicators

How does a city measure economic impact/program/partnership success? Three metrics prevail: increasing economic activity/development, increasing property values, and increasing tax revenue achieved with static tax rates. The outcome section examines results from these categories.

Regarding regional development, the results have proven nothing less than transformational. Regarding these efforts, current mayor and city council members observed that city leadership believes in using cutting edge policies and legal arrangements to create an investment opportunity for the private sector and the public sector. North Texas Municipal Water District has invested $200 million; Trinity Valley Community College invested over $13 million; Terrell Independent School District invested over $40 million; and a combination of Kaufman County and Texas Department of Transportation invested over $30 million. These "partner" public sector investments aren't possible without the city leading the way. These public sector investments simply add to the private investment climate. These steps are making Terrell a great place for developers to buy and rehab existing buildings/properties in our core and a great place for developers to find new customers and new opportunities in Terrell's greenfield areas. Overall, the total development has generated $165 million in total improvements. The developed area currently extends over 350,000 square feet with Baylor Medical Center and Buc-ee's serving as the anchors. The private sector performance (new properties) includes medicine, regional entertainment centers, hotels, and shopping. Additionally, Trinity Valley Community College is creating a Health and Science Hub for training nurses after renovating the 90,000 building which previously housed the local hospital. The public sector is hardly left out as the Terrell police department is moving into a state of the art center that will also house a 911 dispatch center.[27]

Economic data speaks to the depth and scope of the TIF impact. For example, property values and tax revenue have exploded as Table 8–2 illustrates. Housing and overall property values soared during the five year period from 2011–2016.[28] Consequently, tax revenues and tax assessments increased with only a modest tax rate increase. Additionally, sales tax revenue increased by 26 percent during the same period. The

27. City of Terrell, *Building a Sustainable Community*.
28. The TIF actually launched in 2008 but the city and development partners understandably use 2011 as the benchmark given the "Great Recession "of 2008–2009 and its obvious impact on all economic activity.

increased sales tax revenue provides a concrete indicator that the regions is experiencing increased economic activity as well. Specifically, the results speak to retail activity including store purchases, restaurants, and spending at the newer national chains.

Table 8–2

Property Value/Tax Revenue Increases

	2011	2016	Increase	%
Housing Values	$ 70,000	$ 155,000	$ 85,000	121%
Total assessed Property	$ 914,141,372	$ 1,006,227,532	$ 92,086,160	10%
Assessed tax	$ 5,941,919	$ 7,287,099.79	$ 1,345,180.79	23%
Sales Tax	$ 6,810,990.63	$ 8,601,151.62	$ 1,790,160.99	26%

Overall, developers have injected $105 million in private funds since 2010. The economic data excludes future activity. The city has issued over 147 certificate of occupancies through the summer of 2017 that were still in the developmental stage. In fact, the city saw over $2 million in residential permits and $45 million in commercial permits issues during the first half of 2017. Economic development continues at a brisk pace.

Additionally, the TIF structure empowers Terrell development at a manageable incremental cost. Table 8–3 summarizes the taxable value increase in both the city and county TIF structure as well as the annual tax increment which reimburses the private developer. The jurisdictions experienced over $40 million in property value increases while merely reimbursing developers $150,000 annually. For example, Terrell pays the developer who built roads around the Buc-ee's $60,952.38 annually in exchange for $8 million in infrastructure costs. Not a bad ROI.

PART III: POLICY PRESCRIPTIONS

Table 8–3

Property Value Increase and Incremental Reimbursements

	City of Terrell Taxable Value in TIF	Kaufman County Taxable Value in TIF
Base 2007	$ 128,435,437	$ 128,734,320
January 2018 Taxable Value	$ 149,589,418	$ 148,751,263
Captured Value	$ 20,153,981	$ 20,016,943
Property Taxes due to TIF Based on City/County Agreement and Actual Tax Payments	$ 108,356.84	$ 43,016.47

Terrell Report Cards

Did the Terrell water partnership/TIF agreement achieve our goals based on the selected criteria? The criteria assessment actually includes two report cards since the Terrell comprehensive plan altered two government functions: utility delivery and economic development.

Table 8–4 presents the water system report card. The overall policy score is excellent. For example, the water agreement achieved a perfect efficiency score by providing the leveraging regional water sources thus providing scalability, creating a the water source for neighboring communities which eliminated the need for each town to create its own water system while also creating a revenue source for Terrell. Finally, The NTMWD treats water for Terrell thus eliminating steps and standardizing the operations. That said, the new water system also enhanced service quality. Citizens benefit from a larger, cleaner water supply delivered by new treatment technology. Bottom line: Terrell leaders and citizens no longer worry about whether service will happen or if there are service gaps.

The democracy grade falls in the needs improvement range but is hardly failing. The delivery of water remains the responsibility of Terrell leadership which affords citizens the opportunity to engage in the process. Additionally, the city actively provides material related to the agreement. With that said, the city needs to work on the presentation of said materials as documents remain challenging for most citizens to review or examine.

Table 8-4

Water Delivery Report Card

Efficiency	100%
Effectiveness	100%
Feasibility	100%
Accountability	100%
Transparency	83%
Equity/Equalization	50%
Total	89%
Policy Average	100%
Democracy Average	80%

TIF Report Card

Table 8-5 presents the TIF report card. Frankly, assessing the efficacy of the TIF contract proved to be most challenging. Simply put, the goals and objectives for economic development deviate from the other cooperative arrangements subject to a case study. The highest (and perhaps only) economic development objective remains increasing a city or region's economic base, creating jobs, and/or attracting existing businesses. Economic development as a government function lies at the epicenter of the competitive municipal model espoused by Tiebout.

Given these distinctions, how can we assess the efficacy of the Terrell TIF? Well, the contract certainly attracted more businesses and investment capital than a traditional TIF model which makes it more effective than a traditional agreement. Additionally, the TIF reduced the total capital costs which means Terrell experienced efficiencies. Therefore, the TIF scored well on the policy score. However, the nature of a TIF structure is very similar to a special district which impacted the democratic grade.

PART III: POLICY PRESCRIPTIONS

Table 8–5

TIF Report Card

Efficiency	80%
Effectiveness	100%
Feasibility	100%
Accountability	100%
Transparency	67%
Equity/Equalization	0%
Total	74%
Policy Average	92%
Democracy Average	60%

Summary

1. Situated on the outskirts of Dallas but also at the edge of rural East Texas, Terrell's location and population needs demanded economic development that would enhance old infrastructure while also transforming the city economy by attracting employers.
2. City leaders led by the city manager chose tax incremental financing to incentivize developers to do business in Terrell.
3. The TIF structure was unprecedented as Terrell partnered with Kaufman County and unincorporated communities to formalize the public portion of the public-private arrangement. The agreements eventually added a fourth partner as developers and local leaders created a power center, along with an appointed board, to help to enhance further economic incentives to greater incentivize development, dedicating even more county incremental tax base growth to support economic development.[29]
4. The innovative mindset city leadership displayed illustrated how small towns can learn to think like big cosmopolitan cities to create

29. Torry Edwards, phone interview by author, September 14, 2017.

economic wealth.[30] Uniquely, Terrell designed a governance framework model focused on economic development with the alignment of two public board structures. The City of Terrell Mayor, City Council, Kaufman County Commissioners, Power Center Board, and Tax Increment Financing District No. 1 Board all interact together to fuel the way to economic prosperity.[31]

Without the partnership of Terrell to transfer a city owned water facility, in the form of an unused water take point, over to NTMWD, the $200 million cost would have greatly increased while also increasing the time for construction of a new water treatment plant. Overall, the governance structure built by the City of Terrell will lead land development innovation for regional economic growth for years to come.[32]

5. The initial objective was revitalizing the water supply and infrastructure which Terrell accomplished via an interlocal contract with a regional water source and a local source. The contract transformed Terrell from a small rural community with water supply issues (due to aging infrastructure) to retail provider of water to smaller surrounding communities. An issue became a revenue stream.

6. Thus far, both TIFs have led to the development of $165 million worth of retail property. Most importantly, the developers identified and secured commitments from anchor tenants which are already conducting business in Terrell.

---

30. Torry Edwards, phone interview by author, September 14, 2017.
31. Torry Edwards, phone interview by author, September 14, 2017.
32. Torry Edwards, phone interview by author, September 14, 2017.

PART III: POLICY PRESCRIPTIONS

Lessons Learned

1. *Leveraged existing partnerships*
2. *Leveraged existing capacity*
3. *Utilized professional/complex solutions*
4. *Included partners of multiple sizes and jurisdictional types*
5. *Included regional partners*
6. *Municipal Utility Districts (MUDs) and Special Districts (SDs)*

9

Lean Six Sigma & Analysis of the Service Provision Process

NEW TECHNOLOGIES AND METHODS afford forward thinking cities the opportunity to look at old, existing services and resources in a new light. Gainesville, a relatively small city on the cusp of North Texas, committed to Lean Six Sigma as a singular innovation in 2013. The process transformed how the business of government is conducted in the city but also the philosophy staff members bring to work daily. Like contracts and shared services, the method instilled a collaborative and citizen-driven mindset across all departments as well as new levels of cross-departmental respect and appreciation.

The Rise of Efficiency Analysis And Lean Six Sigma

Corporations and private employers targeted operational costs since the industrial revolutions replaced trade industries with mass consumption and production. What Taylorization and assembly lines started, efficiency experts and analytics process management continues.[1] The public/non-profit sectors are adopting what the private sector started as cities and local governments, in general, seek to identify waste, excess steps, duplication, and tools that yield higher service quality.

Lean Six Sigma (LSS) fits snugly in this work as the process is completely dependent on collaborative teams. Six Sigma remains a prominent process management analytics method since the 1980s. The focus is on customer experience and key stakeholders. The method targets systematic

---

1. Bluestone, Stevenson, and Williams, *The Urban Experience*, 82.

process examination and improving the core product. Lean focuses on waste reduction within the process flow and should enhance performance for less.[2] The Six Sigma method emerged in the early 1980s as American companies responded to the Japanese Kaizen era which triggered an economic boom for the tiny island nation.[3] The Japanese economic boom faded but efficiency and quality efforts remain prominent.[4]

LSS leverages analytical phases to improve existing processes. The DMAIC framework spells out said phases below. These phases structure our project examination later in the chapter:

1. Identify a problem
2. Define what needs improving
3. Measure collection of data to enhance understanding of the process (like most research projects, the data collection phase is typically the longest and most labor intensive. However, the method and stakes demand uncovering any and all data sources. Phase three basically provides the definition for phase two as well as setting the table for the project. Priority number one in data collection is determining how the work gets done.)
4. Analyze collected data to identify root causes of performance inhibitors
5. Improve the process by identifying possible solutions (this obviously cannot occur absent identifying the inhibitors during phase four.)
6. Control the improvement by again collecting outcome data which helps determine whether the new process is achieving desired results

Most importantly, the focus remains squarely on the customer and those steps that add value to the customer experience and outcomes. LSS mandates understanding how the work really gets done which demands the inclusion of employees at all levels of the process and collaborative thinking. The ultimate goal is the identification of those factors creating waste in the process and eliminating those factors.[5]

2. Morgan and Brenig-Jones, *Lean Six Sigma for Dummies*, 9–12.

3. According to Morgan and Brenig-Jones, "Specifically, Motorola CEO Bob Galvin guided the development of Six Sigma to compete with the Japanese manufacturing process." Morgan and Brenig-Jones, *Lean Six Sigma for Dummies*, 14.

4. Morgan and Brenig-Jones, *Lean Six Sigma for Dummies*.

5. Morgan and Brenig-Jones, *Lean Six Sigma for Dummies*.

Does Municipal Texas Use Lean Six Sigma or Other Analytic Tools?

Overall, it appears LSS is not widely utilized among Texas cities. However, several large cities practice the method extensively including Tyler (population 120,000), a deep East Texas central hub, and Irving (245,000), an inner ring city outside Dallas. Additionally, Denton (180,000), a county seat in north Texas, recently integrated LSS.[6] Finally, the East Texas Council of Governments offers training for interested jurisdictions.[7]

Gainesville commitment to Six Sigma/Analytics

Gainesville, a community of 16,000 on the edge of the DFW metroplex, committed fully to LSS and the innovative mindset the process nurtures. The city clearly benefits from needed efficiency and cost reduction. Table 10–1 summarizes Gainesville's profile. The MHHI is comparatively low calculated at merely 74 percent of the state level ($53,207). Additionally, the poverty level eclipses state levels and is actually 128 percent of the state poverty level.[8] Indeed, the city profile would place it squarely in the lower socioeconomic cluster of the urban counties. This fiscal profile combined with the relatively remote location demands innovation from city leaders.[9]

Table 9–1

Gainesville Socioeconomic Profile

Population (2010)	MHHI	Poverty	Health Care	High School	Bachelors
16,002	$39,047	22.2%	77%	79.5%	11.3%

Source: U.S. Census Bureau, "American Community Survey."

---

6. Barry Sullivan, interview by author, October 4, 2017.
7. Barry Sullivan, interview by author, October 4, 2017.
8. U.S. Census Bureau. "2010 Census."
9. Census projections for 2015 indicate a stark reduction in the poverty rate for the entire country. We will use the 2010 data since that is an official census result.

PART III: POLICY PRESCRIPTIONS

City manager Barry Sullivan launched Gainesville's LSS commitment by identifying a class offered by Strategic Government Resources (SGR) and itemizing the $10,000 fee to the 2013 Gainesville budget. He proceeded to pitch the idea to the city council by noting that they preached efficiency and this would allow an efficient mindset to permeate the city staff. The council gave its blessing and the first class of fifteen met that year.[10]

Currently, thirty-five staffers that are still working for Gainesville have graduated and obtained their white belt. Some have continued the SGR training and ascended to higher levels. In fact, the staff includes one black, green, and yellow belt each. Sullivan is actually a black belt and teaches the classes combining the customer-focused and waste elimination process of Lean with the Six Sigma DMAIC process.[11]

Project Examples

Given the widespread training, The LSS mindset has broadly permeated city operations. Table 9–2 identifies which Gainesville departments utilize the method and the results. Regarding those results, the figures clearly speak for themselves as the city and taxpayers have experienced significant budgetary savings. With that said, transforming the office culture remains the most valuable benefit which we will discuss later.[12]

Table 9–2

Gainesville LSS Projects

Department	Function	Alteration/Project Summary	Cost-Benefit
Public Safety	Video Equipment	Utilize recording equipment that can electronically build cases and electronically distribute to prosecutors	$16,085 over 5 years (WIP)

10. Barry Sullivan, interview by author, October 4, 2017.
11. Barry Sullivan, interview by author, October 4, 2017.
12. Barry Sullivan, interview by author, October 4, 2017.

LEAN SIX SIGMA & ANALYSIS OF THE SERVICE PROVISION PROCESS

Department	Function	Alteration/Project Summary	Cost-Benefit
Parks	Downtown LED lights	Plan to replace high-pressure sodium lights with more efficient LED	Estimated $81,697 over 10 years (future)
Transportation	LED lights for state roads	See downtown lights	$137,240 over 10 years (implemented)
Public Works/Parks/Fire Department	Gas	Changed contracting method and monitoring method for the city	$3,000 annually (implemented)
Public Works/Solid Waste	Demo Trailer	Used large trailer instead of smaller dump trucks	$22,000 annually (implemented)
Public Works	Work Order system	Used automated system instead of paper	$66,000 (implemented)
Office support (Entire City)	Electronic Filing/Application System	Electronic filing instead of paper	Major barrier to transferring documents to different departments, so done to reduce delays (WIP)
Public Works	Automatic Water Meters	Replace manual read and touch reading meters with fix read meters	$887,696 (WIP/on year 3 of 7 year replacement plan)
Department	Function	Alteration/Project Summary	Savings
Public Safety	Automatic Ticket Writers		
Public Safety	Video Equipment		
Parks	Downtown LED lights	Replaced __ lights with more Efficient LED	CA
Transportation	LED lights for state roads	See downtown lights	$137,240
Public Works	Gas		$3,000 annually
Public Works	Demo Trailer		$22,000 annually

PART III: POLICY PRESCRIPTIONS

Department	Function	Alteration/Project Summary	Cost-Benefit
Public Works	Work Order system		$66,000
Office support	Electronic Filing/Application System		

Source: City of Gainesville, *Lean Six Sigma*, 2010–2015.

The list presents several observation worthy factors. Of course, the overall savings clearly represents value and the table format cannot afford true justice to enhanced service quality. Additionally, note the departmental breadth and scope of the projects. Cities typically provide eight service categories and this list includes five. Additionally, the sewage and wastewater plant project adds the utility category. This broad scope speaks to staff commitment to the LSS process as well as the emerging collaborative service culture reaping benefits for Gainesville residents.

Wastewater Case Study

While the projects list is lengthy, the wastewater treatment plant provides perhaps the largest project example. Sullivan and his staff knew they needed to replace the existing plant as it was entering year twenty-nine even though it was designed for twenty years. The city could not even find parts when repairs were needed as the system was so old no one sold specific parts for that system. When the system broke down due to an effectiveness issue, down time was extended. This mandated purchasing fabricated parts which increased service costs. The bell clearly tolled for the Gainesville wastewater plant but the city team needed to think through the replacement steps. Like all case studies, this chapter examines how the innovation improved the service delivery process.

Typical Wastewater Process

Gainesville achieved higher performance and savings by eliminating wasteful processes achieved via the replacement of three pieces of machinery with one. Figure 9-1 presents the traditional wastewater treatment process.

A treatment plant collects and purifies sewage water from homes, businesses, etc. for recycling back into streams, creeks, or other sources of water. Actually, nature accomplishes the purification process on its own thanks to small organisms within the water that consume the sewage and clean the water. Therefore, the treatment plant provides needed support to the organic process due to the volume growing urban populations "produce," which would lengthen the organic purification process.[13]

This process has two phases: the creatively named primary and secondary phases. While the process map from Figure 9-1 illustrates a complex process, the primary phase is best described as the purification prepping phase while the secondary phase might best be described as the purification acceleration phase. The primary phase utilizes a water pump and primary clarifier to remove mass objects such as rags, rocks, etc. while also turning suspended solids into sludge. The secondary phase relies primarily on the trickling filters which are simply a bed of stones laden with bacteria that consumes most of the organic matter. While the trickling process remains the primary purification activity, there is a growing trend to apply the bacteria filled sludge to accelerate cleaning. Either way, the secondary stage simply accelerates the natural process.[14] Gainesville's treatment plant utilized this typical process that the LSS team scrutinized to determine whether a less expensive, more efficient process that delivered higher service quality existed.[15]

Issues/Challenges

While maintaining a treatment plant past the expiration date created its own set of problems, Sullivan and the public services leadership quickly determined that simply replacing the old system with the same system type was not the optimal solution for Gainesville residents. The leadership team asked Kimley-Horn, the engineering firm building the new plant, to present several treatment system options. This facilitated a LSS project designed to develop a process including steps of critical quality and exclusive of any excess steps or waste. This included removing excess cleaning processes, water pumping, natural gas, utility expenses, and personnel. The desired

---

13. United States Environmental, *How Wastewater Treatment Works*, 1–2.
14. United States Environmental, *How Wastewater Treatment Works*, 2–4.
15. Jeff James, email interview with author, November 10, 2017.

outcome would limit the system to basic operational regulations while achieving high performance with fewer moving parts and personnel.

The Lean Six Sigma Process: Identifying Steps Critical to Quality

The Gainesville LSS commitment has transformed the city staff into a community focused, collaborative team. The treatment plant team included the city manager, the public services director, and the treatment plant supervisor. Again, all three hold LSS certifications. Jeff James from Kimley-Horn and Associates served as a technical adviser. Overall, the team decided to examine the feasibility of the following outcomes:

1. Eliminate any process that was not critical to quality
2. Eliminate touching something more than once
3. Identify potential energy savings

Figure 9–1

Wastewater Treatment Plant Operational Process

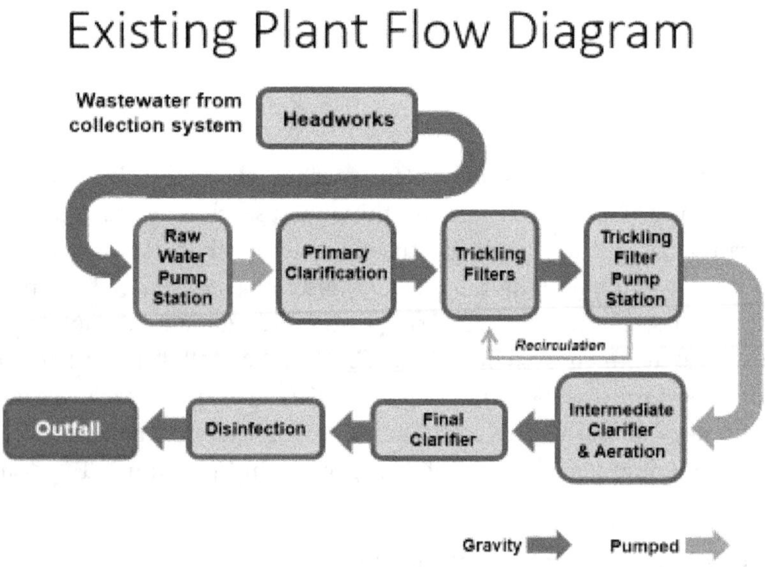

Existing Plant Flow Diagram

Source: City of Gainesville, *Lean Six Sigma*.

The Six Sigma method requires practitioners to separate process steps critical to service quality from steps that do not add value to the customer experience. The process hopefully separates the process wheat from the chaff by identifying process elements that are "critical to quality" and eliminating non-critical elements.[16] The Gainesville team identified three customer groups: residents receiving utility (water, solid waste), property owners, and the Texas Commission for Environmental Quality (TCEQ), which regulates waste removal.[17]

Given this structure, the team identified steps required to adhere to the TCEQ regulations and deliver a high performance system. Data collection and examination is the crux of the LSS method and the team carried out this phase by meeting with employees of the treatment plant to determine how waste system operates on a daily basis. This operational reality remains a critical component of the LSS process as the true picture yields a better understanding of the daily challenges that a broad analysis might miss. The team also analyzed utility bills to determine how to optimize savings.

This research yielded rich data and ultimately direction. The previous process utilized a water pump that required the water to be lifted twice thus requiring more energy.[18] The team replaced the pump with a system that relied on gravity to move water and waste. Most importantly, the team decided to replace the existing four treatment processes (primary clarification, trickling filters, clarification, and aeration) with a sequencing batch reactor (SBR) treatment process. The new SBR construction would yield a single structure with four identical basins treating incoming waste.[19] Figure 9–2 diagrams the proposed plant flow.

This crystallized solution required additional research. Sullivan asked James to provide all available treatment options based on the LSS mandated criteria. The team conducted several meetings with multiple manufacturing companies for headworks, SBR units, and belt presses, which they scored based on lean findings. They also visited a plant in a similar sized Chicago suburb that utilized the same treatment process under consideration.[20] This trip included training on the treatment process.[21]

16. Morgan and Brenig-Jones, *Lean Six Sigma for Dummies*, 10.
17. City of Gainesville, *Lean Six Sigma*.
18. Jeff James, email interview with author, November 10, 2017.
19. Jeff James, email interview with author, November 10, 2017.
20. Jeff James, email interview with author, November 10, 2017.
21. The system manufacturer funded the trip so the LSS did not pass this cost along

PART III: POLICY PRESCRIPTIONS

The extensive research and policy analysis yielded a template for significant savings in every aspect including initial capital investment, construction, daily process efficiency, and electricity costs. Indeed, the energy savings were a key figure in the total operational cost reduction. However, life is full of curve balls and the plant construction presented the Gainesville team with a nasty pitch. During construction, concrete costs skyrocketed as the cement market experienced supply issues. This proved a daunting challenge since the primary raw material for treatment plants is concrete. The construction budget exploded which mandated less excavation and a system that had higher concrete levels to save money.

Leadership ultimately made the decision to raise the elevation of the SBR structure which would reduce the amount of concrete needed to build the structure. Raisin the SBR structure also required moving a water pump from the back of the basin to the front of the basin which slightly increased energy usage and thus costs. However, the overall savings from the concrete still resulted in significant savings for Gainesville.[22]

---

to taxpayers.

22. Jeff James, email interview with author, November 10, 2017.

Figure 9–2
Post-LSS Wastewater Treatment Plant Process

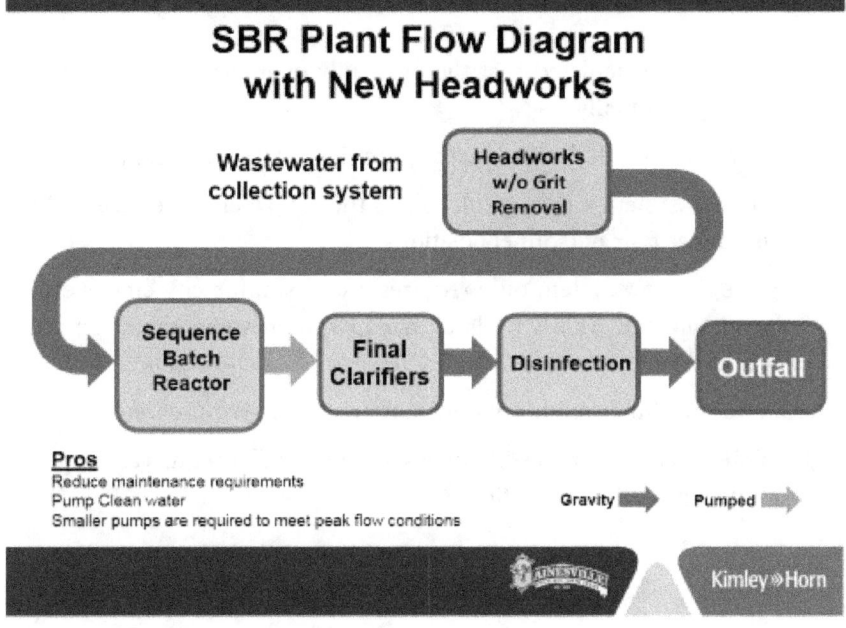

Source: City of Gainesville, *Lean Six Sigma*.

While spiraling concrete costs limited one avenue of savings, Gainesville's response proves instructive. First, the city still experienced big savings overall which heralds the LSS method and their commitment to the process. Additionally, Sullivan and the leadership team found their way through this hurdle via creativity and collaboration. Ultimately, integrating LSS and other methods into organizations and operational processes may seem extraneous but the savings and benefits are real. The team overcame the concrete challenge because embracing LSS has nurtured a staff comprised of problem solvers.

Outcomes[23]

1. The capital investment for the new plant was $13 million while replacing the system with the same treatment process would have cost $16 million.
2. Gainesville calculated that the now fully operational plant will save $214,000 annually.
3. Energy costs will decrease even given the concrete driven alterations.
4. The new system automatically alerts the city when issues arise which eliminates four personnel positions.
5. Since the new system only requires one basin, the city enjoys excess basin capacity. This affords a backup system when the main plant breaks down.
6. Fewer machines reduce maintenance costs and requirements.
7. While the new system still utilizes pumps, smaller pumps are required to meet peak flow conditions.

Report Card

Table 9–3

Gainesville LSS Report Card

Efficiency	60%
Effectiveness	100%
Feasibility	100%
Accountability	100%
Transparency	83%
Equity/Equalization	100%
Total	83%
Policy Average	83%
Democracy Average	89%

23. City of Gainesville, *Lean Six Sigma*.

How did the Gainesville LSS initiative perform based on our chosen criteria? Table 9–3 summarizes the Gainesville report card. While the criteria remains constant, the analysis varied as the innovation focused on an internal commitment to process analysis as opposed to interjurisdictional cooperation. Therefore, regional objectives such as scale are not germane to this approach.

Given that caveat, the Gainesville LSS program achieved high level results. The policy average was 91 percent. The LSS method process saved the city money on all phases of the WWTP construction and operation. The savings emerged via eliminating wasteful steps and processes. Additionally, the cost reductions are sustainable and likely to only increase. The project enhanced effectiveness by reducing needed repairs and downtime for the system. Overall, the new plant easily achieves policy objectives.

The project also scores high in the democracy categories. Gainesville prioritizes transparency with the comptroller's office which is recognized with the platinum designation. Additionally, the LSS method does not create accountability concerns that interlocal contracts might since the innovation never transfers service provision authority. Gainesville citizens continue to receive wastewater service from the same jurisdiction.

Summary

- Public entities are slowly integrating efficiency methods typically reserved for the private sector as budget tightening becomes the new norm.
- Gainesville, a medium sized community on the northeastern edge of the Dallas metropolitan region, embraced LSS culturally.
- The commitment to the method transformed the bottom line and service quality, but also fostered a collaborative culture that transformed staff vision from departmental silos to community service.
- The LSS integration covers several services but the need for a new wastewater treatment plant afforded a singular opportunity for savings and quality enhancement.
- The method ultimately reduced noncritical steps and repair needs.

10

Medstar and Emergency Innovation

ANITA ROLLE KNEW THE drill. She called 911 and was forwarded to one of the dispatchers. They all felt like friends at this point. She heard the sweet, assuring voice of Betty come on the line and asked her what was wrong. Anita calmly replied, "My knee injury is acting up again so I need a ride to the hospital." Betty proceeded to confirm Anita's location and whether she was safe and comfortable. Anita said she was fine. The ambulance and crew arrived ten minutes later just like it had previously. Jeff, the paramedic, helped Anita into a wheel chair and they proceeded to the hospital. Thus, Anita's 150th ambulance ride of 2013 was remarkably similar to the previous 149.

You may have surmised that this suspenseful tale ripe with intrigue is a gripping work of fiction. You are partially correct. The Dallas ambulance team never transported an Anita Rolle as far as I know. However, The City of Dallas Fire-Rescue Emergency Medical Service (EMS) actually transported one person 150 times during 2013. That is almost one trip every two days.[1]

How does this story illuminate the challenges cities face with EMS/ambulance service delivery? First, our tale illustrates the unpredictable nature of emergency service. A city or agency cannot predict emergencies which limits planning much less examining how to make the process more efficient. Also, the call to public service remains a huge factor. An emergency call must receive a response which traditionally required an ambulance trip. Additionally, most agencies are "fire-based" which means they are housed with the fire department at fire stations scattered across the city based on the hope of adequate geographic coverage. Cites that can afford excess capacity pay for it while smaller, poorer jurisdictions make do with

---

1. Norman Seal, interview by author, July 8, 2014.

what they can afford. Therefore, inefficiency is often intentional as cities prepare an effective response to the unexpected.[2]

Most EMS agencies share this burden. For example, Medstar, a regional EMS agency serving fifteen cities in Tarrant County, identified the same issue only on a broader scale. Medstar ambulances provided over 2,000 transports to twenty-one individual patients in 2008. The resulting total cost was $962,429 in ambulance charges. These bills are essentially uncollectible. Stories such as these illuminate the most glaring inefficiency in emergency service: serial users treat ambulance and emergency rooms as their primary care structure which completely subverts the purpose (and cost structure) of emergency medicine.[3]

Dallas realized these challenges (combined with the emerging population growth) could prove toxic to EMS efficacy. Therefore, the city commissioned a study of its EMS bureau service delivery including recommendations in 2012. The study was part of a larger "Vision Process" originated in 2006 to integrate changes in the EMS system. The 2012 study identified several concerns including massive increased call volume and the people and resources responding to the volume. Leaders feared a breaking point where either agency's response efforts suffered via weak performance, or the cost to maintain high levels of performance would become to exorbitant. Dallas residents would be the big losers either way. The agency needed answers and the committee tasked with the study responded with four options:

Option 1: Status Quo

Choose maintaining current performance levels by purchasing needed resources to maintain current response levels. The taxpayer cost would be $12,836,776 while failing to address the heavy workload EMTs/paramedics faced.

2. Norman Seal, interview by author, July 8, 2014.
3. Medstar Mobile Healthcare. "Mobile Healthcare Programs."

PART III: POLICY PRESCRIPTIONS

Option 2: Save Money by Doing Absolutely Nothing

Cost would be next nothing but performance would suffer. Additionally, deferred maintenance issues as well as personnel safety issues would catch up to the agency.

Option 3: High Maintenance

Buy enough resources to fund long-term solutions to performance and population concerns. Final bill would exceed $24,000,000.

Option 4: Innovation Driven by Analytics

Examine the process and completely change it.

Faced with the same options in 1986, Medstar opened door number four. Dallas recently chose the same approach and is currently modifying the business structure.[4]

This chapter examines a regional government that successfully implemented option four decades ago and continues the process. With that said, the regional agency combined an innovative regional structure with data analytics and process management to deliver ambulance services absent the issues that Dallas addressed. The model is highly replicable as we will learn. However, we need to first look at how the EMS industry evolved to this point.

EMS History

The EMS system and structure as we know it is relatively new all things considered. In fact, the history of EMS agencies runs slightly over seventy years.[5] However, ancient historical evidence of the practice exists. For example, the biblical parable of the Good Samaritan includes an explanation of the hero dressing the victim's wounds with oil and wine which indicated that a treatment protocol of some sort existed. While the first utterance of the term "ambulance" traces back to Spanish monarchs King Ferdinand

---

4. Dallas Fire-Rescue Department. *The Future*, 13–18.
5. Dallas Fire-Rescue Department. *The Future*, 13–18.

and Queen Isabella from the fifteenth century, most of the early ambulance history developed as one would expect around treating combat wounds for military personnel during several conflicts over the centuries. The French apparently receive credit for this innovation as Napoleon's chief physician, Baron Dominique-Jean Larrey, presumably developed the first triage and transport system for wounded soldiers. However, there are studies that identify General George Washington as instrumental in developing the same system for revolutionary soldiers while most historical analysis holds that the Americans did little in ambulance transport until the Civil War. Either, the transport process included horse drawn carriages, obviously, but also air transport via balloons.

After the war, several large, urban hospitals still had the equipment used to treat wounded soldiers so they finally decided to provide the same treatment and transport to the civilian population. Cincinnati, Ohio established the first ambulance service for civilians in 1865. While this was definitely the first American public ambulance service, many believe it is the first ambulance department in any country. Atlanta and New Orleans, both hit hard during the war, soon followed Cincinnati's lead. New York unveiled its own ambulance service in 1869 which was quickly followed by the fist dispatch system in 1870.[6]

The industries' development beyond these infant steps was slow prior to 1966 as was the creation of universal standards and benchmarks for existing agencies. However, this phase was not without some landmark events. For example, the Red Cross created almost 900 posts along highways in 1936 to aid motorists suffering from accident injuries. Roanoke Virginia founded the first volunteer EMS unit to serve with the growing number of hospital-based agencies. Still, the military remained the source for enhanced ambulance service and innovations to the process. The Army funded a fleet of new ambulances in time for World War I and maintained transport and treatment protocols. However, civilian ambulance innovation stalled.[7]

One invention, and its greatest unintended consequence, halted the stagnation—the car. Policy experts and the media announced car accidents as a growing epidemic mandating a response. The response was swift. The landmark event heralding the modern EMS era was the National Academy of Sciences section of the National Research Council (NRC) releasing *Accidental Death and Disability: The Neglected Disease of*

6. Robbins, "A History of Emergency," 9–18.
7. Dallas Fire-Rescue Department, *The Future of EMS Service Delivery*, 4–5.

Modern Society in 1964. The NRC paper established goals and structure for fire-based EMS and filled gaps of knowledge and need which created the modern EMS structure. The suggestions flowed from experts that implemented battlefield trauma lessons learned from their tours in the Korean and Vietnam Wars. This model development eventually yielded future studies and funding for the current model.[8]

The Traditional EMS Delivery System

The fire-based model has remained consistent with the addition of several innovative techniques. EMS transports serve as second responders supporting fire engines. The 911 dispatch center remains step one for emergency connections including both crime-based emergencies (or emergencies requiring law enforcement) and fires. Of course, ambulances support both types of emergencies. The normal business model mandates a transport response to all calls regardless of severity as the Dallas and Medstar stories illustrate. In fact, agencies prioritize effective coverage over efficiency which strikes most as a reasonable balance since capacity issues can compromise lives. While this is certainly understandable (even admirable), responding to every call creates inefficiency number one.[9]

Deployment creates number two. Ambulance deploy for on-scene arrival after fire trucks (hence second responder status). Of course, time is of the essence and most agencies track response time. Indeed, the industry created response time (RT) standard (eight minutes) as well as the percentage of all responses meeting the standard (90 percent). Additionally, adequate deployment mandates adequate staffing, training and apparatus.[10]

Overall, geographic coverage perhaps remains the metric that best measures whether an agency will meet RT standards. The best way to explain geographic coverage is to ask whether an ambulance placement and numbers are sufficient to reach every accident within eight minutes. Agencies traditionally house ambulances and the EMT/paramedic staff in fire houses with first responders. Additionally, staffing is constant and does not increase or decrease based on time of day or day of the week. Essentially, meeting geographic coverage standards requires cities with

8. National Academy of Sciences and National Research Council, *Accidental Death and Disability*, 8–10.

9. Matt Zavadsky, interview by author, March 5, 2014.

10. International Association of Firefighters, *Emergency Medical Services*, 39.

the fiscal means to engage in the practice of excess capacity when locating ambulances and staffing said boxes. Granted, cities struggling to meet the cost face different challenges.[11]

This structure requires the city to engage in ambulance acquisition, paramedic hiring, certification, training the 911 dispatch center and staff, and providing the infrastructure to accommodate all emergencies and mass casualty situations. The process also requires a medical director per Texas law who develops emergency protocols and monitors compliance. Additionally, EMS systems include an "online consult" apparatus for respondents, who need to consult doctors or nurses when an emergency requires breaking protocol. However, the traditional hospital-based portion of service has only recognized value of EMS over past two decades. In other words, the typical EMS system is incredibly expensive to maintain and operate.[12]

Medstar

History

What if various cities voluntarily joined or created a regional EMS agency? How successfully could it address these challenges? Medstar provides the answer. The regional cooperative government serves 15 cities through an interlocal contractual agreement between the client cities. Table 10-(1) identifies each partnering jurisdiction and summarizes relevant socio-economic data.[13]

The contract created a governmental body best described as a regional ambulance authority governed by a regional ambulance board comprised of members appointed by the member cities. The governing board enjoys policymaking authority in several areas. First, it sets the overall policy direction and standards for the emergency medical care system in those fifteen cities. The policies are set for a region as opposed to distinct policies or exceptions for individual cities. The board also decided whether or not to contract for ambulance services or provide the ambulance services.[14]

---

11. International Association of Firefighters, *Emergency Medical Service*.
12. Dallas Fire-Rescue Department, *The Future of EMS Service Delivery*, 8.
13. U.S. Census Bureau, "2010 Census."
14. Matt Zavadsky, interview by author, March 5, 2014.

PART III: POLICY PRESCRIPTIONS

Table 10-1 Socioeconomic Profiles of Medstar Client Cities

City	Population	MHHI	Poverty	Health Care	High School	Bachelors
Affluent						
Westover Hills	682	$ 196,250	9%	96%	100%	50%
Blue Mound	2,394	$ 51,208	13%	82%	64%	4%
Forest Hill	12,355	$ 43,949	22%	68%	71%	6%
Fort Worth	741,206	$ 52,492	19%	77%	80%	18%
Haltom City	42,409	$ 43,792	17%	69%	72%	9%
Hurst	37,337	$ 53,488	14%	79%	85%	18%
River Oaks	7,427	$ 42,622	15%	74%	73%	8%
Sansom Park	4,686	$ 38,368	31%	66%	62%	5%
Westworth Village	2,472	$ 53,519	9%	89%	86%	20%
White Settlement	16,116	$ 39,747	22%	76%	76%	7%
Burleson	36,690	$ 69,088	9%	86%	92%	17%
Edgecliff Village	2,776	$ 69,904	11%	83%	91%	13%
Haslet	1,517	$ 89,000	4%	89%	94%	28%
Saginaw	19,806	$ 74,521	8%	86%	91%	15%
Lakeside	1,307	$ 78,750	4%	91%	93%	25%
Dalworthington Gardens	2,259	$ 115,809	2%	94%	93%	29%

Sources: U.S. Census Bureau. "2010 Census"; Medstar Mobile Healthcare. *Community Report for 2013.*

The history of Medstar and the Area Metropolitan Ambulance Authority (the authority) began in 1986. Medstar served mostly as a liaison between the client cities and private companies as the contractors provided EMS deliver under a performance-based contract primarily based on response time. The authority maintained this structure for almost twenty years as it cycled through four contractors. The public-private relationship deteriorated to the point that in 2005 the authority and client cities decided to provide ambulance service directly to the cities.

MEDSTAR AND EMERGENCY INNOVATION

Matt Zavadsky, Medstar Chief of Public Affairs, explains the decision:

In 2005, after a series of failed contractors, the authority decided that it's time to have our hand at doing this ourselves. The primary reasons for the contracting strategy in the beginning for this public utility model system, was that most of the brain trust for operations, on how to make the system efficient and clinically sound, rested in the private sector.

Over time, as these public utility model cooperatives, like we have in Fort Worth, became more mature, the former executives at the contractors that were providing some of these services began to work for the authorities, instead of working for the contractor. The expertise that came along with that, came with them.[15]

The Area Metropolitan Ambulance Authority made the decision to self-operate in 2005 with approval from all fifteen member cities. Currently, all of the system employees, as well as the ambulance component, are assets of a public entity. Table 10-2 summarizes the personnel and emergency apparatus assets.

Table 10-2

Medstar Resources

Ambulances	54
RLS	
ALS	
FT EMT	100
FT paramedics	100
Coverage (square miles)	421
Residents	880,000
Square Mile ratio	7.8
Resident Ratio	16296.3

Source: Medstar Mobile Healthcare. *Community Report for 2015.*

---

15. Matt Zavadsky, interview by author, March 29, 2014.

PART III: POLICY PRESCRIPTIONS

The system utilizes fifty-four ambulances, 100 certified EMT, and 100 certified paramedics. These assets and personnel serve 880,000 citizens over an area of 421 square miles. Ambulance per capita and coverage per square miles are both valuable effectiveness benchmarks for determining whether an EMS provider provides adequate coverage. This equates to one ambulance for every 7.8 square miles and every 16,296 citizens. This report compares these results for each case study.

Like private providers, Medstar leverages the first response resources of client cities. This reality can potentially render evaluations of efficiency and effectiveness suspect given the fire-based wholly inclusive structure. However, a regional agency manages a comprehensive emergency apparatus with significant support staff as well as the infrastructure including the ambulances, the telephony, the 911 communications component, and the most importantly, the accounts receivable.[16]

Therefore, while, Medstar provides ambulance service for any calls in the regions, the authority also bills for the service just like any health care provider. The ambulance transport, potential treatment on the scene, and release from the hospital are billed to either the patient or, if the patient has insurance, to the insurance company. The patient and/or the insurance company pays the bill. The accounts receivable service is also property of the authority. The authority, for twenty years, used the accounts receivable to pay the contractor the monthly fee for hiring employees that operate the ambulances and operate the 911 call center. The employees were limited to the billing process. Every other employee and resource, including the EMTs, paramedics, ambulances, maintenance people, and those who worked in executive offices were private employees. Medstar has permanently altered that structure.[17]

Innovative Solutions

Medstar is essentially a regional government that operates like a private company. Agency leadership, including the executive team and the Board of Trustees, prioritized strict reliance on operating revenue with the cities providing zero tax support. This scarcity has conditioned leadership, staff, and emergency personnel to pursue innovation, technology, and analytic tools to find ways for achieving high performance for less money. However,

16. Medstar Mobile Healthcare. *Community Report for 2017.*
17. Matt Zavadsky, interview by author, March 29, 2014.

the EMS agency is still a public service/government entity which refuses to compromise service quality or transparency.[18]

How does a public entity achieve high performance levels while receiving zero public funding? The leadership team identified four realties of the EMS business model that compromised efficiency and potentially performance. Solving the following challenges became the basis for the cycle of innovation:

1. Decreasing system "abuse" by patients who do not truly need emergency response without compromising public safety.[19]
2. Managing the over-saturation of EMS geographic coverage based on demand while maintaining adequate coverage.
3. Related to number two, reducing excess staffing based on demand without compromising performance or increasing stress for emergency personnel.
4. Bottom line: develop a system with proactive process management that aligns resources with actual demand as opposed to reactively deploying excess resources which increases operational costs.

Solutions

1. Develop four emergency levels based on response. Train 911 personnel to identify severity level and act accordingly. Successful implementation reduces transport deployment for patients that do not require emergency treatment.
2. Identify when and where accidents or emergency events historically occur. Adjust ambulance locations and staffing levels accordingly.
3. Create a response process that leverages technology to monitor emergency demand and response.[20]

Bottom line, what were the results? Did the strategies work? A fiscal and performance review measured against our chosen criteria sheds light

---

18. Matt Zavadsky, interview by author, March 29, 2014.
19. Matt Zavadsky, interview by author, March 29, 2014.
20. Matt Zavadsky, interview by author, March 29, 2014.

on Medstar's operational efficacy. We should review each starting with asking whether the agencies' innovative mindset saved money.

Efficiency

Our efficiency analysis simply asks whether the agency's efforts reduced the cost to taxpayers and is the efficiency sustainable. Table 10–3 summarizes the amount Texas cities of various sizes paid annually for EMS provision. The list includes a large major hub (Dallas) as well as several suburbs and outer ring rural towns. These profiles are similar to the clients which provides an indication of the amount each city would individually pay for its own fire-based EMS agency.

However, The EMS partnership serves the entire region without charging nary a subsidy for the honor. The agency staffed over 230,000 unit hours, responded to over 137,000 calls, and performed over 98,000 transports for 2016 alone. The collective cost to the cities for all this activity was zero.[21]

Regarding sustainability, Table 10-4 also compares the cost per response for Medstar to other EMS units. Cost per unit provides a glimpse into the productivity of organizations. In fact, for profit industries from airlines to banks spend many hours and dollars reducing per unit costs. It is the most detailed process efficiency metric. Amazingly, the ambulance system actually produced per unit profit (or surplus revenue) during this three year period. Additionally, the agency produced a profit during each year even though the table does not provide this data. The three year results highlight the consistency of the Medstar method.

Table 10–3

Medstar Budgetary Comparison

Government	Total Transports 2014–2016	3 Year Average	3 Year Budget	Cost/ Transport
Medstar	318,996	106,332	$ 116,339,326	$ 364.70
Revenues	318,996	106,332	$ 148,806,073	$ 466.48
Net per Transport		0		$ 101.78
Dallas	585,213	195071	$ 85,921,692.00	$ 146.82

21. Medstar Mobile Healthcare. *Careholders' Report for 2017.*

Government	Total Transports 2014–2016	3 Year Average	3 Year Budget	Cost/ Transport
Waxahachie	7977	2659	$ 354,332	$ 44.42
Pilot Point	1200	400	3753334	$ 3,127.78

Source: Area Metropolitan Ambulance Authority, 2012-2016

Effectiveness

How does the EMS industry measure effectiveness? The International Association of Firefighters (IAFF) published a list of generally accepted industry-wide benchmarks agencies prioritize in determining performance levels. The handbook included fifteen benchmarks or system performance measures including eight core standards along with seven considered to be in the developmental stage. The IAFF adopted safety and quality standards developed by the National Fire Prevention Association (NFPA) to agency response and preparedness. With that said, the IAFF adapted the standard for fire-based agencies such as the Dallas unit.[22] Regional systems such as Medstar and private contractors utilize a different process infrastructure. For example, regional systems will most likely not house ambulances in fire stations while private contractors possess narrower responsibilities.[23] Still, every EMS system faces performance expectation regardless the type. Additionally, the criteria examination does not require measuring every core standard as some overlap while others fall outside the daily process standards.[24]

Response Time

Response time provides perhaps the most basic metric for EMS preparedness and resource allocation. Response time is obviously fairly simple to define. The "timer" starts when the ambulance wheels commence rolling toward the incident until the unit actually reaches the emergency scene.

22. International Association of Fire Fighters. *Emergency Medical Services*, 29–47.
23. Norman Seal, interview by author, July 8, 2014.
24. International Association of Firefighters, *Emergency Medical Services*, 36–46.

PART III: POLICY PRESCRIPTIONS

The NFPA 1710 standard for second responders is eight minutes.[25] Agencies ultimately maintain two measurements: average response time (total transports/responses/total minutes) and the percentage of timely responses (total responses/timely responses or responses that took eight minutes or less.[26] Most agencies utilize the latter metric.[27]

Medstar provides performance and productivity data as part of the agenda for every monthly meeting of the board of directors. The author researched response time results for the five year period from 2012–2016 which Table 10-4 summarizes. To be frank, this was hardly the work of combing through dusty archival data as the regional unit posts the minutes/agenda online. Overall, the ambulance operation system exceeded industry benchmarks over the half decade and failed to meet the standard in only one year (2015 which was a near miss at 89.6 percent). Medstar responded to well over half a million calls during this period.

Table 10-4
Response Time/Staffing Results 2012–2016

Year	Calls	Response Time Met	Average	Staffing Scheduled	Produced	Average
2012	108,089	99,815	92.3%	209,446	191,887	91.6%
2013	111,727	102,482	91.7%	218,006	200,149	91.8%
2014	91,142	82,712	90.8%	179,249	168,717	94.1%
2015	106,274	95,205	89.6%	189,969	173,277	91.2%
4 Year Total	417,232	380,214	91.1%	796,670	734,030	92.1%

Source: Area Metropolitan Ambulance Authority, 2012–2016

---

25. The NFPA/IAFF developed separate standards for first and second responders with four minutes serving as the first responder standard. Additionally, agencies are developing different standards based on incident severity.

26. International Association of Firefighters, *Emergency Medical Services*, 37.

27. Matt Zavadsky, interview by author, May 10, 2014.

Staffing

NFPA standard 1710 requires a level of preparedness built on both the quantity and quality of personnel. The standard calls for a minimum number of qualified personnel and resources available to ably manage call volume effectively and safely for patients and crew alike. With that said, the standard does not reference a quantitative benchmark to evaluate staffing effectiveness.[28]

Medstar developed quantitative benchmarks built on historic demand trends. The regional authority determines call and transport volume based on the twenty year history of emergency activity. This data includes quantity as well as call severity and determines staffing and available resources for each hour. This creates a benchmark called "unit hour production" which is the level of support needed to meet emergency demand based on historic patterns plus two standard deviations. The system benchmark requires staffing needs are met for 90 percent of the unit hours. Additionally, Medstar measures a benchmark for personnel capacity which tracks whether the authority staffed the required paramedic and EMT personnel for active shifts. Again, the standard is 90 percent of all shifts experiencing adequate staffing for these key, certified professionals. Granted, both benchmarks were developed internally as opposed to utilizing an industry standard. However, the measurements are sufficiently rigorous and would most likely meet or exceed the industry standard which remains in the developmental stage.

Table 10–4 also includes staffing results. The regional authority exceeded overall staffing quantity standards for shifts during every year of operation, in addition to obviously eclipsing the standard for the five year period. Again, historic data determined staffing demand on an hourly basis. For example, predictive data indicated that the EMS operation would experience 230 transports for a twenty-four hour operation period reviewed by the author. The authority actually had 257 transports during that timeframe but the system adapted by creating a production goal that included two standard deviations. This approach clearly deviates from standard urban fire-based operations which staffs based on crisis level preparedness for each fire station.

---

28. International Association of Firefighters, *Emergency Medical Services*, 38.

PART III: POLICY PRESCRIPTIONS

Analysis

The results are impressive. Medstar provides high performing EMS provision to taxpayers for free. Additionally, the unit costs speak to operational sustainability and continued efficiency. How does the regional jurisdiction accomplish said results?

The answer lies in a continuous cycle of innovation, analytics, and operation examination, or reflection emerging from the solutions mentioned earlier in the chapter. Readers may recall the two pervasive efficiency issues plaguing EMS operations: oversaturation or overdeployment of assets (emergency personnel and ambulances), and abuse of the emergency system by patients whose condition does not require an ambulance nor an ER trip. Agency leadership searched for tools that would address these issues. The Marvilis software package emerged as a solution to the saturation predictive problem.[29]

Marvilis essentially structures daily Medstar operations via analytics. The system analyzed twenty years of accident data to identify event trends and proceeded to "crunch" the data. The result is the daily operational schedule in the form of a PULSE report.

Marvilis and the PULSE report govern asset deployment based on "demand" or emergency event data. As you can see from the illustration, operational supervisors utilize the analytic tools to determine staffing levels on half hour shifts which reduces personnel costs. Additionally, the system replaces geographic coverage with demand coverage as the deployed emergency field staff positions the ambulances geographically according to historic trends. Like the saturation approach, the ambulance numbers and placement objective targets adequate geographic coverage to ensure response times within industry standards.[30]

While Medstar builds operational deployment based on demand, it is perhaps somewhat ironic that its most impactful innovation targets demand reduction. The chapter began with true stories of ambulance abuse by patients better served by a trip to a primary physician or specialist. While the issue is far more complex than this book can could possibly express, such waste remains perhaps the largest cause of rising costs for ambulance service and even the larger health care market.

---

29. Matt Zavadsky, interview by author, May 10, 2014.
30. Matt Zavadsky, interview by author, May 10, 2014.

Given these concerns, the EMS provider launched the Mobile Integrated Healthcare (MIH) program in 2009. The program pursues a decrease in ambulance trips and emergency room visits by targeting high volume EMS patients, low acuity triage cases, and readmission issues. Additionally, an innovative home health partnership provides EMT personnel to help discharged patients adhere to medical advice such as taking prescribed medication and avoiding certain activities. Bottom line: MIH decreased the burden facing emergency personnel by avoiding 3,760 emergency room visits, 553 hospital admissions, and 7,162 ambulance transports. It is vital to note that the program did not cause emergency personnel to ignore these patients but rather it redirected said patients to a more appropriate treatment outcome which saved them valuable time and money. Additionally, the financial impact was palpable as the redirected process saved $12,222,205 in healthcare costs.[31] Overall, patients received proper treatment (while avoiding ER charges), the emergency infrastructure could focus on actual high acuity patients, and the taxpayer burden was alleviated.

Transparency

Table 10–5

Medstar Transparency Rubric

Transparency Available Data		Clarity	
Finances	1	Summaries	1
Contracts	1	Visualizations	1
Procurement	1	Downloads	1
Economic Development		Other	1
Pensions		Staffing	1
Debt	1		
Total	4		5

---

31. Medstar Mobile Healthcare, *Careholders' Report for 2017*; Medstar Mobile Healthcare. "Mobile Healthcare Program."

PART III: POLICY PRESCRIPTIONS

Medstar excels in providing data and decisions for public consumption. Interested citizens enjoys online access to monthly board meeting minutes which includes the following data:

1. A monthly update to the annual budget including revenue and costs
2. Monthly expenses including emphasis toward capital expenses such as new ambulances, defibrillators, etc.
3. The monthly performance results by city including number of calls by severity, number of transports, response time, and staffing productivity results (including coverage hours).

Additionally, the agency also produces annual reports with the following data: annual budget including cost/transport, annual performance results, and staffing cost plus turnover

The public affairs staff prioritizes clarity especially when developing the annual report structure. Readers can review financial data via easily understood charts or graphs.[32]

Table 10–6

Medstar Report Card

Efficiency	100%
Effectiveness	100%
Feasibility	67%
Accountability	100%
Transparency	100%
Equity/Equalization	50%
Total	91%
Policy	92%
Democracy	90%

32. Area Metropolitan Ambulance Authority, *Board of Directors Meeting Packets*, 2012–2016.

Report Card

Medstar emerged as the only regional government to earn straight As. Leadership leveraged a combination of innovation, analytics, and the regional structure to eliminate wasteful steps and excess staffing which yielded a revenue driven, subsidy-free operation that actually delivers profits or surplus revenues. Additionally, performance results easily eclipse industry benchmarks. Tax free governments also tend to enjoy high public approval ratings.

With that said, Medstar truly distinguishes itself with a democracy score of ninety. The organization's website includes data from every monthly board meeting. This is not limited to mere meeting minutes but budgetary data, capital spending, personnel turnover, performance results, and decisions. Finally, citizens can access clear charts and tables free of jargon. Medstar obviously prioritizes transparency.

Summary

1. Fifteen cities including Fort Worth founded Medstar in 1986 via an interlocal contract. The Area Metropolitan Ambulance Authority served as a liaison between the client cities and private contractors that actually delivered ambulance services.
2. The regional government eventually replaced the private providers with "in-house" service provision due to performance issues.
3. The client base barely eclipses national MHHI standards. Additionally, nine of the fifteen cities fall in the low socioeconomic cluster.
4. The regional government has self-funded since 2009 which was the last year cities subsidized the EMS agency. The agency operates like a private for-profit entity which mandates waste eradication. However, leadership remains committed to providing high quality emergency response.
5. Two innovative tools enhanced process efficiency: reducing ambulance abuse (non-emergency use) and replacing a geographic coverage model which promoted resource oversaturation with a demand model.

6. Six sigma collaborative analysis yielded a systemic process that produced a transactional surplus as well as an annual budget surplus while maintaining performance results eclipsing industry standards.

7. Innovation remains constant as they focus on creating alternatives to ambulance transport for populations prone to EMS abuse.

8. Medstar prioritizes transparency as interested parties enjoy access to budgetary data, policy decisions, and performance online. Reports include focused graphics which enhances clarity.

Part IV: Changing the Landscape

A Checklist for Reform

WHAT HAVE WE LEARNED? What have the case studies taught us? Are the lessons replicable to other Texas regions and counties? Which innovations remain optimal and which government functions should local leadership target for regional innovation?

Valuable Partnerships argues that voluntary cooperative regional structures, or functional regionalism, provides the optimal strategy for maintaining the benefits of fragmentation while also introducing the benefits of regionalism including greater efficiency, higher performance, and networking.

Part IV addresses whether the argument was successful. Chapter 11 synthesizes the case study findings to develop a report card (checklist) to help determine whether the programs achieved the criteria standards defined in chapter 5. That chapter identifies what worked, what failed, and offers suggestions for improvement.

The analysis unveiled in chapter 11 segues into the conclusions structuring chapter 12, which compares the profile of cities and regions participating in successful case study partnerships. The regional profiles from chapter 3 determine whether the model can be replicated across the state and what the regional structure might look like. We also consider what municipal Texas look like in twenty to thirty years. The final chapter builds on the presented evidence to develop a feasible, workable structure that addresses the challenges facing the state.

11

Synthesis of Results

PART III ILLUMINATED THE innovations Texas municipalities are adopting. Each chapter explores the challenges facing Texas municipal leaders and the innovative solutions they developed to save taxpayer dollars while still providing high quality service. Each study presented how innovative structures, partnership, technology, and analytics transformed service provision for an array of government functions as well as potentially transforming the structure of municipal America. Each contract/regional government adapted a multi-party or regional structure as opposed to a transactional two party model to determine if voluntary, functional consolidation yields the same benefits as actual consolidation allegedly provides save Gainesville.

Granted, the chapters hardly qualified as light reading given the density of budget data and performance benchmarks. Now what? Avid readers often use analogies to describe the joys of book reading. Some books are like marathons requiring patience and pacing. Some works are like roller coasters taking the reader on a fast-paced, page-turning thrill ride. How would readers describe this work?[1] Well, government contracts would be a poor name for a roller coaster although city managers probably envision their job as one. This work flows like a game (video or board) that requires the player to successfully complete several stages before reaching the final destination which brings the biggest challenge to the player's skills.[2]

---

1. Be gentle. I have feelings too.
2. For example, fight/war games where you, the antagonists, cannot fire accurately or are meek. You finish with an Arnie/Rock combo platter scripted for annihilation. Good times.

PART IV: CHANGING THE LANDSCAPE

What are the "stages" of this work? Chapter 1 identified the questions framing each section and the chapters occupying those sections. These are the structural stages for this journey:

Part I

1. What is the historic American municipal structure?
2. Why is the model in dire need of innovative change?
3. Which factors are driving said need?
4. How is local government in Texas different?
5. Why is the need perhaps most dire in Texas?

Part II

6. How are local leaders responding?

Part III

7. Are the responses innovative?
8. Are the responses working?

Part IV

9. Are the responses replicable in other urban regions?
10. Are the responses sustainable?

Part III addressed questions (stages) seven and eight with case studies examining whether citizen-centered results/outcomes are based on policy and democratic criteria. Therefore, we are left with the final, most challenging stage: determining whether cities can replicate these great ideas. For example, could Houston or Harris county initiate a regional EMS service that mimics Medstar's success? Could less populous, more rural regions adapt the Terrell ED/water model? Which regions possess the capacity to integrate Six Sigma and analytic tools in general? Finally, are these models sustainable? This chapter serves as the pivot form describing the challenges and the innovative solutions some leaders have developed to prescribe a plan for urban Texas.

A word on the proper prescription and reform, in general, recalls chapter 6. Social science textbooks always finish with a prescription which chapter 1 alluded to quite strongly (IMHO). Those prescriptions (like real world solutions) typically fall under one of two categories: the idealistic, normative-driven,pie-in-the-sky/save-the-world approach juxtaposed with the incremental, realistic approach tinged by seasoned experience and wisdom. While you, the dear reader, might accuse me of making fun of the idealistic plans (you would be correct although many realistic plans suffer from bitter sourness or the hopeless, "that is the best we can possibly hope for," mantra. Indeed, experience can cloud judgment and render leaders blind to both opportunities and warning signals.) The world needs both types and people committed to fighting for them. However, the realists carry most days which is why I wrote and included chapter in the introduction of Part III. Most dreams die with the dreamer.

With that in mind, allow me to inject Tiebout back into the discussion. Public choice theory builds on the rational economic approach to posit that public actors are really no different than private actors. They make decisions that maximize their own self-interest. Tiebout applies this mindset to local citizens or voters who can "vote with their feet" by moving to the community (thanks to fragmentation for creating the municipal market) which provides the optimal bundle of goods and services at the optimal price.

What if we combined the two concepts to better predict whether city council members, mayors, and city managers are more or less likely to pursue regional cooperation?[3] Both my 2013 survey and logical conjecture find the proposition that large cities with middle to low income tax bases benefit from sharing services and cooperation. If so, both aging "suburbs" with smaller populations and fringe rural towns (they possess similar economic profiles) need cooperation. The motivation for these categories essentially runs the gamut from saving money to providing services at performance levels that are simply not affordable given their own devices.

Conversely, what about affluent or upper middle class suburbs with relatively large populations? Or the communities that can afford high level

---

3. Analytic tools and software designed to help those of us who cannot calculate the analytic tools on our own exist to develop probability/predictive models based on a set of variables. This sounds like an awesome project. We will rely on conjecture for now.

services and control over service delivery? What motivates the city leadership to contract? Well, saving money appeals to everyone from elected officials to citizens. Granted, the vast majority of the suburbs fitting these profiles contract for services as well as sharing capacity with smaller units. However, these jurisdictions obviously enjoy leverage when entering into contracts and would more likely crave control.

Additionally, the citizens might find certain agreements unattractive based on a variety of characteristics.[4] The NIMBY charge seems appropriate here. Would this citizen base approve of sharing their police force with lower income communities closer to the inner city, or of receiving service from the central city? Party partisanship is instructive as most Texas hubs are Democratic power bases while suburbs fuel the Republican machine.

What if we removed high income services as a partner option just for fun? Could cooperation still yield the needed benefits for the other jurisdictions? This thesis (affluent suburbs are less likely to enter into regional cooperative agreements) serves as the framework for chapter 11.

Synthesizing the Results

Our ten chapter journey still leaves several unanswered questions such as whether the innovations were successful. Chapter 11 answers this question with a composite report card. Finally, are the models replicable and sustainable for all Texas counties or urban regions? The final section of the chapter addresses this question by comparing the partnering profiles from each agreement to the county profiles from chapter 4.

Table 11–1 summarizes the composite results. We will examine the broad, cumulative categories of policy and democracy first. The structured contracts clearly benefitted partnering cites and residents as the average fell in the A minus range. This makes sense as participating municipalities targeted results based outcomes. Indeed, the scores are solid across all eight contracts. Conversely, democratic averages are mixed. Some contracts, such as Medstar, exceeded transparency expectations while others struggled. Both results call for a deeper examination of each report card category.

---

4. Yes, this assumes they would actually show interest in government contracts. Cynics.

SYNTHESIS OF RESULTS

Table 11-1

Composite Report Card Results

Efficiency	96%
Effectiveness	100%
Feasibility	93%
Accountability	100%
Transparency	76%
Equity/Equalization	60%
Total	86%
Policy	98%
Democracy	81%

Regarding the policy categories, this work has frequently referenced saving money as the highest contracting priority and these results support that thesis. Every service provision/government function driven contract scored highest in efficiency with only the Terrell TIF contract and the PRPC service producing modest savings at best. However, partnering cities entered the agreement to achieve higher performance or create benefits that could not exist absent shared service arrangements.

Interestingly, the effectiveness average not only eclipsed the efficiency average but scores were consistently high across the board. These results speak volumes to the refusal of leaders compromising quality to save money. Additionally, every partnership either prioritizes performance, or even identified service quality, as the main priority. Most importantly, causation remains a vital piece of the research puzzle and each contract provided direct evidence of either contributing to, or directly improving service. Many contracts (such as Terrell and PRPC) provided services cities could not afford, while others (such as Medstar and Gainesville) leveraged scale and analytics.

Finally, feasibility never emerged as an issue. Granted, state law affords local government the capacity to cooperate absent electoral approval and public sentiment which is hardly critical, given the result. With that said, the culture remains highly suspect of government actors and activities; conservative state officials are promising new efforts to strip local authority. Given these realities, leaders are wise to prioritize working with their elected leaders and the public in crafting policy solutions. The Glenn Heights story proves instructive. City manager and staff only help their cause by keeping stakeholders aligned, engaged, and supportive of prevailing strategy.

Indeed, 47 percent of city managers responded that their county was the primary contracting partner with 43 percent indicating that the county was also their preferred partner. Additionally, a regional partner (county, COG, or special district) was the primary contracting partner with 54 percent listing a regional partner as the preferred option. Granted, these findings do not indicate if these relationships involved multiple contracting partners.[5] Additionally, the Tarrant County EMS authority provided effective service to fifteen cities, including nine municipalities with a struggling tax base.

A deeper review of the democracy results explains the lower categorical scores. Specifically, many contracts struggled in presenting transparent data and decision-making to the public. Accountability concerns actually proved unfounded as citizens still enjoyed direct access to responsible officials. However, reporting proved subpar. Citizens motivated to the point of reviewing budget, policy, and personnel decisions enjoy access to the information by law. In fact, the data remains readily available via the internet. However, clarity remains the primary issue as jurisdictions typically provide public access to budgetary data or city council meeting minutes, as opposed to present results and expenses in tables or charts that citizens can more readily comprehend and access. Hopefully, municipalities will leverage the many tools available that transform canned quantitative data reports into more digestible charts or infographics.

The purpose of this work is prescribing a solution to the budget woes and challenges facing numerous cities of all sizes and categories. The contracts under examination clearly helped participating cities save money, increase revenue, and improve service quality. However, can local government across the state replicate the models successfully? More to the point, can urban Texas replicate the contracting success on a regional scale, including agreements that involve at least ten partners? This question addresses both political and fiscal feasibility issues. We examine feasibility for cooperation, analytics, and Six Sigma.

---

5. Sullivan, *Valuable Partnerships*, 188.

Barriers/Questions

One approach would compare the fiscal mix of the largest urban regions to the contract mix. The counties serve twenty-eight cities on average with populations averaging 1.5 million. The cumulative numbers were 280 cities or towns serving 16,000,000 Texans. Overall, the cluster analysis identified 65 percent of the urban Texas municipalities (185) as low socioeconomic with 20 percent falling under the middle class cluster. Merely 15 percent or forty-two of the cities were upper class or affluent. The cooperative agreements served a similar mixture. For example, Terrell falls squarely in the lower socioeconomic category. The larger contracts (at least based on number of clients) also adhere to this profile.

In fact, what if we created a super county comprised of all cooperative clients discussed in Part III? The agreements serve thirty-four cities with a combined population of 1.3 million which exceeds the population of half of the counties listed in Table 11–2. Bottom line: twenty-one cities serving 800,000 residents fall under the lowest socioeconomic cluster. That is 61 percent of the served population. The financial structure of these contracts indicates the counties possess the fiscal profile to initiate and sustain contracts on a regional scale.

What is the optimal profile mix and is that attainable? Most leaders regardless of population, type, region, or affluence level openly entered into cooperative agreements or shared service arrangements. The only barriers carrying any significance were geographic remoteness and fear over loss of control. This would especially make sense for affluent suburbs that possess the fiscal capacity necessary for staffing, capital investment, etc., although little to no data exists to support this sentiment. With that said, this assumption harkens back to Tiebout and the rational expectations for each jurisdiction based on its status and proximity to other units.

The mix must balance a modicum of affluence with lower income if we assume most rich, densely populated suburbs would opt out. How does one calculate the proper mixture? The Medstar model presents perhaps the most thorough example. The region deftly balances affluent/middle class cities with the lower income communities to achieve a profile that meets both national and statewide averages. The system remains proof that regional partnerships can flourish with the inclusion of lower income cities, and the right mix creates a sustainable government program.

Table 11–2 compares the cluster distribution for the five most populous counties with the Medstar distribution. The regional ambulance jurisdiction serves a higher percentage of lower socioeconomic cities (93 percent) than any listed county save Harris (94 percent). In fact, the system largely serves middle and lower class populations. This illustrates the true balance and leveraging of scale that only a multi-jurisdictional relationship can achieve. Wealthier municipalities with greater health insurance coverage essentially fund high performance service provision to an entire region or county.

Table 11–2

Cluster Distribution for Five Largest Texas Counties

Profile	Medstar	Tarrant	Dallas	Harris	Bexar	Travis
Affluent	0.1%	0.04%	1%	1%	0.1%	0.00%
Upper Middle	0.2%	6%	1%	1%	2%	2%
Middle	6.7%	19%	16%	4%	7%	7%
Lower socioeconomic	93.0%	75%	82%	94%	91%	90%

In conclusion, the optimal financial structure that facilitates regional cooperation exists at some level in most every county. However, does Texas house regions that would struggle in providing the model? Which counties fall below the Cooperative County profile in other words? Both the Hidalgo and El Paso counties grapple with staggering poverty levels eclipsing 20 percent (35 percent in the case of Hidalgo). These clearly represent the largest challenges to regional models. Could the regional model work in areas with concentrated poverty?

El Paso County and many of the governments it serves certainly believes it can work. The county hosted a "Shared Service Summit" in 2008 to facilitate communication and collaboration among the general purpose jurisdictions such as cities, school districts, community colleges and the Universities of Texas at El Paso. The summit focused on three service arenas: purchasing, information technology, and facilities planning. The meeting objectives included determining which agreements were in place, identifying new cooperative opportunities, discussing the benefits and challenges related to interlocal agreements, and finally, developing both short- and long-term collaboration goals with responsible personnel. Additionally, while the existing contracts were more transactional, long-term goals included several regional agreements such as insurance pools, purchasing alliances, GIS, professional development and a regional data center.

Summary

Chapter 11 synthesized the case study findings in order to help determine whether intergovernmental agreements provide the benefits as laid out by the policy criteria. The overall policy results were stellar with high marks for efficiency and effectiveness specifically among the examined agreements. However, the democratic results left room for improvement with a particular focus on clarity.

Additionally, the chapter identified the lessons leaders gleamed from their cooperative experience. Most successful partnerships leverage existing capacity and the wisdom of seasoned professionals and experts. Innovation requires an understanding of the old process. However, leaders should utilize LSS or other analytical tools to possibly alter the entire service delivery model. For example, Medstar examined which elements of the ambulance delivery process created waste in the emergency infrastructure.

Finally, the work transitioned into prescriptive mode by determining whether Texas urban regions could replicate the cooperative regional structure utilized by the partnering jurisdictions from Part III. The socioeconomic analysis indicates eight of ten urban counties possess the needed socioeconomic mix to produce successful regional agreement structures. This appeared to be the case even when removing affluent suburbs that might opt out of regional opportunities due to the desired outcomes of both leadership and citizens.

With that said, two counties presented problematic profiles: El Paso and Hidalgo. However, El Paso County has aggressively pursued regional cooperation for nearly a decade. In fact, the county led shared service summits facilitating ideas, networking, and, ultimately, regional agreements.

The final chapter considers how the state of Texas and urban regions could promote regional cooperation among local governments. Does the El Paso summit provide a model for future regional agreements? Would such meetings prove to be the optimal networking and collaboration tool leading to a regional cooperative explosion? The final chapter addresses this possibility.

12

Lessons Learned, Success, and the Future of Innovation

Lessons Learned

WHAT HAVE WE LEARNED about the cooperative craft? Also, what lessons did partnering leaders learn? Which practices work, which require refinement, and which are best discarded to the ashbin? This chapter proceeds to compile lessons gleamed from the process/development section of each case study. While this compilation clearly includes some best practices, others serve as reminders of the unique hurdles innovators face in the public square.

1. Reject Silo Thinking by Building Alignment Between Stakeholders
   Silo thinking refers to the propensity for department or organizations to withhold vital information or ideas from other departments or entities. A competitive environment tends to exacerbate such insular thinking. (Please do not read that as a critique of competition directly. My comment is empirical as opposed to normative.)

2. Keep All BBs in the Box
   Public sector innovation requires alignment between all stakeholders which is very difficult. It is hard (impossible, really) to strategically innovate when drama rules the day. Interviewee Torry Edwards spends an enormous amount of time making sure city council members get along. Smart local leaders identify political forces and manage egos.
   This includes achieving staff alignment. Indeed, maintaining an aligned environment integrates the hiring and training process. Smart organizations, in general, practice the "hire slow, fire fast" philosophy.

LESSONS LEARNED, SUCCESS, AND THE FUTURE OF INNOVATION

Hiring in a public sector context requires examining whether applicants fit both politically and within the community.

3. Stability and Tenure/Continuity

   Research indicates that organizational stability maximizes alignment while reducing political drama. Granted, tenure alone does not guarantee high performance or tranquility. We all know successful leaders who succeeded via manipulation or threats. However, long-term strategic planning is long-term. Tenure affords the needed time for strategy, execution, and fruition.

4. Engage in Structured Mental Exploration with Innovative Thinking

   Torry Edwards coined the phrase mental exploration which involves sitting down with stakeholder from various jurisdictions, positions, and career phases to explore the possiblities. Exploration requires breaking barriers by conceptualizing ideas and honing them into viable policy initiatives. Mental exploration require many skills including grasping whether it is the time and place for innovation. The primary objective involves integrating new, young ideas with wise experience

5. But Always Connect Innovative Exploration with Community Knowledge

   Terrell utilizes an apt phrase: "The council is losing memory here." Memory loss occurs when new members join the council. This happens frequently as Terrell has term limits.

   Terrell leadership firmly believes that the staff possesses the responsibility to give voice to the historical context in any policy discussion. The decision-making process requires the frame of reference which explains why certain decisions were made in the past.

   Most importantly, policy and partnering should flow from the community distinctive. Each community has its own culture and initiatives should leverage the culture. This especially true with economic development programs that directly impact the city's image.

6. Think "Rationally" (in Economic Terms) by Leveraging Your Strengths and Identifying Benefits For Potential Partners

   Terrell had little in the way of economic development assets. However, the city owned acres of developable land adjacent to an interstate highway. Additionally, the town location in close proximity to Dallas and addictive destinations (Shreveport for gambling and

Canton for antiques) guaranteed traffic loaded with shoppers. Terrell leveraged this asset and paired it with value for each partner they approached including the county, the state, unincorporated communities, and private developers.

This lesson could also be titled "Remember Tiebout" as it hammers home the vision of the rational-minded, utility-maximizing leader. Bottom line: local leaders desiring to partner with other jurisdictions should identify the benefits of partnering for each.

7. Leverage Private Sector Processes but Maintain Public Sector Outcomes

    Public sector innovation affords the savings to taxpayers that private organizations provided to shareholders. Both city and citizens benefit from identifying inefficiencies in service delivery. Everyone wins. With that said, leaders must marry the innovative process with public outcomes that involve saving lives, public safety, or utilities (as opposed to profits).

8. Micro-Innovation/Incrementalism

    The political, legal, and logistical challenges create hurdles to success before cities reach the point of analyzing how effectively the agreement met goals. Micro-innovation provides an incremental approach to reaching said goals within the prevailing political framework. Capital in its fiscal and political form remains scarce and baby steps afford an avenue for discount spending in case the agreement results are not optimal. Some jurisdictions, such as the North Texas Council of Goverments, go one step further by implementing temporary pilot agreements to determine if goals are met as well as facilitating an easier route for reversing course in the need arises.

9. Include Subject Matter Experts (SME) to Utilize Professional Solutions

    The optimal innovative process pairs efficiency concepts with operational realities. Subject matter experts inject said realism challenging the process analysts to develop new approaches only after gaining a full understanding of the old approach as well as everyday realities that only the grizzled veteran has dealt with.

10. Project Champions Are Necessary

    This lesson permeates every agreement and regional structure. The technology officers crystallized and promoted the software sharing idea. Terrell led the Tax Incremental Funding (TIF) recruitment via Mike Sims and Torry Edwards. Medstar staff pitched moving operation fully in-house and bringing private executives along with the change. Project champions explain the benefits of partnering but also recognize the concerns stakeholders have in relinquishing control.

11. Include Partners of Multiple Sizes and Jurisdictional Types

Most city managers preferred partnering with regional jurisdictions given their scope, scale, and cooperative capacity. Indeed, every profiled partnership included a county or Council of Government (COG). Additionally, jurisdictions of every size or socioeconomic capacity bring something to the table.

How Can Texas Advance Innovation?

Finally, how can state and local leaders increase contracting frequency and improve the effectiveness of interlocal agreements and their implementation? What are the policy implications? The proper response may well reside in financial incentives. States such as New York and New Jersey initiated competitive grant programs that fund feasibility studies or defray implementation and start-up costs.[1] The state of Texas should analyze the long-term benefits of incentive policy.

The effective collection and dissemination of communication among local political subdivisions provides affordable shared service empowerment. Texas previously had a center dedicated to archiving active contracts, advising local administrators and elected officials, and monitoring performance.[2] Reviving this approach could benefit the state and save money. Local entities could benefit from cost/benefit analyses, modeling successful examples, and the development of a performance measurement tool that includes a citizen feedback and other efficiency measures. The National Center for Public Performance at Rutgers University provides these tools for New Jersey municipalities.[3] The primary fiscal gap remains capital investment which would serve as the best target for grant programs.

---

1. Holzer, Sadeghi, and Schwester. "State Shared Services," 451–56.
2. Tees and Stanford, *Handbook for Interlocal Contracting,* 14–16.
3. Holzer, Sadeghi, and Schwester. "State Shared Services and Regional Consolidation,"451–56.

PART IV: CHANGING THE LANDSCAPE

The Lean Six Sigma (LSS) infrastructure is far less developed although some support currently exists. Chapter 10 serves as perhaps the only research on the subject matter. However, certain programs exist. For example, one council of government offers LSS training for city staff much like the SGR program Gainesville utilized.[4] Cities are increasingly stressing innovation. For example, Austin recently created a chief innovation office position. The expansion most likely falls to the same statewide associations (Texas Municipal League [TML], Texas City Managers' Association [TCMA], Texas Association of Regional Cooperation [TARC]) to foster growth and commitment on a larger scale. Overall, this remains a fertile research area this author will continue to explore.

Several states remain ahead of the curve in promoting LSS. For example, LeanOhio offers training and project grants primarily for state agencies but also for municipalities and local jurisdictions. Local staff participate in a "LeanOhio Boot Camp lead by local training partners. The boot camp lasts four days providing students with practical approaches to process improvement and efficiency. While most trainees work for cities, housing association, school districts, country commissioners, and utilities have improved customer experience and reduced costs the LSS way."[5] Municipal Texas could benefit from such state support.

Finally, the investigation clearly extends beyond Texas borders. A similar examination of other states facing the same challenges would yield dividends. For example, a comparison of the Texas approach with California could provide fascinating results and clues for future innovation. Overall, a study comparing commitment to innovation and cooperation within the cultural and political context of states would benefit decision makers.

Furthermore, what about global exploration? An examination of city management in developed nations could shed light on the extent of model integrated cooperation. Granted, several European nations operate regional governments with significant policy authority which reduces the need for cooperation. Still, comparing results from these countries with the Texas cooperative model would afford compelling data.

The global context also speaks to the needs of the developing world. Non-governmental organizations (NGOs) spend millions annually supporting these struggling regions. Additionally, the private sector constantly combs developing regions for untapped sources of wealth. Both sectors, as

4. Council for Six Sigma Certification, "Provider Directory."
5. https://lean.ohio.gov/.

well as diplomatic efforts, benefit from analysis probing how to provide better, safer public goods to the population as well as increasing affordability of service provision for developing municipalities.

Quick Summary

This journey began with the Chicago River. City leaders resolved a crisis with innovative thinking. The crisis facing Texas municipalities (and beyond) is hardly as pressing as contaminated drinking water and the epidemics it caused. However, the long-term consequences of doing nothing are very real and a cause for concern. Failure to act compromises public service quality while also not addressing escalating costs and reduced funding.

The solutions this work illustrates provides real, measurable results that saved money and lives. Most importantly, the innovations remain politically feasible and viable. The book introduces readers to several urban reform efforts since the industrial revolution. The plans that actually produced positive results found approval (or at least acceptance) from vested stakeholders and residents alike. Recall the lessons of Chicago, the Texas Urban Commission, and the case studies. Compare those to the Bureau for City Betterment. The successful plans leveraged existing resources.

What about EMS response time or the safe delivery of various utilities? Students cringe when terms such as "public" and "administration" are combined. This is not the stuff of passion or fiery screaming! The scholarly exchange of ideas promulgates by the likes of CNN, MSNBC, or Fox rarely (never) strays into this arena (note-there was a solid amount of sarcasm in that sentence).

Why Discuss This Topic? Why Write About It?

This work essentially dealt with federalism. Like many political concepts, federalism certainly existed prior to the United States yet the USA was the first modern federation success story. Federalism above all things heralds that quaint democratic notion that decision making and governing policymaking is not a top-down enterprise. The "subnational" leadership enjoys a say in how to run their little piece of the 90,000+ government puzzle. They possess what I like to call "policy autonomy" which remains a good thing given the diversity of the American population.

However, as most any adults will tell you, autonomy is an expensive proposition. Governments make the same deal. Local towns, suburbs, school district, community colleges, etc. may yearn for the opportunity to serve their citizens as they deem proper but can they "tote the note" service provision requires of them? Local leadership also bears the performance burden. Voters expect results whether it involves functioning traffic lights or school quality.

Hopefully, the 200+ pages comprising this work helped advance concepts and ideas for reducing the note toting burden for taxpayers. My fervent hope is that leaders implement the innovations and that both lives and money are saved. However, a lingering purpose of this book is to introduce readers to municipal management and all its complexities. Readers should also finish the book with a greater appreciation of the work city managers and other local personnel perform and the dynamic nature of local governance. Perhaps this journey opened your eyes a bit.

Most importantly, my hope is that this work ingrained an appreciation for the challenges local leaders face. The scope is broad and daunting from service provision to economic development. Additionally, the career remains far more dynamic and interesting than even the most ardent followers of politics can appreciate. City managers possess one of the few jobs balancing policy advocacy, development, and implementation. Additionally, the capacity for innovation is as vast as the municipal marketplace. My most fervent desire is that this work plays even a nominal role in motivating leaders at the state and local level to consider and possibly embrace innovation driven policy.

Bibliography

"About LeanOhio." LeanOhio, "Home" page, accessed November 11, 2017, http://lean.ohio.gov/.

American Planning Association. "Planning for Smart Growth: 2002 State of the States." Chicago: Smart Growth Network, 2002.

American Public Works Association. "Top Ten Public Works Projects of the Century" American Public Works Association. http://www2.apwa.net/about/awards/toptencentury/chica.htm.

Area Metropolitan Ambulance Authority. *Board of Directors Meeting Packets*, 2012–2016, http://www.medstar911.org/board-of-directors.

Ashbacher, Dawn. "Managing Effective Interlocal Economic Development Networks. (A 28E Management Report prepared for the Department of Administrative Services, Ames, IA, Iowa State University, 2005.)

Auger, Deborah A. "Privatization, Contracting, and the States: Lessons From State Government Experience." *Public Productivity & Management Review* 22 (1999) 435-54.

Arvidsen, Enid, Rod Hissong, and Richard L. Cole. "Tax Increment Financing in Texas: Survey and Assessment." In *Tax Increment Financing and Development: Uses, Structures, and Impacts*, edited by Joyce Y. Man and Craig L. Johnson, 137-54. Albany, NY: State University of New York Press, 2001.

Babbie, Earl R. *Survey Research Methods, Second Edition*. Belmont, CA: Wadsworth, 1990.

Baker Tilly. "Local Governments Scramble for Budget Solutions." *Insights* (blog), *BakerTilly.com*, January 2012, http://www.bakertilly.com/insights/local-governments-scramble-for-budget-solutions/.

Baumle, Amanda K., Mark Fossett, and Warren Waren. "Strategic Annexation Under the Voting Rights Act: Racial Dimensions of Annexation Practices." *Harvard BlackLetter Law Journal* 24 (2008) 81-114.

Boadway, Robin and Anwar Shah. *Fiscal Federalism: Principles and Practice of Multiorder Governance*. New York: Cambridge University Press, 2009.

Blodgett, Terrell. *Current City-County Consolidation Attempts*. Washington, DC: National Association of Counties, 1996.

_____. *City Government That Works: The History of Council-Manager Government in Texas*. Austin: Texas City Management Association, 2008.

BIBLIOGRAPHY

Bluestone, Barry, Mary Huff Stevenson, and Russell Williams. *The Urban Experience: Economics, Society, and Public Policy*. New York: Oxford University Press, 2008.

Boddy, Trevor. "New Urbanism: 'The Vancouver Model' [Speaking of Places]." *Places* 16 (2004) 14-21.

Boyne, George A. and Michael Cole. "Revolution, Evolution, and Local Government Structure: An Empirical Analysis of London," *Urban Studies* 35 (April 1998) 751-69.

———. "Competition and Local Government: A Public Choice Perspective." *Urban Studies* 33 (1996) 703-21.

———. "Is There a Relationship Between Fragmentation and Local Government Costs? A Comment on Drew Dolan," *Urban Affairs Quarterly* 28 (December 1992) 317-23.

Brewer, Garry D. and Peter DeLeon. *The Foundations of Policy Analysis*. Homewood, IL: The Dorsey Press, 1983.

Brooks, David. "Patio Man and the Sprawl People." *The Weekly Standard* (blog), *Weekly Standard.com*, August 12, 2002, https://www.weeklystandard.com/david-brooks/patio-man-and-the-sprawl-people.

Buchanan, James M. and Gordon Tullock. *The Calculus of Consent: Logical Foundations of Constitutional Democracy*. Ann Arbor: University of Michigan Press, 1962.

Campbell, Richard W. and Sally C. Selden. "Does City-County Consolidation Save Money?: The Unification of Athens–Clarke County Suggest It Might." *Public Policy Research Series* 1 (March 2000) 1-2.

Caro, Robert. *The Power Broker: Robert Moses and the Fall of New York*. New York: Alfred A. Knopf, 1974.

Carr, Jered B. and Richard C. Feiock. *City-County Consolidation and Its Alternatives: Reshaping the Local Governance Landscape*. New York: Taylor & Francis, 2004.

Cisneros, Henry, ed. *Interwoven Destinies: Cities and the Nation*. New York: Norton, 1993.

City of Dallas. *2010-2011 Fiscal Year Budget: General Financial Overview for Dallas Fire Department*. Dallas, TX: Controller's Office, 2010. http://www.dallasfirerescue.com/pdf/Budget_Information.pdf.

———. *2011-2012 Fiscal Year Budget: General Financial Overview for Dallas Fire Department*. Dallas, TX: Controller's Office, 2011. http://www.dallasfirerescue.com/pdf/Budget_Information.pdf.

———. *2012-2013 Fiscal Year Budget: General Financial Overview for Dallas Fire Department*. Dallas, TX: Controller's Office, 2012. http://www.dallasfirerescue.com/pdf/Budget_Information.pdf.

City of Burleson. *Annual Operating budget and Plan of Services for 2013-2014*. Burleson, TX: City Manager's Office, August 19, 2013.

City of Gainesville. *Lean Six Sigma Wastewater Treatment Plant Report*. Gainesville, TX: City Manager's Office, 2015.

City of Palo Pinto. *2010-2011 Fiscal Year Budget*. Palo Pinto, TX: City Manager's Office, October 2010.

———. *2010-2011 Fiscal Year Budget*. Palo Pinto, TX: City Manager's Office, August 2, 2013.

City of Terrell. *2002 Comprehensive Plan*. Terrell, TX: City of Terrell Planning and Zoning Commission, 2002.

———. *TIF Budget Overview with Project Details*. Terrell, TX: City Manager's Office, 2007.

———. *Building a Sustainable Community*. Terrell, TX: Terrell Office for Economic Development, 2011.

———. *Public-Private Project Overview.* Terrell, TX: Terrell Office of Economic Development, 2007.

City of Waxahachie. *2010-2011 Fiscal Year Budget: General Financial Overview for Dallas Fire Department.* Waxahachie, TX: Controller's Office, 2010.

Council for Six Sigma Certification. "Provider Directory." https://sixsigmacouncil.org/six-sigma-certification/business-directory/862/east-texas-council-of-governments/ (accessed October 13, 2017.)

Creswell, John W. *Research Design: Qualitative, Quantitative, and Mixed Method Approaches.* London: Sage, 2009.

Dallas County (Tex.). Health and Human Services, Parkland Health & Hospital System. Community Health Institute, New Solutions (Firm). "Horizons: The Dallas County Community Health Needs Assessment." Dallas: Dallas County Health & Human Services, 2013.

Dallas Fire-Rescue Department. *The Future of EMS Service Delivery to the City of Dallas.* Dallas, TX: Dallas Emergency Medical Services Bureau, August 2013.

Dehoog, Ruth Hoogland, David Lowery, and William E. Lyons. "Citizen Satisfaction with Local Governance: A test of Individual, Jurisdictional, and City Specific Explanations." *Journal of Politics* 52 (1990) 807-37.

Denton, Nancy A., and Douglas S. Massey. *American Apartheid.* Boston, MA: Harvard University Press, 1993.

Dill, Jennifer. "Final Technical Report: Travel and Transit Use at Portland Area Transit-Oriented Developments (TODs)." (Prepared for TransNow, University of Washington, May 2006.)

Dillingham, Gerald Lee. "Airport Privatization: Issues Related to the Sale or Lease of US Commercial Airports." United States General Accounting Office, 1996.

Dodge, W.R. *Regional Excellence: Governing Together to Compete Globally and Flourish Locally.* Washington, DC: National League of Cities, 1996.

Dolan, Drew. "Local Government Fragmentation: Does it Drive Up the Cost of Government?" *Urban Affairs Review* 26 (1990) 28-45.

Downs, Anthony. *New Visions for Metropolitan America.* Washington, DC: Brookings Institution, 1994.

———. "Some Realities About Sprawl and Urban Decline." *Housing Policy Debate* 10 (1999) 955-74.

Duany, Andres, Elizabeth Plater-Zyberk, and Jeff Speck. *Suburban Nation: The Rise of Sprawl and the Decline of the American Dream.* New York: North Point Press, 2000.

Duncombe, William and Yinger, John. "An Analysis of Returns to Scale in Public Production, With an Application to Fire Protection." *Journal of Urban Affairs* 52 (1993) 49-72.

Dye, Thomas. *Top Down Policymaking.* New York: Chatham House, 2001.

Eisenberg, Mickey. Lawrence Bergner, and Alfred Hallstrom. "Cardiac Resuscitation in the Community: Importance of Rapid Provision and Implications for Program Planning." *JAMA 241* (May 1979) 1905-07.

Elazar, Daniel. *American Federalist.* 3rd ed. New York: Harper Row, 1984.

———. *American Federalism: A View from the States.* New York: Thomas Y. Crowell, 1966.

El Paso County. *2009 El Paso Shared Services Summit: Summit Findings.* El Paso, TX: El Paso County, 2009.

———. *2010 El Paso Shared Services Summit: Summit Findings*. El Paso, TX: El Paso County: 2010.

"Family Budget Calculator." Economic Policy Institute. Accessed February 21, 2017. https://www.epi.org/resources/budget/.

Featherstun, Donald G., D. Whitney Thornton, and J. Gregory Correnti. "State and Local Privatization: An Evolving Process." *Public Contract Law Journal* 30 (2001) 643-75.

Finney, Miles. "Scale Economies and Police Department Consolidation: Evidence from Los Angeles." *Contemporary Economic Policy* 15 (1997) 121-26.

Fleischmann, Arnold. "Regional and City-County Consolidation in Small Metro Areas." *State and Local Government Review* 32 (2000) 213-26.

Forum of Federations. "Partnering Countries." http://www.forumfed.org/.

Foster, Kathryn Ann. *The Political Economy of Special-Purpose Government*. Washington, DC: Georgetown University Press, 1997.

Fowler, Floyd. *Survey Research Method*, 4th ed. Thousand Oaks, CA: Sage, 2009.

Fox, David. "Halting Urban Sprawl: Smart Growth in Vancouver and Portland." *Boston College International and Comparative Law Review* 33 (2010) 43-59.

Frederickson, George H., et al. *The Public Administration Theory Primer*. New York: Westview Press, 2003.

Frederickson, George H. "The Repositioning of American Public Administration." *Political Science and Politics* 32 (1999) 872-84.

Freilich, Robert H. *From Sprawl to Smart Growth: Successful Legal Planning, and Environmental Systems*. Chicago: American Bar Association, 1999.

Frierson, Jack S. "How Are Local Governments Responding to Student Rental Problems in University Towns in the United States, Canada, and England?" *Ga. J. Int'l & Comp. L.* 33 (2004) 497-542.

Frug, Gerald E. *City Making: Building Communities without Building Walls*. Princeton, NJ: Princeton University Press, 1999.

Fruth, Darrell A. "Economic and Institutional Constraints on the Privatization of Government Information Technology Services." *Harvard Journal of Law & Technology* 13 (1999) 521-46.

Gaines, James P. "Looming Boom: Texas Through 2030," *Tierra Grande* 1841 (January 2008) 1-6.

Gall, Meredith D., Joyce P. Gall, & Walter R. Borg. *Educational Research: An Introduction*. Boston: Pearson, 2007.

Gay, Lorraine R., Geoffrey E. Mills, and Peter W. Airasian. *Educational Research: Competencies for Analysis and Applications*, 8th ed. Columbus, OH: Pearson Education, 2006.

Greene, Jennifer C. *Mixed Methods in Social Inquiry*. San Francisco: Jossey Bass, 2007.

Griffith, Janice C. "Smart Governance for Smart Growth: The Need for Regional Governments." *Georgia State University Law Review* 17 (2000) 1019-62.

Harrison, Brigid Callahan, and Jean Wahl Harris. *American Democracy Now*, 2nd ed. New York: McGraw-Hill, 2011.

Hamilton, David K. "Regimes and Regional Governance: The Case of Chicago." *Journal of Urban Affairs* 24 (2002) 403–23.

Handbook of Texas Online. Terrell Blodgett, "COUNCIL-MANAGER FORM OF CITY GOVERNMENT," accessed April 10, 2012, http://www.tshaonline.org/handbook/online/articles/moco2.

Hardy, Pat, "The Consolidation of City and County Governments: A Look at the History

And Outcome-Based Research of These Efforts." Metropolitan Technical Advisory Service, The University of Tennessee, 2005. http://www.mtas.tennessee.edu/.

Hawkins, Brett W., Keith Ward, and Mary P. Becker. "Governmental Consolidation as a Strategy for Metropolitan Development." *Public Administration Quarterly* 15 (Summer 1991) 253-67.

Hill, Libby. *The Chicago River: A Natural and Unnatural History*. Carbondale: Southern Illinois University Press, 2000.

Holzer, Marc, Leila Sadeghi, and Richard W. Schwester. "State Shared Services and Regional Consolidation Efforts." In *The Book of States 2007*, edited by Keon S. Chi, 451-456. Lexington, KY: The Council of State Governments, 2007.

Hosenfeld, Carol. "Case Studies of Ninth Grade Readers." In *Reading in a Foreign Language*, edited by J. Charles Anderson and Alexander H. Urquhart, 231-49. New York: Longman, 1984.

Hueglin, Thomas O., and Allan Fenna. *Comparative Federalism: A Systematic Inquiry*. Toronto, Canada: Broadview Press, 2006.

International Association of Fire Fighters. *Emergency Medical Services: A Guidebook for Fire Based Systems*, 4th ed. Washington DC: International Association of Firefighters, 2008.

Jackson, Kenneth T. *Crabgrass Frontier: The Suburbanization of the United States*, 1st ed. New York: Oxford University Press, 1987.

J.R. Henry Consulting. *Calculating Your EMS Service's "Average Cost of Service" and "Unit Hour Analysis."* Pittsburgh: J.R. Henry Consulting, 2011.

Kain, John F. "Housing Segregation, Negro Employment, and Metropolitan Decentralization." *The Quarterly Journal of Economics* 82 (May 1968) 175-97.

Kimball, Justin F. *Our City—Dallas: A Community Civics*. Dallas: Kessler Plan Association of Dallas, 1927.

Kincaid, John. "Values and Tradeoffs in Federalism." *Publius: The Journal of Federalism* 25 (January 1995) 29-44.

Kingdon, John. *Agendas, Alternatives, and Public Policies*, 2nd ed. New York: Longman, 2003.

Kraft, Michael E. and Scott R. Furlong. *Public Policy: Politics, Analysis, and Alternatives*. Washington, DC: Congressional Quarterly Press, 2004.

Kuntsler, James Howard. *The Geography of Nowhere: The Rise and Decline of America's Man-made Landscape*. New York: Simon & Schuster, 1993.

Kushner, James A. *Healthy Cities: The Intersection of Urban Planning, Law and Health*. Durham, NC: Carolina Academic Press, 2007.

Leland, Suzanne, and Christopher Cannon. "Metropolitan City-County Consolidation: Is There a Recipe for Success?. In *Annual Meeting of the Midwest Political Science Association*, Chicago, 1997.

Leland, Suzanne M., and Kurt Thurmaier. *Case Studies of City County Consolidation*. Armonk, NY: M.E. Sharpe, 2004.

Leland, Suzanne, and Kurt Thurmaier. "Lessons from 35 Years of City-county Consolidation Attempts." Municipal Year Book (2006) 4-10.

Leo, Christopher. "Regional Growth Management Regime: The Case of Portland, Oregon." *Journal of Urban Affairs* 20 (1998) 363–94.

Leslie, L. L. "Are Higher Response Rates Essential to a Valid Survey?" *Social Science Research* 1 (1972) 323-334.

BIBLIOGRAPHY

Levin, Jonathan and Stephen Tadelis. "Contracting for Government Services: Theory and Evidence from U.S. Cities." *Journal of Industrial Economics* 58 (September 2010) 517-541.

Levy, John M. *Contemporary Urban Planning*, 9th ed. London & New York: Routledge, 2011.

Lindblom, Charles E., and Edward J. Woodhouse. *The Policy-Making Process*, 3rd ed. Englewood Cliffs, NJ: Prentice Hall, 1993.

Lyons, W. E. "Government Fragmentation Versus Consolidation." *Public Administration Review*, (Nov–Dec, 1989) 533-44.

Martin, Richard. *A Quiet Revolution: The Consolidation of Jacksonville-Duval County and the Dynamics of Urban Reform*. Jacksonville, FL: White Publishing, 1993.

McCabe, Barbara Coyle. "Special-District Formation Among the States." *State and Local Government Review* 32 (2000) 121-31.

McDavid, James C. "The Impacts of Amalgamation on Police Services in the Halifax Regional Municipality." *Canadian Public Administration* 45 (December 2002) 538-65.

McDonough, Jo, and Steven McDonough. *Research methods for English language teachers*. New York: Routledge, 2014.

Medstar Mobile Healthcare. *Community Report for 2017*. Fort Worth, TX: Medstar Mobile Healthcare, 2018.

———. *Community Report for 2013*. Fort Worth, TX: Medstar Mobile Healthcare, 2014.

———. *Community Report for 2015*. Fort Worth, TX: Medstar Mobile Healthcare, 2016.

———. "Mobile Healthcare Programs - Overview." Accessed June 25, 2017. http://www.medstar911.org/mobile-healthcare-programs.

Mercer, Monte. "Shared Services & Cost Saving Collaboration Deserce Respect." *Public Management* (May 2011) 9–12. https://icma.org/sites/default/files/35_MAY 2011 · VOLUME 93 · NUMBER 4.pdf.

Metro Regional Government. *Portland: Transit Oriented Development and Centers Program, 2007*. Metro Annual Report for 2007. Portland: Metro Regional Government, 2007.

Mills, Edwin S. and Bruce W. Hamilton. *Urban Economics*, 5th ed. Upper Saddle River, NJ: Pearson, 1994.

Morgan, David R., and Michael W. Hirlinger. "Intergovernmental Service Contracts: A Multivariate Explanation." *Urban Affairs Quarterly* 27 (1991) 128-44.

Morgan, John, and Martin Brenig-Jones. *Lean Six Sigma for Dummies*, 3rd ed. West Sussex, England: John Wiley & Sons, 2016.

Morse, J.M. "Approaches to Qualitative-Quantitative Methodological Triangulation." *Nursing Research 40* (1991) 120-23.

National Academy of Sciences and National Research Council. *Accidental Death and Disability: The Neglected Disease of Modern Society*. Washington, DC: The National Academies Press, 1966. https://doi.org/10.17226/9978.

National Highway Transportation Safety Association. *EMS A Historical Perspective*. Reprinted from *EMS Agenda for the Future*. National Highway Transportation Safety Association, August, 1996.

National League of Cities. "City Fiscal Issues for 2010," accessed September 15, 2013, https://www.nlc.org.

Nesbary, Dale K. *Survey Research and the World Wide Web*. Boston: Allyn & Bacon, 2000

BIBLIOGRAPHY

North Texas Municipal Water District, "Our Water System," https://www.ntmwd.com/our-water-system.

Oberlander, Judy. "History of Planning in Greater Vancouver." In *The Greater Vancouver Book: An Urban Encyclopedia*, edited by Chuck Davis, 247. Vancouver, BC: Linkman Press, 1997.

Olson, Mancur. "The Principle of 'Fiscal Equivalence': The Division of Responsibilities Among Different Levers of Government." *American Economic Review* 59 (May 1969) 479-87.

Orfield, Myron. *American Metropolitics: A Regional Agenda for Community and Stability.* Washington, DC: Brooking Institution, 1997.

———. *American Metropolitics: The New Suburban Reality.* Washington, DC: Brooking Institution, 2002.

Osborne, David and Ted Gaebel. *Reinventing Government.* Hoboken, NJ: John Wiley & Sons, 1993.

O'Sullivan, Arthur. *Urban Economics*, 6th ed. New York: McGraw-Hill, 2007.

Owen, James and York Wilbern. *Governing Metropolitan Indianapolis: The Politics of Unigov.* Berkeley: University of California Press, 1985.

Pennsylvania Economy League of Southwestern Pennsylvania. *A Comparative Analysis of City/County Consolidations.* Pittsburgh: Pennsylvania Economy League, 2007.

Perlman, Bruce J., and J. Edwin Benton. "Going It Alone: New Survey Data on Economic Recovery Strategies in Local Government." *State and Local Government Review* 44 (2012) 5S-16S.

Pierce, Neal R., Curtis W. Johnson, and John Stuart Hall. *Citistates: How Urban America Can Prosper in a Competitive World.* Washington, DC: Seven Locks Press, 1993.

Pons, Peter and Vincent J. Markovchick. "Eight Minutes or Less: Does the Ambulance Response Time Guidelines Impact Trauma Patient Outcomes?" *The Journal of Emergency Medicine* 23 (2002) 43-48.

Potter, Lloyd. *Population Projections for the State of Texas.* San Antonio: Texas State Data Center, 2006.

Prager, Jonas. "Contracting-Out: Theory and Policy." *New York University Journal of International Law & Politics* 25 (1992): 73-111.

Pyecha, J. *A Case Study of the Application of Noncategorical Special Education in Two States.* Chapel Hill, NC: Research Triangle Institute, 1988.

Putnam, Robert D. "Bowling Alone: America's Declining Social Capital." *Journal of Democracy* 6 (1995) 65-78.

Regional Planning Commissions. Texas Local Government Code Title 12, Subtitle C Chapter 391. 70th Texas States Legislature, September 1, 1987.

Robbins, Vernon D. "A History of Emergency Medical Services & Medical Transportation Systems in America." *American College of Healthcare Executives* (March 2005) 1-38. Accessed June 15, 2014. https://www.monoc.org/bod/docs/history american ems-mts.pdf.

Rose, Albert. *Governing Metropolitan Toronto: A Social and Political Analysis, 1953-1971.* Berkeley: University of California Press, 1972.

Rosenbaum, Walter A., and Gladys M. Kammerer. *Against Long Odds: The Theory and Practice of Successful Governmental Consolidation*, vol. 2. Beverly Hills: Sage, 1974.

Rosentraub, Mark S. "City-County Consolidation and the Rebuilding of Image: The Fiscal Lessons From Indianapolis's UniGov Program." *State and Local Government Review* 32 (Fall 2000) 180-91.

Rusk, David. *Cities Without Suburbs: A Census 2000 Update*, 3rd ed. Baltimore, MD: Woodrow Wilson Center Press, 2003.

———. *Baltimore Unbound: A Strategy for Regional Renewal*. Baltimore, MD: The Abell Foundation, 1996.

———. *Cities Without Suburbs*. Baltimore, MD: Johns Hopkins Press, 1993.

———. *Inside Game/Outside Game: Winning strategies for Saving Urban America*. Washington, DC: Brookings Institute, 1999.

Salant, Priscilla, and Don A. Dillman. *How to Conduct Your Own Survey*. New York: John Wiley & Sons 1994.

Samuelson, Paul, A. "The Pure Theory of Public Expenditures." *The Review of Economics and Statistics* 36 (April 1954) 387-89.

Savitch, Hank V., and Ronald K. Vogel. "Suburbs Without a City Power and City-County Consolidation." *Urban Affairs Review* 39 (July 2004) 758–90.

Savitch, H. V., et al. "Ties That Bind: Central Cities, Suburbs, and the New Metropolitan Region." *Economic Development Quarterly* 7 (1993) 341-57.

Soja, Edward W. *Seeking Spatial Justice*. Minneapolis: University of Minnesota Press, 2010.

Song, Yan, and Gerrit-Jan Knaap. "Measuring Urban Form: Is Portland Winning the War on Sprawl?" *Journal of the American Planning Association* 70 (2004) 210–25.

Stake, Robert, E. "The Art of Case Study Research." *Thousand Oaks, Sage* 10 (1995) 85-91.

Staley, Samuel R., Dagney Faulk, Suzanne Leland and D. Eric Schansberg. "The Effect of City-County Consolidation: A Review of the Recent Literature." Fort Wayne: Indiana Policy Review Foundation, 2005.

Staley, Sam. *Bigger is Not Better: The Virtues of Decentralized Local Government*. Washington, DC: Cato Institute, 1992.

Statewide Land-Use Planning Act of 1973. Senate Bill 100. 59th Oregon Legislative Assembly, 1973.

Steele, Tom. "Boom! Dallas-Fort Worth Population Growth Only Beaten by One City." *News* (blog), *Dallasnews.com*, March 2016, https://www.dallasnews.com/news/news/2016/03/24/boom-dallas-fort-worth-population-growth-beaten-by-only-one-city.

Stone, Clarence. *Regime Politics: Governing Atlanta, 1946-1988*. Lawrence: University Press of Kansas, 1989.

Sue, Valerie M., and Lois A. Ritter. *Conducting Online Surveys*. Thousand Oaks, CA: Sage, 2007.

Sullivan, R. J. "Valuable Partnerships: The Regional Benefits of Interlocal Contracts for Texas Cities." PhD diss., The University of Texas at Arlington, 2015.

Tannahill, Neal. *Texas Government: Policy and Politics*, 12th ed. Upper Saddle River, NJ: Pearson Education, 2013.

Tashakkori, Abbas, and Charles Teddlie. *Mixed Methodology: Combining Qualitative and Quantitative Approaches*. Thousand Oaks, CA: Sage, 1998.

Tax Foundation. "Center for State Tax Policy." Accessed March 18, 2016, https://taxfoundation.org/center/state-tax-policy/.

Tees, David W., and Jay G. Stanford. *Handbook for Interlocal Contracting in Texas*. Arlington: University of Texas at Arlington, 1972.

Tees, David W., Richard Cole, and Seth S. Searcy. *Durable Partnerships in Texas: The Interlocal Contract at Mid-Decade*. Arlington: University of Texas at Arlington, 1995.

Texas City Management Association. *Texas City Management Association 2012-2013 Directory*. Austin: Texas City Management Association, 2012.

BIBLIOGRAPHY

Texas Legislative Council. *Amendments to the Texas Constitution Since 1876.* (Prepared by the *Research Division.* Austin: Texas Legislative Council 2012.)

Texas State Data Center and Office of the State Demographer. *Population Projections for the State of Texas.* Austin: Texas State Data Center and Office of the State Demographer, 2006.

Texas State Legislature. Senate Committee on Intergovernmental Relations. (Written Testimony submitted to Texas Senate Committee on Intergovernmental Relations hearing. 82nd legislative session, 2010.)

Texas Urban Development Commission. *A Texas Advisory Commission on Intergovernmental Relations: A Report Prepared for the Texas Urban Development Commission by James F. Ray.* Austin: Texas Urban Development Commission, 1970.

Texas Urban Development Commission. *Toward Urban Progress: A Report to the Governor and the 62nd Legislature.* (Report by the Texas Urban Development Commission. Austin: Texas Urban Development Commission, 1971.)

———. *Summary of Recommendations from Urban Texas: Policies for the Future by. Report of the Texas Urban Development Commission.* Austin: Texas Urban Planning Commission, 1971.

———. *Urban Growth in Texas: A Report Prepared for the Texas Urban Development Commission* by Joe B. Harris. Arlington: Texas Urban Development Commission, 1970.

The Bureau for City Betterment. *How Manhattan is Governed: Facts you Should Know about the Administration of the Borough of Manhattan.* New York: The Bureau of City Betterment of the Citizens of New York, 1906.

Thurmaier, Kurt, and Curtis Wood. "Interlocal Agreements as an Alternative to Consolidation." In *City County Consolidation and Its Alternatives: Reshaping the Local Government Landscape,* edited by Jered B. Carr and Richard C. Feiock, 113-30. New York: M.E. Sharpe, 2004.

Thurmaier, Kurt. "Elements of Successful Interlocal Agreements: An Iowa Case Study." *Working Group on Interlocal Services Cooperation* (2005) 2.

Tiebout, Charles M. 1956. "A Pure Theory of Local Expenditures." *The Journal of Political Economy* 64 (May 1956) 416-24.

United States Environmental Protection Agency. Office of Water. *How Wastewater Treatment Works . . . the Basics.* Washington, DC: Environmental Protection Agency, 1998.

United States Government Accountability Office. "Patient Protection and Affordable Care Act: IRS Managing Implementation Risks, but Its Approach Could Be Refined." *United States Government Accountability Office* (June 2012). http://purl.fdlp.gov/GPO/gpo25481.

U.S. Census Bureau. "American Community Survey." American FactFinder, accessed June 12, 2013, https://factfinder.census.gov/faces/nav/jsf/pages/index.xhtml.

U.S. Census Bureau. *Interim State Population Projections.* Washington, DC: Government Printing Office, 2005.

U.S. Census Bureau. "2010 Census." *Community Facts* (blog), *American FactFinder,* April 21, 2016, https://factfinder.census.gov/faces/nav/jsf/pages/community_facts.xhtml.

U.S. Census Bureau. "2017 Population Estimates." *Community Facts* (blog), *American FactFinder,* May 5, 2016, https://factfinder.census.gov/faces/tableservices/jsf/pages/productview.xhtml?pid=PEP_2017_PEPANNRES&src=pt.

BIBLIOGRAPHY

U.S. Census Bureau. *Government Organization: 1992 Census of Governments*, Washington, DC. 2012. https://www.census.gov/data/tables/2012/econ/gus/2012-governments.html

U.S. Census Bureau. *Interim State Population Reports*. Population Division, 2006.

U.S. Department of Health & Human Services. "Effects of Healthcare Spending on the U.S. Economy." *Basic Report* (blog), *ASPE*, February 22, 2005, https://aspe.hhs.gov/basic-report/effects-health-care-spending-us-economy.

Voith, Richard. "Do Suburbs Need Cities?" *Journal of Regional Science* 38 (1998) 445-64.

Watts, Ronald. *Comparing Federal Systems*, 2nd ed. London: McGill-Queens University Press, 1999.

Wheeler, Stephen M. 2000. "Planning for Metropolitan Sustainability." *Journal of Planning Education and Research* 20 (December 2000) 133–45.

Wilson, William Julius. *When Work Disappears: The World of the Urban Poor*. New York: Alfred Knopf, 1996.

Yin, Robert K. *Applications of Case Study Research*, 2nd ed. London: Sage, 2002.

———. *Case Study Research: Design and Methods*, 4th ed. London: Sage, 2009.

Yockey, Ronald D. *SPSS Demystified: A Step-By-Step Guide to Successful Data Analysis*, 2nd ed. Boston: Prentice Hall, 2011.

Young, Raymond. "Vancouver: Made in America, Eh?" *Georgia State University Law Review* 17 (2000) 1109-18.

Zainal, Zaidah. "Case Study as a Research Method." *Jurnal Kemanusiaan* 9 (2007) 1-6.

Index

academic attainment, in Texas, 40, 41
accessibility, of transparency data, 88
Accidental Death and Disability: The Neglected Disease of Modern Society (1964), 155–56
accidents or emergency events, identifying likely occurrence of, 161
accountability
  on the composite report card, 177
  compromising government, 79
  described, 87
  regional/consolidated results regarding, 96
  table of criteria, 91
affluent clusters, 51, 59
affluent suburbs, less likely to enter into regional cooperative agreements, 176
Affordable Healthcare Act (2012), 49
agencies, competing to provide higher-quality service, 27–28
agenda setting stage, of the policy process, 83
ambulance service delivery, challenges, 152
ambulances, 155, 156
American federal map, with thousands of governing layers, 71
American municipal model, 14, 18
Anchorage, Alaska, consolidation with Greater Anchorage, 72

Area Metropolitan Ambulance Authority, 158, 159, 169
assessment, 83, 84
assumptions, driving analysis and research, 14
Athens, Georgia, consolidation with Clarke, 72
Austin, Texas
  chief innovation office position, 186
  population growth (1940-2010), 33–34
autonomy, as an expensive proposition, 188
average response time, 164
"average up" scenario, 94

Baton Rouge, Louisiana, consolidation with East Baton Rouge Parish, 72
beliefs, identifying distinctive, 35
benchmark(s)
  effectiveness for EMS providers, 160
  government effectiveness, 84
  International Association of Firefighters (IAFF), 163
  for Medstar personnel capacity, 165
  spatial equity, 69–70
Bexar County
  cluster distribution for, 180
  population increase 2000 to 2015, 45–46
  socioeconomic characteristics, 47
  socioeconomic profile, 56–57

INDEX

"bias," as unavoidable, 14
binary questions, developing a list of, 84
booming populations, taxing government resources, 26
budget and finance officers, maximizing tax revenue, 94
budget woes, of American municipalities, 25–26
budgetary data, using to measure efficiency, 85
budgetary savings, from LSS in Gainesville, 142–44
budgeting, as a major area of CMP focus, 114
burden, reducing to taxpayers, 14
businesses, in the Terrell TIF, 128

California
  comparable population but less fragmented than Texas, 21
  with fewer local jurisdictions, 20
  population growth (2010-2015), 32, 33
Canada
  fragmentation ratios, 22
  property and land use zoning powers, 70
cars
  decisions required for buying, 82
  growing epidemic of accidents, 155
case studies
  examining regionally structured interlocal agreements, 13
  of individual culture in Illinois, 36
  Medstar, accountability in, 87
  policy analysis or evaluation methodology, 12
  report cards for each, 92
  wastewater treatment plant in Gainesville, 144–46
causation question, failing to address, 83–84
Central Texas Triangle, population growth projected for, 33
change, managing for, 3–17
Chesapeake-South Norfolk, Virginia, consolidation with North Norfolk, 72

Chicago, Illinois
  cost of living, 39–40
  Fire in 1871, 3
  population growth from 1840-1890, 3–4
  process modeled by, 5–7
  public services failed, 3–4
Chicago River, pollution of, 3–5
child care, costs in three cities (Washington DC, Chicago, and Houston), 39–40
Cincinnati, Ohio, established the first ambulance service for civilians, 155
cities
  benefiting from sharing services and cooperation, 175
  consolidating with their counties, 71
  facing challenges, 5, 7
  fighting for citizens and businesses, 7
  with low MHHI facing struggles, 47–48
  merging with the regional jurisdiction, 71
  overcoming hurdles to provide critical services, xiv
  partnering with counties, 68
  providing both city and county level services, 73
  providing the same service as suburbs, 9
  staff keeping all of the BBs in a box, 111
  struggling with funding basic and essential goods and services, xiv
citizens
  expecting municipalities to accomplish more with less, 7
  mistrusting government activity in Texas, 37
  as perfectly mobile, 28
  shopping around for preferred tax-service packages, 27
  supporting smaller jurisdictions, 94
  "voting with their feet," 175
city council members, cannot devote entire attention to city operations, 109

INDEX

city management, 10, 16, 112
city management model, 107
city manager/council-manager structure, reasons for the emergence of, 107–8
city managers
    answering to elected officials and citizens, 110
    avoiding friction among city council and staff, 90
    balancing policy advocacy, development, and implementation, 188
    benefits for citizens, 111
    compensation of, 111
    contracting with counties, 178
    duties of, 109–11
    finding regional cooperation attractive, 68
    greater appreciation of, 188
    innovative structure for providing, 113–15
    leveraging networks and alliances, 9
    maintaining high service quality despite dwindling resources, 108
    offering professionalism and a singular focus, 109
    partnering with regional jurisdictions, 185
    scope of, 108–9
    strategic role of, 110
city reform movement, 4–5
city-county consolidation, 68, 71–73
civic activities, as exhausting, 71
clarity, remaining the primary issue, 178
cluster analysis, 44, 179
cluster model, statewide results for, 50–52
CMP. *See* Contract Management Program (CMP)
COGs (Council of Governments), 112
college, graduation rates, 50
college-educated parents, in the traditional suburban population, 23
Collin County
    meeting the national average of population holding health care coverage, 50
    population and population increase 2000 to 2015, 45–46
    poverty rate, 48
    socioeconomic characteristics, 47
    socioeconomic profile, 58–59
commissioner model, 107
communication efforts, pursuing successful transparency, 88
commuting distance, from suburbs, 24
competitive environment, exacerbating insular thinking, 182
competitive grant programs, 185
competitive pressures, forcing response to citizen preferences, 27
composite report card, results of, 176–78
comprehensive plan, for Terrell's water system, 124
concentrated poverty regions, 48
conditional stand-by arrangements, 77–78
consolidated jurisdictions, types of, 73
consolidation
    allowing citizens to choose elected officials and communicate, 96
    benefits of, 73–74
    elections rarely successful, 97
    including separate service provision districts for the central city and the outlying suburbs, 95
    mixed results in regard to efficiency, 94
    as really about saving money, 93
    resulting in an increased cost of production, 93
constitutional limits, special districts skirting, 75
Contract Management Program (CMP), 113, 116–17, 118
contracts
    center dedicated to archiving active, 185
    comparing long-term and short-term from CMP, 113
    contributing to, or directly improving service, 177
    providing needed services, 79
    rate for CMP client cities, 116
    struggled with transparency, 178

INDEX

cooperation, "suburbs" with smaller populations and fringe rural towns needing, 175
cooperative agreements, barriers to, 179
cooperative city management, 107–18
cooperative experience, lessons gleaned from, 181
cooperative options, 11, 74
cooperative structures, inability to provide on an equal level of quality, 90
cost of living, in Texas, 38–40
cost per unit, indicating productivity of organizations, 162
cost reduction, as the top contracting priority, 91
cost/efficiency, in CMP client cities, 116
cost-per-unit, as a simple efficiency analytical tool, 85
council members, receiving minimal compensation, 109
"Council of Governments" (COGs), 112
council-manager form of government, 107, 108
counties
    non-affluent, 61
    ten largest Texas by population, 45
crime rates, relationship and correlation with poverty, 48
criminal punishment, in Texas, 35
crises and challenges, modern, 7–8
criteria
    accoountability, 91
    applying to each option, 13
    democratic, 87–92
    described, 84–87
    equity/equalization, 92
    evaluating and comparing options, 12
    examining alternatives, 12
    feasibility, 91
    optimal varying of government services, 83
    recognizing local jurisdictions practicing transparency, 88–89
    for the suburban identification model, 24
    transparency, 92

Crossroads shopping center, developing, 131
culture
    categories identified by Elazar, 36–37
    crucial to widespread reform, 97
    initiatives leveraging, 183
    suspect of government actors and activities, 177
    traditional advocating for the status quo, 36–37
customer groups, identified by the Gainesville team, 147

daily commute, to work from suburbs, 24
Dallas, Texas
    low socioeconomic cluster in, 54
    population growth (1940-2010), 33–34
Dallas County
    cluster distribution for, 180
    low health care coverage rates, 50
    population and population increase 2000 to 2015, 45–46
    sheriff's department contracting with for police services, 89–90
    socioeconomic characteristics, 47
    socioeconomic profile, 54
Dallas/Fort Worth (DFW) metroplex, 119
Dallas/Fort Worth/Arlington Metropolitan Statistical Area (MSA), 46
data collection, 140, 147
death penalty, in Texas, 35
decision-making process, 183
decisions, maximizing self-interest, 175
democracy
    on the composite report card, 177
    grade for the Terrell TIF, 135
    grade for the Terrell water system, 134
    table of criteria, 91–92
democratic accountability, compromising, 87
democratic averages, mixed across all eight contracts, 176
democratic criteria, 13, 87–92

INDEX

democratic participation and decision-making approach, 36
Denton County, 45–48, 61–62, 141
deployment, of EMS, 156
developed nations, city management in, 186
developers, in the Terrell TIF, 128
development, creating inefficiency, 156
disparities, regionalism remedying, 67
diversity
    of the coming population boom, 43
    examining in suburbs, 24
    increasing demanding on infrastructure and social services, 29
DMAIC framework, spelling out phases of LSS, 140
doing absolutely nothing option, for EMS services, 154
duplication of service, 86

East Texas Council of Governments, offering training in LSS, 141
economic benefits, for Terrell, Texas, 120
economic characteristics
    dividing municipalities into clusters, 46
    for fiscal fitness of municipalities, 47–50
economic cycles, remaining a permanent fixture, 26
economic development, 110, 113, 133
economic growth, accompanied by increasing population, 8
economies of scale, as a standard, 86
economy, political culture impating in Texas, 38–41
education, xiv, 40–41, 42, 50
educational attainment, 50
Edwards, Torry, 110–11, 119, 182, 183
effective coverage, prioritizing over efficiency, 156
effectiveness
    benchmarks measuring government, 84
    on the composite report card, 177
    policy checklist, 87
    regional/consolidated results regarding, 94
    separating from efficiency, 84
efficacy, assessing for the Terrell TIF, 135
efficiency
    analysis of, 139–41
    on the composite report card, 177
    considering the process or how things are done, 85
    experts, 85
    perfect for Terrell water system, 134
    policy checklist, 86–87
    reducing the cost of doing business, 85
    regional/consolidated results regarding, 93–94
    as the victim of political expediency, 109
El Paso County
    hosted a "Shared Service Summit," 180–81
    population and population increase 2000 to 2015, 45–46
    poverty levels, 180
    poverty rate, 48
    pursuing regional cooperation, 181
    socioeconomic characteristics, 47
    socioeconomic profile, 59–61
Elazar, Daniel, 30, 36
elected officials
    loath to raise taxes, 27
    more responsive in small towns, 94
electoral reality, prioritizing minimal government spending, influence, or innovation, 42
emergencies and mass casualty situations, providing the infrastructure for, 157
emergency calls, responding to, 152, 156
emergency infrastructure, focusing on actual high acuity patients, 167
Emergency Medical Service (EMS)
    bureau service delivery, 153–54
    business model, 161
    challenges with ambulance service delivery, 152, 156
    delivery system, 156–57

INDEX

Emergency Medical Service *(continued)*
    effectiveness, 160, 163
    expensive to maintain and operate, 157
    facing performance expectation, 163
    geographic coverage, 161
    history of, 154–56
    inefficiency of serial users of ambulance and emergency rooms, 153
    in non-emergency medical situations, 48
    "online consult" apparatus, 157
    unpredictable nature of, 152
eminent domain, constitutional protection against, 70
employees, including at all levels of LSS, 140
employment opportunities, in Terrell, 129
energy savings, reducing cost in Gainesville, 148
equitable transportation solutions, in Portland, 70
equity
    on the composite report card, 177
    providing, 90–91
    regional/consolidated results, 95–96
    table of criteria, 92
ethnic statistics (or homogeneity), pairing with socio-economic status, 24
European nations, regional governments with significant policy authority, 186
evaluation criteria and methodology, in this book, 12–13
exclusionary zoning, as racially motivated, 19
"exclusive" powers, within designated areas of responsibility, 68–69
experts, measuring effectiveness using bechmarks, 84
externalities, eliminating, 93
extraterritorial jurisdiction (ETJ), MUDs situated within Terrell's, 125

families
    expressing preferences, 63
    migrating toward jobs and career opportunities, 33
Farm to Market Road 148 expansion, 130–31
feasibility
    on the composite report card, 177
    regional/consolidated results regarding, 97
    study by the PRPC, 117
    table of criteria, 91
federalism, 11–12, 19
federations, 19, 22
fee-based or retainer services, involving interlocal collaboration, 78
Film Alley development, focusing on, 130–31
financial incentives, by states, 185
financial structure, facilitating regional cooperation, 180
"fire-based" emergency services, 152
fiscal wellness, 49
Florida, 20, 32, 33
food, costs in three cities (Washington DC, Chicago, and Houston), 39–40
Fort Bend County, 45–48, 62–63
fragmentation
    challenges of, 25–28
    in Collin County, 59
    comparison for largest American states, 21
    county profiles illuminating the impact of, 63
    of Dallas and Tarrant counties, 54
    definition for governmental, 18
    as economically inefficient and unfair, 10
    elimination of, 95
    as a federalism issue, 19
    in Fort Bend County, 62
    fostering ineffective government performance, 29
    of jurisdictions, xiii, 28–29
    measurements of, 20
    of municipal America, 7

INDEX

providing costs and benefits, 15
referring to the number of local governments, 19
stimulating competition and lowering spending, 27
in Tarrant County, 55
in Travis County, 57
"framing era," of Texas, 37
functional consolidation, 68
functional regionalism, 74–80. *See also* voluntary regionalism

Gainesville, Texas
  commitment to Six Sigma/analytics, 139, 141–44
  LSS report card, 150–51
  socioeconomic profile, 141
  wastewater plant treatment outcomes, 150
Galvin, Bob, 140n3
gap filling, 118
General Service Districts (GSD), 73
geographic coverage, for EMS, 156–57, 166
Germany, fragmentation ratios, 22
Glenn Heights, Texas, 89, 90
globalized economy, breeding fiscal uncertainty, 25
Good Samaritan, biblical parable of, 154
governance framework model, 137
governing units, relationships among, 77–78
government services, criteria for optimal, 83
governments
  federal and state providing little support to struggling regions, 123
  in the Terrell TIF, 128
"Great Recession," effects of, 26
Greater Vancouver government, developed the Livable Region Strategic Plan in 1972, 70–71
growth pattern, re-shaping the Texas population, 41

Hampton City, Virginia, consolidation with Elizabeth City, 72
Harris County
  cluster distribution for, 180
  health care coverage rates, 50
  population and population increase 2000 to 2015, 45–46
  socioeconomic characteristics, 47
  socioeconomic profile, 53
Health and Science Hub, Trinity Valley Community College creating, 132
health care
  costs in three cities (Washington DC, Chicago, and Houston), 39–40
  coverage included in the profile, 49–50
  individuals or families without insurance, 49
  low coverage, leading to increased use of emergency medical services, 48
  in ten largest Texas counties, USA, and Texas, 47
health insurance, 49
Hidalgo County
  population increase 2000 to 2015, 45–46
  poverty levels, 180
  poverty rate, 48
  socioeconomic characteristics, 47
  socioeconomic profile, 60–61
high growth city, urban economists describing, 46
high maintenance option, for EMS services, 154
high school, graduation rates, 50
Hill Country Village, in Bexar County as affluent, 57
"hire slow, fire fast" philosophy, in smart organizations, 182
Hispanic population, growth in Texas, 41
historic American municipal structure, in need of reform, 16
home health partnership, providing EMT personnel, 167
homeownership/owner occupied dwellings, in suburbs, 23

INDEX

homogenous groups, based on chosen characteristics, 44
housing, costs in three cities (Washington DC, Chicago, and Houston), 39–40
housing and property values, soaring, 132–33
Houston, Texas
    as the corporate epicenter of the American energy industry, 34
    cost of living, 39–40
    MHHI of, 53
    population growth (1940-2010), 33–34
Houston Channel, adjacent to critical locations, 35
hub city residents, looking to escape urban blight, 29
human capital, 46, 50

Illinois
    individual culture of, 36
    population growth (2010-2015), 32, 33
    state and local tax burden, 38
immigration, effect on population increase, 26
improvement, 6–7, 11–12
income tax, none in Texas, 35
Indianapolis, Indiana, consolidation with Marion, 72
individual actors, Tiebout's assumptions regarding, 28
individualism, public choice resting on, 27
individualistic culture, 36, 41
infrastructure, xiv, 114, 123
Ingham, Kyle, 113, 116
innovation
    capacity for, 188
    driven by analytics option, 154
    driven by professional expertise and technology, 5
    mandated in municipal America, 8
    marrying with public outcomes, 184
    requiring an understanding of the old process, 181
    ways for Texas to advance, 185–87
innovative exploration, connecting with community knowledge, 183
innovative responses, 10–11
innovative thinking, engaging in, 183
intergovernmental agreements. See also interlocal contracting
    policy and democratic results, 181
intergovernmental collaboration, 76
intergovernmental cooperation. See voluntary regionalism
interlocal agreements, 15, 77, 79–80
interlocal contracting, 77–79, 87, 117
interlocal cooperation, 78–80
International Association of Firefighters (IAFF), industry-wide benchmarks, 163
Irving, Texas, practicing LSS, 141

Jackson, Kenneth, 23
Jacksonville, Florida, consolidation with Duval, 72
James, Jeff, 146
joint agreements, 77, 78
Jones, Ken, 112
jurisdiction levels, merging, 93

Kansas City, Kansas, consolidation with Wyandotte County, 72
Kaufman County and Texas Department of Transportation, investment by, 132
Kimball, Justin, authored "Our City Dallas," 107
Kimley-Horn engineering firm, 145

Lafayette, Louisiana, consolidation with Lafayette Parish, 72
Lake Tawakoni project, of North Texas Municipal Water District, 124
Larrey, Dominique-Jean, 155
leaders. See local leaders
leadership, clarion call for, 17
Lean Six Sigma (LSS)
    dependent on collaborative teams, 139

INDEX

identifying steps critical to quality, 146–49
infrastructure, 186
leveraging analytical phases, 140
not creating accountability concerns, 151
not widely utilized among Texas cities, 141
other states ahead of the curve in promoting, 186
project examples in Gainesville, 142–44
yielded a systemic Medstar process, 170
LeanOhio, offering training and project grants, 186
lessons learned, 182–85
Livable Region Strategic Plan, developed in Vancouver, 70–71
living expenses, in three cities for a family of four, 38–41
local government
    appearing to cut budgets, 75
    axioms driving this book, 15
    battling for revenue, 7
    facing multi-jurisdictional policy challenges, 74
    innovative tweaking in the real world of, 16
    leveraging regional cooperation and innovation, 14
    service side of, xiii
    serving a very unique populous, 12
    in a structure nurturing cooperation, 67
    vital to every American citizen, 6
local issues, rarely falling along partisan lines, xiii
local jurisdiction per capita, indicating the existence of fragmentation, 20
local jurisdictions
    embracing regional cooperation, 14
    enduring budget shortfalls, 29
    examining consequences from thousands of, 19
    facing problems with a reduced budget, 7
    functions of taken for granted or ignored, 6
    over 5,000 in Texas, 7
local leaders
    answering to the people, 90
    broad scope of, 16
    challenges faced by, 188
    identifying benefits of partnering, 184
    identifying political forces and managing egos, 182
    implementing innovations, 188
    looking for opportunities to save money, 7
    refusing to compromise quality to save money, 177
local planning, as critical, 9, 42
local public goods and service, as essential, 15
local services
    as boring, xiii
    labor intensive nature of, 93
    remaining largely ignored, 6
Lone Star State. *See* Texas
Louisville, Kentucky, 72, 95
low socioeconomic cluster
    in Bexar County, 56
    in Collin County, 59
    in Denton County, 62
    described, 52
    in El Paso County, 61
    in Fort Bend County, 63
    in Harris County, 53
    in Hidalgo County, 61
    in Tarrant County, 55
    in Travis County, 57
    of urban Texas municipalities, 179
low socioeconomic families, as problematic, 48
lowest socioeconomic cluster, twenty-one cities falling under, 179
LSS. *See* Lean Six Sigma (LSS)

majority party, as always the safe, conservative party in Texas, 37
managing, for change, 3–17
market knowledge, creating a competitive market, 28

INDEX

market-driven Tiebout model, 29, 110
Marvilis software package, 166
matrix structure, of municipal America, 16
mayor and council, leading five major consolidations, 73
mayor-council form of government, compared to council-manager, 108
mayors, 109
measurements, for fragmentation, 20
measuring, improvement, 6–7
median household income (MHHI)
    of CMP client cities, 115
    of Gainesville, 141
    as the most macro of measures, 47–48
    in ten largest Texas counties, USA, and Texas, 47
    of Terrell, Texas, 119
    Texas experiencing a shift in, 8
Medstar
    accountability in, 87
    ambulance system produced per unit profit, 162
    analysis of results, 166–67
    balancing affluent/middle class cities with lower income communities, 179
    bills for ambulance service, 160
    budgetary comparison table, 162–63
    building operational deployment, 166
    cluster distribution for, 180
    effectiveness of, 163–65
    efficiency analysis, 162–63, 164
    exceeded transparency expectations, 176
    fiscal and performance review, 161–65
    founding of, 169
    governing board of, 157
    history of, 157–60
    innovation remaining constant, 170
    innovative solutions, 160–61
    leveraging first response resources of client cities, 160
    online access to board meeting minutes, 168
    providing performance and productivity data, 164
    quantitative benchmarks, 165
    regional ambulance jurisdiction serving a higher percentage of lower socioeconomic cities, 179–80
    a regional EMS agency serving fifteen cities in Tarrant County, 153
    report card, 168–69
    resources of, 159–60
    response time, 163–64
    socioeconomic profiles of client cities, 158
    solutions developed, 161–68
    staff pitched moving operation fully in-house, 185
    staffing, 165
    structuring daily operations via analytics, 166
    transparency of, 167–68, 169
mental exploration, requiring many skills, 183
Metro
    as the elected regional government for Portland, Oregon, 69
    governance model, 70
metro-level challenges, in a rural area with rural resources, 119
metropolitan or regional governments, possessing all municipal powers codified by state law, 68–71
metropolitan regions, establishing and maintaining an urban growth boundary, 69
metropolitan renewal/social equity advocates (neo-progressives), 73–74
MHHI. *See* median household income (MHHI)
micro-innovation, providing an incremental approach, 184
middle class cluster
    Bexar County, 56–57

INDEX

Collin County, 59
Dallas County, 54
described, 51
Fort Bend County, 63
Travis County, 58
of urban Texas municipalities, 179
middle-class socioeconomic status, of suburbs, 23
Midwest, as most fragmented, 20
Mobile Integrated Healthcare (MIH) program, targeting high volume EMS patients, 167
mobility, of citizens, 27, 28
monocentric or de facto monocentric regions, in the western US, 20
moralist political culture, 69
moralistic culture, viewing government as a force for good, 36
multi-jurisdictional public issues, local governments increasingly facing, 9
multi-party contracts, built on a regional structure as the optimal framework, 15
municipal market, concept of difficult to grasp, 28
municipal operations, fiscal challenges impacting, 25
municipal Texas, new challenges for, 8–9
municipal utility districts (MUDs), developer-created, 125
municipalities. *See also* cities
  challenges facing, 5
  enforcing comprehensive plans in Canada, 70
  experiencing challenges putting service delivery at risk, 6
  having no history of regional consolidation, 15
  losing the capacity to manage complex policy issues, 9
  transferring assets or developing managed competition, 76
  wealthier funding high performance service provision, 180

Nashville, Tennessee, consolidation with Davidson, 72
National Association of Counties, report on funding shortfall, 25
National Center for Public Performance at Rutgers University, 185
National Fire Prevention Association (NFPA), standards developed by, 163, 164, 165
National League of Cities, report on funding shortfall, 25
natural growth, of population, 31
"net commuters," from suburbs, 24
"net migration," setting Texas apart from the rest of the country, 31
"New Urbanist" approach, pursuing spatial equity benchmarks, 69–70
New York, 20, 32, 33
Newport News, Virginia, consolidation with Warwick, 72
NIMBYistic (not in my backyard) worldview, 19
911 dispatch center, 156
non-governmental organizations (NGOs), supporting the developing world, 186
North Texas Council of Governments, 131, 184
North Texas Municipal Water District (NTMWD), 125, 132, 134
Northeast, as most fragmented, 20

Ohio, population growth (2010-2015), 32, 33
one-party state, Texas as, 37
"online consult" apparatus, to consult doctors or nurses, 157
Open Records Act, 114
operational supervisors, determining staffing levels, 166
Oregon Land Conservation Development Commission, 69
Oregon State Legislature, 69
organizational stability, maximizing alignment, 183
"Our City Dallas" (Kimball), 107

INDEX

outcome data collection phase, of LSS, 140

outcomes and results, as critical, 11

outsourcing, by city staffers questioned, 90

Panhandle Regional Planning Commission (PRPC)
  clients not able to afford to pay a city manager, 112
  Contract Management Program client list, 114–15
  developed a regional contract program, 112
  efficiency of service, 177
  leveraged the Local Government Services staff, 113
  report card for, 117–18

partners, multiple sizes and jurisdictional types, 185

partnerships, 125, 181

patients, decreasing system "abuse" by, 161

Pennsylvania, population growth (2010-2015), 32, 33

performance, mattering for local agencies, 8

performance analysis, of CMP client cities, 116

performance inhibitors identification phase, of LSS, 140

performance issues, from sprawl-driven fragmentation, 25

personal relationships, small town governance building, 94

personnel, contracting for needed additional, 78

personnel capacity, Medstar benchmark for, 165

personnel searches, rate for CMP client cities, 116

physical wellness, impacting the burden on several services, 49

police services, improving in Glenn Heights, 89–90

policy, on the composite report card, 177

policy adoption stage, of the policy process, 83

policy analysis process
  presuming a rational decision making model, 12
  steps in, 82–84

policy checklist, for efficiency and effectiveness, 86–87

policy criteria, 84–87

policy decisions, 12, 36

policy evaluation model, 81–98

policy evaluation stage, of the policy process, 83

policy evaluation structure, following, 65

policy evaluations, of case studies, 13

policy formulation stage, of the policy process, 83

policy implementation stage, of the policy process, 83

policy process, conclusion stage of, 13

policy solutions, crafting with elected leaders and the public, 178

"policy window," merger process providing, 74

political culture
  compared to ideology, 36
  impact on the Texas economy, 38–41
  maintaining government status quo, 42
  shaping city structure, 109
  of Texas, 30, 34–38, 97
  traditionalistic/individualistic, 10, 42, 123

political feasibility, 89–90, 97

political intrigue, in Texas reserved for primary season, 37

politics and governing history, challenging government innovation, 10

polycentric fragmented municipal model, versus regional jurisdictions, 11

population
  aging of, stressing social services, 26
  of CMP client cities, 115
  divided by every county, city/town, school district, and special

INDEX

district in each metropolitan
region, 20
of Texas as second largest among the
states, 8
trends in Texas, 32
population conundrum, of decreased
revenue combining with
increased demand, 26–28
population density
of suburbs, 23
in Texas as low, 21
population explosion, in Texas, 1–2, 46
population growth
for Dallas, Houston, and Austin
(1940-2010), 33–34
escalating demand for public goods
and services, 9, 26, 42, 43
explosive in Texas, 30–34
indicating positive economic growth,
46
for the ten largest American states
(2010-2015), 32–33
for Texas and United States (1950-
2010), 30–31
population trends, projections for Texas,
32
Port of Houston, foreign and domestic
tonnage, 34
Portland, Oregon, 36, 68, 69
poverty
Gainesville, 141
Harris County, 53
as a key problem, 15
regional model in areas with
concentrated, 180
in ten largest Texas counties, USA,
and Texas, 47
Terrell, Texas, 119
poverty rate
of CMP client cities, 115
of the ten largest counties, 48–49
poverty threshold, defined, 48
Power Center, Terrell partnership
created, 130–31
power center agreement, 131
private concerns, trumping public or
community concerns, 36

private contractors, outsourcing to, 76
private investment, promoting, 120
private investors, funding the FM 148
expansion, 130–31
private partners (developers), developing,
131
private sector, 184, 186
privatization/outsourcing options, 76–77
proactive analysis, of both opportunities
and challenges, 6
problem definition phase, of LSS, 140
problem identification phase, of LSS, 140
process elements, identifying "critical to
quality," 147
process management, developing a
system with proactive, 161
process model, step or stages of, 12
procurement officers, in central cities, 94
professional solutions, utilizing, 184
project champions, necessity for, 184–85
property value/tax revenue increases, in
Terrell, 132, 133, 134
provinces and local governments, role of
Canadian, 70
public actors, really no different than
private actors, 175
public administrators, managing
dynamic organizations, 7
public agencies, serving an entire
community, 8
public choice theory, 27, 175
public entity, achieving high performance
levels, 161
public executives, leveraging networks
and alliances, 9
public goods, optimum expenditure level
for, 27
public partners (cities and counties),
collecting tax revenue and
reimbursing private partners, 131
public policy evaluation process,
providing a clinical approach, 13
public revenue streams, demographics
impacting, 8
public safety, xiv, 9
public sector, 132, 184
public service, 26, 36

INDEX

public services, 28, 41
PULSE report, governing asset deployment, 166
"A Pure Theory of Local Expenditures" (Tiebout), 27
purification phases, of wastewater treatment, 145

quality public goods and services, access to, 13
quantitative standards, for suburbs, 24–25

racial segregation, fragmentation facilitating, 29
racism, 60
reactive response, to crises, 6
regional agency, delivering ambulance services, 154
regional agreement structures, socioeconomic mix to produce, 181
regional ambulance authority, 157
regional and consolidated structures, examples of, 68–71
regional balancing act, described, 49
regional development, as transformational for Terrell, 132
regional EMS agency, Medstar as, 157–60
regional government
    addressing regional issues, 74
    as more efficient, 15
    only elected in the United States, 69
    Portland as an example, 68–71
    potentially serving a larger population, 86
regional jurisdictions, 10, 68
regional models, 10, 125
regional partner, as the primary contracting partner, 178
regional partnerships, 125, 179
regional solutions, leveraging high and middle income communities and cities, 48–49
regional structures
    equalizing the quality of public services, 67

    transitioning to, remaining unfeasible politically, 15
regional systems, not housing ambulances in fire stations, 163
regional/cooperative checklist, 92
regionalism. *See also* structural consolidation
    benefits of, 67, 73–74
    condemning social stratification among cities, 60
    report card results, 97
"Remember Tiebout" lesson, 184
repairs/improvements, of Terrell's water infrastructure, 122
report card
    composite, 176–78
    for each case study including a grade for every criteria, 92
    Gainesville LSS, 150–51
    Medstar, 168–69
    method, 84
    regionalism results, 97
    Terrell water partnership/TIF agreement, 134–36
research and policy analysis, into wastewater treatment, 148
residential units, in suburbs, 23
response, to crises, 5, 6
response time (RT), 156, 163–64
results, synthesis of, 173–81
revenue
    displacing fragmentation as an urban Texas reality, 63
    issues due to a small, lower income tax base, 25
    special districts creating multiple options, 75
rugged individual climate, in Texas, 10, 37
rural land, preservation for agricultural purposes, 69
rural populations, seeking access to the urban economic engine, 29
rural towns, struggling with modernizing infrastructure, 122–23

INDEX

Sabine River Authority, partnership with Terrell, 125
sales tax revenue, increased in Terrell, 133
San Jacinto Battleground, 35
saving money, appealing to everyone, 176
SBR. *See* sequencing batch reactor (SBR) treatment process
scalability, of the Terrell water system, 134
scalable economies, leveraging, 93
scalable operations, possessing greater growth potential, 86
school consolidation, yielding greater government efficiency, 73
school districts, 9, 42
schools, adapting to booming populations, 26
scoring and reporting tools, developing, 92
self-interested utility maximizers, 27
sequencing batch reactor (SBR) treatment process, 147, 148, 149
service delivery, 78, 79, 184
service duplication, 78, 86
  eliminating, 93
service performance, Texas governments increasing, 14
service provision, efficiency and effectiveness in, 78
service quality, as the main priority, 7–8, 91, 177
services, provided for a fee, 77
severity levels, identifying, 161
"shadow governments," 74
shared service arrangements, barriers to, 179
"Shared Service Summit," in El Paso county, 180–81
shared services. *See also* interlocal contracting
  accountability of, 87
"Shark Tank," 86
silo thinking, rejecting, 182
Sims, Mike, 120
single family homes, in suburbs, 23
Six Sigma. *See* Lean Six Sigma (LSS)

small towns, learning to think like big cosmopolitan cities, 136–37
Smart growth policies, in Vancouver similar to the Portland model, 71
social equity issues, failing to appear as priorities for interlocal agreements, 78
social issues, rational-comprehensive approach to, 82
social problem, defining or analyzing, 12
social services, ever increasing stress on, 7
socioeconomic analysis, of ten urban counties, 181
socioeconomic characteristics, for the ten largest Texas counties, 47
socioeconomic profile
  Bexar County, 56–57
  Collin County, 58–59
  Dallas County, 54
  Denton County, 61–62
  El Paso County, 59–61
  Fort Bend County, 62–63
  Harris County, 53
  Hidalgo County, 60–61
  Tarrant County, 55–56
  Travis County, 57–58
solutions identification phase, of LSS, 140
south, traditional culture dominating, 37
Spain, fragmentation ratios, 22
spatial equity benchmarks, pursuing, 69–70
special districts, 74–76
"special taxing service districts," in the Louisville-Jefferson county merger, 95
staff alignment, achieving, 182–83
staffing, reducing excess based on demand for EMS services, 161
stakeholders, 15, 182, 183
state and local governments, appearing to cut budgets, 75
state and local tax burden, comparison between DC, Illinois, and Texas, 38
state regions, comparing fragmentation, 20

213

INDEX

state taxation policy, limiting government influence in Texas, 38
State Water Supply Districts, solutions for water acquisition, 122
states, fragmentation comparison for largest, 21
status quo, maintaining current EMS performance levels, 153
statutes, layering for maximum revenue, 127–34
storage tanks, pumping water to, 121
Strategic Government Resources (SGR), LSS class offered by, 142
strategic planning, 113, 116, 183
strengths, leveraging, 183
structural approach, as more transparent, 98
structural consolidation, 68
structural efficacy, measuring, 13
structural government reform, failing to yield spatially equitable results, 95
structural regionalism, 14, 97
structured mental exploration, engaging in, 183
Subject Matter Experts (SMEs), including, 184
"subnational" leadership, possessing "policy autonomy," 187
suburban dwellers, fairness of taxing, 95
suburban families, benefitting from the economic core of the large city, 23
suburban identification model, including additional criteria, 24
suburban proliferation, moving jobs, training, and opportunity to the outer ring, 19
suburban sprawl, impact on local governance, 22
suburban units, substantive profile of, 24
suburban wasteland, facilitating cooperative agreements, 9
suburbs
    affluent less likely to enter into regional cooperative agreements, 176, 179
    commuting to and from on a daily basis, 24
    consolidation agreements not mandating participation from, 96
    deciding not to avoid consolidation, 73
    existing because people are escaping from something, 28
    identifying, 22–25
    incorporated cities or towns in Texas as, 7
    jurisdictions as, 28
    majority of the new Texans flowing into, 8
    as soul-sucking, racist, mall magnets destroying America, 22
Sullivan, Barry, 142
Sunbelt region, experiencing massive migration, 33
super county, comprised of all cooperative clients, 179
support staff, for city managers, 109
sustainability, of Medstar, 162

"Takings" clause, of the Fifth Amendment to the United States Constitution, 70
Tarrant County
    cluster distribution for, 180
    described, 55
    EMS authority, 178
    population and population increase 2000 to 2015, 45–46
    as a prime example of public safety bloat, 9
    socioeconomic characteristics, 47
    socioeconomic profile, 55–56
tax base, expanding to include wealthy suburbs, 95
tax increment reinvestment zone (TIRZ), 127
Tax Incremental Funding (TIF) agreement
    benefits of programs, 127
    depth and scope of impact, 132–33
    efficiency of the contract, 177
    goal/objectives of, 128–31
    largest rural, 126

INDEX

outcomes benefits/economic
    development indicators, 132–34
process, 127, 130
as public/private business
    partnerships, 131–32
recruitment led by Mike Sims and
    Torry Edwards, 185
report card for Terrell, 135–36
specific objectives driving, 126
structure empowering development
    at a manageable incremental cost,
    133–34
structure unprecedented, 136
uniqueness of, 128
zone #1 agreement became TIRZ #1,
    131
tax revenue, 126, 132
taxes
    costs in three cities (Washington DC,
    Chicago, and Houston), 39–40
    new or increased weakening
    economic growth, 27
technology, leveraging, 161
tenure, not guaranteeing high
    performance or tranquility, 183
Terrell, Texas
    aging water infrastructure of, 122
    comprehensive plan, 134
    falling under rural Texas category,
    120
    geographic location of, 119
    innovation by leaders, 124–26
    keeping people from leaving, 128–29
    leveraged assets and described value
    for each partner, 184
    leveraged complex financial
    instruments, 127
    leveraged the water plan to establish
    a tax incremental financing zone,
    126
    location and population needs
    demanding economic
    development, 136
    in the lower socioeconomic cluster,
    179
    memory loss when new members
    join the council, 183

    population growth of, 119, 123
    receiving water from a regional
    source, 125
    transformed to retail provider of
    water to smaller surrounding
    communities, 137
    water delivery process, 126
    water source options, 124
Terrell Independent School District,
    investment by, 132
Terrell Public-Private Partnership (PPP),
    127
Terrell TIF (Tax Incremental Funding)
    agreement. See Tax Incremental
    Funding (TIF) agreement
Terrell water delivery system, innovative,
    125–26
Terrell water partnership/TIF agreement,
    report cards, 134–36
testing, of water, 121
Texas
    advancing innovation, 185–87
    changes demanding attention, 41–42
    comparing with other states, 186
    consequences for twenty-first
    century, 28–29
    culture not prioritizing equalizing
    service quality, 91
    experiencing a dual independence
    boost, 35
    health care coverage rates lagging
    behind other regions, 49–50
    high school graduation rates, 50
    independence shaping traditions,
    culture, and political norms, 35
    largest land mass in the continental
    United States, 21
    most cities employing a council-
    manager structure, 108
    passing the fragmentation test, 21
    political culture, 34–38
    population and socioeconomic
    characteristics, 47–50
    population growth, 1–2, 8, 30–34, 45
    preferring limited government with
    limited pay for elected officials,
    109

INDEX

Texas *(continued)*
    remaining highly fragmented and suburbanized, 29
    remaining in the middle, 20
    state and local tax burden, 38
    unique characteristics, 35
Texas Association of Regional Cooperation (TARC), 186
Texas City Managers' Association (TCMA), 186
Texas Commission for Environmental Quality (TCEQ), 147
Texas counties
    five largest, 180
    health care coverage rates, 49–50
    socioeconomic profiles, 53–63
    ten largest, 44–46, 47
Texas Department of Transportation (TxDot), 131, 132
Texas Interlocal Cooperation Act, 77
Texas Municipal League (TML), 186
Texas Open Meetings Act, 114
Texas Revolution, with Mexico, 35
Tiebout, Charles, discussion of, 27–28
Tiebout competitive municipality model, 29, 110
timely responses, percentage of, 164
Toronto/Vancouver, as a structured regional government, 68
towns
    in remote regions, 111–12
    rural, struggling with infrastructure, 122–23
    small, building personal relationships, 94
    small, learning to think like big cosmopolitan cities, 136–37
transactional leadership, 37
transparency
    benefits from, 14
    on the composite report card, 177
    enabling accountability, 88
    Gainesville prioritizing, 151
    Medstar prioritizing, 170
    model for determining the existence of, 88–89
    regional/consolidated results regarding, 96
    separating democracy from more authoritative forms of government, 88
    table of criteria, 89, 92
"Transparency Stars" program, honoring local governments, 88
transport response, to all calls regardless of severity, 156
transportation, costs in three cities (Washington DC, Chicago, and Houston), 39–40
transportation and economic development districts, 75
transportation networks, 9, 26–27, 42
Travis County
    cluster distribution for, 180
    population and population increase 2000 to 2015, 45–46
    socioeconomic characteristics, 47
    socioeconomic profile, 57–58
treatment, of water, 121
treatment plant, 144–46, 147, 148
Trinity Valley Community College, 132
Truth in Taxation, 114
Tyler, Texas, practicing LSS, 141

U. S. Census Bureau, projecting Texas population to increase, 32
Unigov, as the only successful, large-scale consolidation not requiring voter approval, 73
"unit hour production" benchmark, defined, 165
United States
    as the first modern federation success story, 187
    fragmentation, 20, 22
    population and socioeconomic characteristics, 47–50
    population growth (1950-2010), 30–31
    population growth (2010-2015), 32, 33
    by population with population increase (2000 to 2015), 45

INDEX

University and Highland Park, in the affluent cluster, 54
upper class cluster
  in Fort Bend County, 63
  in Travis County, 58
  of urban Texas municipalities, 179
upper middle class cluster, 51
urban affairs disciplines, addressing fragmentation, 19–20
urban and suburban counties, dichotomy existing between, 63
urban areas, experiencing more growth in Texas, 33
urban core, maintaining to avoid urban sprawl, 70
urban economists, on the ability of municipalities to fund services, 20
urban region consolidations, since 1947, 72–73
Urban Service District (USD), including the old central city, 73
urban sprawl, attacking and eliminating, 71
urban Texas, 17, 44–64
urban Texas population, 58, 63
utilities, 9, 93

Vancouver, pursuing the same goals as Portland, 70
Virginia Beach, Virginia, consolidation with Princess Anne, 72
"Vision Process," integrating changes in the EMS system, 153
voluntary cooperation, bias toward, 80
voluntary regionalism, 11
voter turnout numbers, confirming the irrelevance of general elections in Texas, 37

walkability, Metro prioritizing and quantifying, 70
Washington, DC, 38–40
Washington, George, ambulance transport developed by, 155
wastewater treatment plant, 144–46, 147, 149
water delivery process, 120–26
water delivery report card, for Terrell, 135
water source/acquisition, in Texas, 122–23
water supply
  for Chicago, 3–4
  inadequate in several regions of Texas, 9, 42
water system report card, 134–35
water treatment plant, built by the NTMWD, 125
West Texas, PRPC serving sixty-three towns in, 112
worker productivity, enhancing, 50
workforce, well-trained attractive to firms, 40

Zavadsky, Matt, 159

www.ingramcontent.com/pod-product-compliance
Lightning Source LLC
Chambersburg PA
CBHW070313230426
43663CB00011B/2114